Joy in Mudville

Joy in Mudville

Essays on Baseball and American Life

Edited by JOHN B. WISEMAN
with a foreword by Benjamin G. Rader

McFarland & Company, Inc., Publishers
Jefferson, North Carolina, and London

Chapter 4, "Tinkers to Evers to Chance: Poetry in Motion," was originally published in *Nine: A Journal of Baseball History and Culture* 14:1 (114–129).

Chapter 5, "The Adventures of Spike and Smoky Joe," is based on information from *Tris Speaker: The Rough-and-Tumble Life of a Baseball Legend* by Timothy M. Gay, published by the University of Nebraska Press.

Chapter 9 originally appeared in *Maryland Historical Magazine* 87:2 (Summer 1992).

Chapter 15 was presented at Baseball Forever at Frostburg State University in November 2006 by Jules Tygiel. It is used here by permission of Curtis Brown, Ltd.

LIBRARY OF CONGRESS CATALOGUING-IN-PUBLICATION DATA

Joy in Mudville : essays on baseball and American life / edited by
   John B. Wiseman with a foreword by Benjamin G. Rader.
      p.   cm.
   Includes bibliographical references and index.

   ISBN 978-0-7864-4228-7
   softcover : 50# alkaline paper

   1. Baseball — United States — History — 19th century.
   2. Baseball — Social aspects — United States — History — 19th century.   I. Wiseman, John B., 1938–
   GV863.A1J685   2010
   796.357097309034 — dc22   2009036595

British Library cataloguing data are available

©2010 John B. Wiseman. All rights reserved

No part of this book may be reproduced or transmitted in any form or by any means, electronic or mechanical, including photocopying or recording, or by any information storage and retrieval system, without permission in writing from the publisher.

Front cover design by Steve Neffield

Manufactured in the United States of America

McFarland & Company, Inc., Publishers
   Box 611, Jefferson, North Carolina 28640
      www.mcfarlandpub.com

For my dad,
Earleen Wiseman,
Caroline Brady,
Elizabeth Alves—
My baseball family

Acknowledgments

Let me first acknowledge my father, who taught me the game and then took me to watch Earl "Hi Ho" Silverthorne, the centerfielder of the Idaho Falls Russetts in the late 40s. His daring play enthralled me. Later, my boyhood teammates on the Rapid City, South Dakota Dodgers taught me the value of teamwork. Then there were Minnie Minoso and Willie Mays, who reminded me that baseball was meant to be fun. My daughters, Caroline and Elizabeth, subsequently revived my interest in the game in the 1970s as we watched the Orioles play so intensely. My wife, Earleen, who fell in love with the Brooklyn Dodgers in the 1950s and later rooted for the Atlanta Braves, has been my household baseball companion. She remains an enduring testament to one of the hallmarks of baseball in its prime — loyalty to one team.

I would be remiss not to mention my indebtedness to Thomas Cripps, a steadfast advisor and friend, who put me up in his "hotel" on my many trips to Baltimore. He simply wouldn't let me quit on this project. So would I be neglectful in failing to mention Catherine Gira, whose generous support of my 2006 conference on baseball at Frostburg State University provided the foundation for this book. Frank Peto, Colleen Stump, and Steve Simpson were also helpful. And since this is a paean to baseball, I simply must pay tribute to Clyde King, perhaps the finest Christian gentleman of the game since Christy Mathewson. Few people have been as supportive of me in my many historical endeavors with baseball as this former teammate of Jackie Robinson and later coach, manager, and general manager of several major league teams, and special advisor to George Steinbrenner — sixty-five consecutive years in all. Most importantly, my wife, Earleen, has been my Sancho Panza on this quixotic journey, taking care of the homefront, correcting my grammar, and shortening my sentences.

I am also grateful to the many fine historians whose pioneering research into baseball informed the contributors to this volume, thereby legitimatizing the study of baseball as serious history. The late Jules Tygiel was the most recent example of such scholarship.

His remarkable book on the Jackie Robinson "experiment" was a scholarly breakthrough as important to social historians of baseball as his subject was to the game. Tygiel continued to write on the racial history of baseball. For this volume, he brought his superb knowledge, perspective, and skills to a magisterial analysis of Curt Flood's seminal contribution to the liberation of players from economic servitude.

This book has truly been a team effort. All of the contributors, far better versed in their subjects than I, have given the best of themselves and have supported my editorial interventions. Some of them have edited my own writing. Burt Solomon sharpened my essay and introductions, Peter Morris corrected some of my mistakes, Bill Akin did all of the above and gave me great moral support. Tom Cripps critically reviewed my concluding essay and helped me in a search for a publisher, as did John Eisenberg. Ted Patterson made available to me photographs from his personal collection and two unusual interviews he conducted with Jackie Robinson and Carl Erskine. Shelley Drees, a great baseball fan and my departmental secretary for thirty-six years, typed part of the manuscript, alerted me to some of its critical omissions, and helped me prepare the index. While Susan Eisel, another faithful university department secretary, transcribed the interviews with Jackie Robinson and Carl Erskine. Danny Filer, a former student, helped me navigate the technological waters that accompany modern manuscripts. For any mistakes in this book I bear full responsibility.

I am grateful to Elaine Maruhn at the University of Nebraska Press, Shawn Herne and Greg Schwalenberg at the Sports Legends Museum in Baltimore, Laura Cleary at the Hornbake University of Maryland Library, and Susan Reyburn at the Library of Congress for their assistance in locating photographs. Bob Constanza and Jennifer Brekke from Scout Marketing in Atlanta and San Diego were helpful in other important matters.

Table of Contents

Acknowledgments	vii
Foreword by Benjamin G. Rader	1
Introduction	3

PART I: BASEBALL'S RISE AND A CAST OF CHARACTERS   11

  1. Becoming the National Pastime:
      The Crucible of Change (PETER MORRIS)   15

  2. The Science and Business of Baseball:
      The First Baltimore Orioles (BURT SOLOMON)   25

  3. The Birth of Modern Baseball (FRANK DEFORD)   34

  4. Tinker to Evers to Chance: Poetry in Motion
      (PAUL D. STAUDOHAR)   44

  5. The Adventures of Spoke and Smoky Joe (TIMOTHY M. GAY)   58

  6. Honus Wagner and Jimmie Foxx: Baseball and the
      Lives After (A. FRANKLIN PARKS)   68

  7. The Tenth Man: Baseball and Radio Broadcasting
      (TED PATTERSON)   78

PART II: BEYOND THE MAJORS   95

  8. West Virginia Coalfield Baseball, 1921–1941 (WILLIAM E. AKIN)   97

  9. Boom and Bust: The Elite Giants and Black Baseball
      in Baltimore, 1936–1951 (ROBERT V. LEFFLER, JR.)   107

PART III: TRANSCENDING RACE   121

  10. Jackie Robinson in Baltimore: History and Memory
       (THOMAS CRIPPS)   123

  11. Jackie Robinson Interview (TED PATTERSON); and Speech
       (JACKIE ROBINSON)   136

  12. An Interview with Carl Erskine (TED PATTERSON)   144

  13. Minnie Minoso and His Footsteps (TIM WENDEL)   150

PART IV: THOSE DAMN YANKEES AND THE REBELLIOUS CURT FLOOD — 157

14. The New York Yankees, 1949–1964: The Price of Dynasty (HENRY D. FETTER) — 159
15. Revisiting Curt Flood (JULES TYGIEL) — 176

PART V: THE GLORY YEARS IN BALTIMORE AND THE GAME'S DECLINE — 197

16. The Baltimore Orioles: How They Built a Winner (and Tore It Down) (JOHN EISENBERG) — 199
17. Fall from the Pedestal (JOHN B. WISEMAN) — 211

Chapter Notes — 223
About the Contributors — 233
Index — 237

Foreword
by Benjamin G. Rader

Mention baseball and it evokes memories. For me, one memory is the voice of Harry Caray as he melodramatically described the games of the St. Louis Cardinals in the 1940s and early 1950s on radio station KWPM in West Plains, Missouri. I remember trying futilely as a ten-year-old to catch a curve ball thrown by my father, and I recall my father's stories of pitching for a rural community team in the depressed 1930s. My memories are of playing catch with my younger brother, of endlessly discussing baseball with him, and later of playing on teams with him. For me, baseball evokes playing ball on cow pastures, of driving a pickup truck to ball fields with bare infields on Sunday afternoons, of playing in dusty towns that had only a single street, a filling station, and perhaps a church. Some recollections are painful: I remember muffing an easy pop fly, even though the error was of no consequence in terms of winning or losing the game, and, to this day, I wince from the memory of taking a called third strike with the bases loaded and two outs in the last of the ninth inning to lose the game. Each of us has his own fund of baseball memories.

Reading this book not only triggers such personal recollections but also offers rich opportunities for expanding one's understanding and appreciation of the role of baseball in the fabric of American life. On the local level, one learns of baseball in the grim coal towns of West Virginia in the 1920s and 1930s, of the Elite Giants and of black baseball in Baltimore from 1931 to 1951, and of Jackie Robinson's debut in Baltimore in 1946. We learn from the words of Robinson himself what the experience was like to be the first African American to break through baseball's color barrier. Dip into these pages and you will encounter the Bunyanesque players of yesteryear: Honus Wagner, Jimmie Foxx, Christy Mathewson, Tris Speaker, and "Smoky" Joe Wood. Here one finds how the Baltimore Orioles of the 1890s developed and perfected modern baseball tactics and strategies, how the New York Yankees established yet another dynasty in the post–World War II era, and how the modern Baltimore Orioles rose to preeminence only to decline into mediocrity.

All of this and more adds up to praise for John B. Wiseman's book, and a defense of one of its themes—the game's resiliency. Despite untrammeled commercialism and player strikes and misbehavior, baseball endures. "We've tried and tried to ruin this game," remarked Sparky Anderson, manager of the Detroit Tigers in 1990, "and we just can't do it." Unique among American team sports, baseball, the late commissioner A. Bartlett Giamatti remind us, it is a "strenuously nostalgic" game. It is a game of memories. It is this, the experience of baseball's past and present that gives the game its special appeal, a power that transcends the game itself. For American society, it is even more than this. In the apt words of English novelist Virginia Woolf, baseball is "a centre, a meeting place for the diverse activities of a people whom a vast continent isolates [and] whom no tradition controls."

Introduction

When a group of middle-class young men began to play a game called "base ball" in the heart of New York City in the 1840s, they hardly knew they were organizing a sport that would become synonymous with American life. They simply wanted outdoor physical recreation and fellowship. The game they chose required athletic skills, cunning, and individual exploits, as well as team play. To expand, baseball needed organization of its rules as well as its teams. A set of rules was developed, fraternal societies produced the teams, and American culture supplied the drive for competition. In the Philadelphia area and in Massachusetts, young men devised versions of the game they called base ball. All that was missing to bring teams from different places together to compete was a rail transportation system that would carry teams from city to city. Before the Civil War began, this last link in the chain of events necessary to produce a national sport was in place. Northeastern amateur teams blossomed. They soon met in convention to create standardized rules, an association of baseball players was formed, and fans were occasionally charged admission to the game. The outline of organized baseball was complete by the Civil War.

Soon after the Civil War the game spread like wildfire. By 1869, as many Civil War veterans joined other migrants to the West and a railroad linked the nation, the game was described by the Cincinnati *Enquirer* as "a national craze." The railroad facilitated a more mobile population that spread people across the country. College students brought the game home from school as baseball became a national pastime, one that that mirrored the whims and will of the American people — all of them. Some teams included whites and blacks, and soon young women would play, too. In 1871 the first professional league — the National Association — was formed. Five years later in the nation's centennial year of 1876, the National League was created. It had teams in eight cities, from Boston to St. Louis and Chicago, and as far south as Louisville.

This was how baseball became the national game. But then how did it last so long as the nation's pastime? This volume is meant to answer that question and others in essays that recognize baseball as a mirror of American society, warts and all. The opening chapter goes a long way in explaining why the game earned its title. Peter Morris reveals how experimentation with the rules of the game during a temporary lapse in the game's popularity in the 1870s restored its public momentum. The changes were jointly decided by players, umpires, managers and fans alike, which gave everyone a sense of ownership in how it would be played. This was an act of democracy that reflected the nation's underlying beliefs and its willingness to experiment.

American inventiveness, another late nineteenth century trait displayed in various technological breakthroughs, found its baseball equivalent in its highly imaginative Baltimore Oriole manager, Ned Hanlon, in the 1890s. Burt Solomon describes how Hanlon and his team invented new ways to win games—"scientific baseball"—before the club's business success was ruined by another national trend, monopolistic business practices that moved their operations from one city to another without mercy. Not lacking mercenary skills themselves, Oriole owners transplanted their club to New York.

The National League survived rupture, an earlier gambling scandal, economic warfare between owners and players, and the depression of the 1890s. It then faced a formidable organizational challenge as the new century began. Using anti-monopolistic arguments and shrewd tactics, a former Cincinnati sportswriter, Byron "Ban" Johnson, spread baseball's fortunes and his own in 1901 by producing another league. It was aptly named "American." More than 70 National League players jumped to the new enterprise.

As the country entered the twentieth century, baseball entered an era of unprecedented prosperity and a half-century of stability. The game also began to create a pantheon of heroes, demigods in uniform. Few players have ever been so heroic in so many way as Christy Mathewson, the ace of the mighty New York Giants. He set performance records that no one may ever surpass, and he was revered as "The Christian Gentleman" while doing it. Frank Deford's examination of Mathewson and his manager, John McGraw, within the context of the larger sporting world of the nation, illuminates the larger renaissance of sport as well as the birth of modern baseball. Americans wanted both spotless heroes and combative ones in their game. Mathewson personified purity of behavior on the field, while his manager and close friend, McGraw, waged a personal war on it. Winning was everything to McGraw. Who can say which of them was most typically American? The English writer George Bernard Shaw, after meeting McGraw, chose him for this distinction.

Some of the players' exploits in the early twentieth century evoked poetry and song worthy of the national game. The enduring battle between the batter and the pitcher inspired Ernest Thayer to write "Casey at the Bat" in the 1880s. It became the most widely recited poem in the nation's history. Later, someone who had never seen a game, Jack Norworth, heard enough about it to write the game's anthem, "Take Me Out to the Ball Game," in 1908. Almost as familiar to fans before World War I was an eight-line poem that Franklin Adams dashed off to finish a newspaper column so that he could attend a game between the Cubs and the Giants in New York. Now popularly known as "Tinker to Evers to Chance," the rhyme was based on the great defensive skills of Chicago Cub infielders—shortstop Joe Tinker, second baseman Johnny Evers, and first baseman Frank Chance—during the deadball era when the balls were often scruffed up, the fields rough, and their gloves small. Paul D. Staudohar's essay explains the importance of these three players—each from a different part of the country—who mastered the play that all pitchers pray for, the double play that stops an opponent's rally. These players remained on the same team from 1902 to 1912, winning four pennants and two World Series. The poem the trio inspired helped win all three of them a place in the Hall of Fame. Baseball, then and now, produced special literature.

The national game called for a diverse cast of players who embodied the sprawling nation—its diverse temperament and its ideals. A part of this volume is devoted to some great performers often neglected in baseball histories. Tris Speaker and "Smokey" Joe Wood are two of them. Westerners who carried their adventuresome spirit and Protestant beliefs to Irish Catholic-ruled Boston in the early twentieth century, "Smoke" and "Spoke," as they were dubbed by their teammates, became, in Timothy M. Gay's word, close "pals." But they were openly hostile to Catholics and African Americans, as were many of their contemporaries. They also became embroiled in the gambling culture of the time. Still, during his short career on the mound with the Red Sox, Wood performed brilliantly and tirelessly. His supreme athleticism later made him a starting outfielder and superb hitter for the Cleveland Indians. Speaker was simply the best centerfielder of his time and rivaled Ty Cobb as the era's best hitter. Some of his records, at the plate and in the field, have never been matched.

Honus Wagner and Jimmie Foxx were equally dominating players who reflected their times. Unmatched as a shortstop, Wagner also hit so well and so consistently that statisticians rank him in the top ten in fielding and batting. Like so many players of the late nineteenth, and early twentieth centuries, Wagner's German lineage and working-class background mirrored the predominant economic and ethnic segments of society. In his essay on Wagner and Foxx, A. Franklin Parks aptly describes Foxx's subsequent rise from a small-town background on the Eastern Shore of Maryland, through the burgeoning minor leagues in the mid-1920s, to finding his way to the Philadelphia Athletics in 1928. His astounding batting power was his trademark—some of his home runs measured 600 feet. These performances easily carried him to the Hall of Fame. They also earned Wagner a statue at the front gate of the new Pittsburgh Pirates' stadium while Foxx's home town of Sudlersville did the same for him at a park.

Even more important than the printed word in sustaining the game's popularity was the voice of radio broadcasters who superbly communicated the play on the field to the millions of fans at home. Beginning in the 1920s, when radio and sports celebrities became a dominant part of the nation's leisure culture, baseball broadcasters became what Ted Patterson calls "the Tenth Man" for people in their living rooms. You didn't have to go to the park to watch your team play. You could see them in your mind's-eye through the descriptive powers of broadcasters whose voices became as familiar to fans as members of the family. Before major league parks stretched across the county after World War II and Americans became more mobile, and before the arrival of television, the radio was the only ticket to a major league game for most fans. Patterson poignantly brings that audio world home to us.

In the flourishing minor leagues, the players became part of the extended family of baseball lovers. The West Virginia coalfields were awash with teams between the two world wars. They spread to virtually every coal patch, camp, and town through the southern half of the state. Since miners worked six days a week, baseball games followed church services on Sundays—both "precious times," as William E. Aikin carefully explains. Black teams were also formed, but, as was the custom of the times, they normally played other teams of color. West Virginia also mirrored another national phenomenon of the 1920s—welfare capitalism. Company managers stamped out rising unions with the help of federal troops, then co-opted miners with subsidized teams and special favors to its best players to produce a reliable labor force.

Major League Baseball owners had long kept their employees, the players, subservient as a labor force and enjoyed, after 1923, special exemption from federal anti-trust prosecution. They also denied black players a chance to perform and compete alongside their white peers. Jim Crow custom was thus as deeply imbedded in the "majors" as it was in American life. So blacks formed their own equivalent leagues. Often lacking the financial resources to stabilize their teams and generally dependent on their white counterparts to lease their stadiums, black owners, for these reasons and others, faced an uphill struggle to endure. In his essay on the Baltimore Elite Giants, Robert V. Leffler, Jr., traces the ownership history of the team and its relationship with the city's black community. His wistful conclusion about the effect of the Giants' demise had its parallel in other cities where the Negro Leagues performed.

While they survived their players performed remarkably well, often after all-night bus rides, followed by day games on rough fields. They sometimes played three or four games in a day. The brand of play on black teams was faster, tougher, and more ferocious than it was in the white major leagues. Jackie Robinson, who played the 1945 season with the Kansas City Monarchs, brought these qualities—and much more—to the Brooklyn Dodgers two years later.

This watershed event in the life of the nation and its most illustrious game deserves a special place in this volume and requires a special social historian to describe the larger sociological context that made it possible. Thomas Cripps describes the emerging racial liberalism in the nation in the 1930s, how World War II strengthened it, and how a thoroughly segregated southern city, Baltimore, provided a good testing ground for racial change. Jackie Robinson's appearances there in 1946 with a Brooklyn Dodger farm team, the Montreal Royals, provided a glimpse of how baseball's reformist racial drama would play out. Looking back on his life with baseball twenty-five years later, Robinson, in an interview with sportscaster Ted Patterson transcribed for this book, as well as in an edited transcript of a speech Robinson made in receiving the *Sport Magazine* reward as the outstanding athlete over twenty-five years, pays tribute to the role his family and Brooklyn teammates made in making the breakthrough successful. In a later Patterson interview with Robinson teammate, Carl Erskine, also published here, we learn about how the black pioneer helped his white teammates become better Americans by his moral courage.

Until recently, historians have slighted the importance of Latinos to baseball and have largely ignored the difficulties they faced in playing the game in a new country where not only their language was foreign, but where their skin color was suspect. The legendary Roberto Clemente described the unique position of the Latino player in the years after Jackie Robinson as being "a double minority." Tim Wendel has done much to rectify the gap in our knowledge of this dilemma of Latino baseball in his writings. In this volume he highlights the role of Orestes "Minnie" Minoso as a pioneer for a quiet Hispanic revolution in major league baseball that would follow him. The rapidly growing number of Hispanic players in the majors and their cultural assimilation into their adopted country is just another example of how baseball continues to serve as a mirror image of, and perhaps as a model for, a nation experiencing an expanding wave of immigrants from South of our border.

Baseball's multiracial integration took years to complete and it was unevenly adopted by major league teams. Some clubs, such as the Red Sox and the Yankees, held off for years. In his essay for this volume, Henry D. Fetter attributes Yankee racial smugness during its postwar dynastic era to its subsequent decline. Fetter also provides charts to demonstrate why ideals converged with self-interest. The National League teams that bent with the integrationist movement were rewarded with championships and higher attendance. Another sociological trend, the nation's demographic shift to the West after World War II, became an important factor in the migration of two rival National League teams there in 1958. Fetter explains the decision-making dynamics that resulted in the movement of the Brooklyn Dodgers to Los Angeles and the New York Giants to San Francisco.

A more fundamental transformation in major league baseball occurred on the economic front where the game's purse would become more evenly divided between owners and players. No one deserves more credit for this transformation and few transforming agents have been so forgotten as Curt Flood. Inspired by the civil rights upheavals in the 1960s, Flood challenged the game's reserve clause that had held players in economic servitude to the owners since the Players' League collapsed in 1890. A child of the '60s who regarded the Rev. Martin Luther King, Jr., and Jackie Robinson his moral mentors, Flood faced an uphill battle in his personal economic war against the baseball establishment. Jules Tygiel, who wrote the classic history of Robinson's experiment twenty-five years ago, fully describes this new turning point — the redistribution of economic power in the business of baseball. Flood's challenge to Major League's Baseball's exemption from anti-trust action in the U.S. Supreme Court proved unsuccessful, but it signaled a strengthened players' union that would collide with the owners in a 1994 strike that contributed to baseball's decline.

Baseball has always been subject to the ebb and flow of popular affection, whether caused by its own mistakes or by the nation's changing tastes in entertainment. At all times the game provided a window to social trends. When radio gave way to television in providing entertainment for the home, the new mass medium catapulted professional football into the forefront of the sports viewing world for reasons explained by Fetter (and by the editor in the concluding essay). Whenever the public's enthusiasm for baseball faltered in the past, an infusion of new energy resuscitated it. (Consider Babe Ruth's exploits in the aftermath of the Black Sox scandal). At the end of World War II the game faced a different challenge that was met by invigorating it with players of color.

Teams also need to be energized in their own ebbing times following their flow of success. Nowhere is this more true than in contemporary Baltimore. John Eisenberg recounts the Oriole championship formula that produced a modern dynasty second only to that of the Yankees. The recipe may well have been taken from pages of the numerous tracts of "the organization man" written in the late 1950s about corporate America. Building a successful baseball enterprise, a large service corporation by any standards, required skillful executive leadership that built a strong system from the bottom up. During its heyday, Oriole executives kept the field filled with the best talent available—and they won. When that system was abandoned, a decade of losing seasons followed.

So did the Major Leagues lose many of its fans in the 1990s. Being an Oriole fan during the team's good years was ecstasy for two young girls in Western Maryland, Caroline and Elizabeth Wiseman. The 1994 strike ended the romance for one of them, as it did for millions of other baseball loyalists in the game's fall from the pedestal described by the editor at the end of this book. Resilient as always, the game regained the support of some and won the interest of new fans with a home run barrage and aesthetic new parks that recaptured some of the historic closeness of fans to the field of play. However, the emphasis on home runs and the extravagant salaries gained by the players who hit many of them planted the seeds for yet another cycle of fans' dismay in the widespread use of drug enhancements to greater strength and longer careers. The belated and weak response of the baseball establishment—owners, players, and commissioner—to this latest cheating crisis, unlike the firmer stance the commissioner took after the World Series was fixed in 1919, has left many traditional fans disheartened. So has the frequent movement of stars from one team to another dampened fan loyalty to teams. If that were not enough to diminish the attraction of attending one of its games, the high price for doing it, along with the multiplicity of many other sport venues, surely has. While the overall attendance at major league games keeps rising, many disaffected fans are forming a parade to minor league parks. Baseball is no longer the national pastime, but it remains forever a significant part of our culture. It is hard to imagine America without it.

Part I

BASEBALL'S RISE AND A CAST OF CHARACTERS

Organized baseball became a national craze two decades after its formation in the mid–1840s only to fall on hard times by the 1870s. In his "Becoming the National Pastime: The Crucible of Change," Peter Morris explains the multitude of decisions that not only produced the game's revival, but enabled it to endure. Morris' thorough research provides a fascinating view of how the rules of baseball evolved and how the roles of its participants changed on its way to becoming the signature sport of the nation. The reader will also learn how ground keepers affected the game, how the role of umpires changed, and how the dynamics between them and the fans evolved. The trial-and-error nature of these changes mirrored the life of the nation during this period of rapid urbanization and industrialization. At the end of his essay, Morris, who has written extensively about nineteenth century baseball, suggests how team play would spread. From its beginnings baseball provided a window into the changing life of the nation.

Nowhere was this more apparent than the emergence of major league baseball as a big business, similar, though not equal to that in industries by the end of the nineteenth century. Organized baseball at the highest level had become a major business enterprise by the 1890s, one in which players and owners wanted to make as much money as possible. As Burt Solomon notes in his essay on the Baltimore Orioles in the 1890s, "The Science and Business of Baseball: The First Baltimore Orioles," the owners, then as now, "acted like owners and the players acted as players and the fans were basically an afterthought." During their heyday in the mid–1890s the Orioles were the best team that the game had produced. Their dominance rested on the scientific management of the team by its manager and part owner, Ned Hanlon. His mastery of the details of how baseball should be played during its slow ball era led to what would be called the "inside game," one that rested on speed, aggressive play, and "hitting them where they ain't." Nothing about his team and the weaknesses of its opponents escaped the attention of Hanlon. His inventiveness was for baseball what Thomas Edison was for technology during that age of rapid change.

Matching skillful field management with inspiring play was necessary to sustain the game's popularity. Two of the stars of New York Giants provided these qualities. John McGraw and Christy Mathewson led their team to greatness in the early twentieth century and would become as widely known as presidents. As different as night and day in their temperament on the field, these two unlikely cohorts became celebrities during an age that also elevated another famous athlete, John L. Sullivan, and during which college football and other sports preoccupied many Americans. Frank Deford takes us back to the turn of the century and bustling Manhattan and its mania for sports in his essay, "The Birth of Modern Baseball." He also explains why baseball was so well suited for America and describes the making of the game's anthem, "Take Me Out to the Ballgame."

What fans saw at the game at the beginning of the twentieth century was very different from what we see now. Home runs were scarce in a dead ball age dominated by pitching, defense, speed on the bases, and place hitting. In a decade with the Chicago Cubs, their three great infielders, Joe Tinker, Johnny Evers, and Frank Chance, individually averaged about one home run a year. The home run king of the era, Frank Baker, hit ninety-six in thirteen years. What earned Tinker, Evers, and Chance a place in the Hall of Fame was their special defensive skills, their overall ability, their knowledge of the game, and their fierce competitiveness. Their temperaments clashed off the field, but their collective playing skills produced the greatest era in Cub history—four pennants and two World Series from 1902 to 1912. Paul D. Staudohar's essay "Tinker to Evers to Chance: Poetry in Motion" also contains rich information on other teams of that period, recounts in detail one of the greatest bloopers in baseball history, and describes the making of a legendary baseball poem.

While most of the early major league players came from the Northeast and the South, the game's popularity had spread everywhere by the early 1900s. Two of the greatest players of that era, Tris Speaker and Joe Wood, grew up in the West. They also soon became fast friends and roommates, first with the Boston Red Sox and then the Cleveland Indians. In his cameo treatment of these two colorful players, "The Adventures of Spoke and Smokey Joe," Timothy M. Gay remedies the inattention they have received by many baseball historians. They surely merit ours, based on their records as outfielders, batters, and, in the case of Wood, a pitcher at the start of his career. His fastball earned him the nickname Smokey Joe for no pitcher threw it better. While Wood wore out his arm after less than a decade, Speaker remained healthy for his twenty-two-year career as a centerfielder where he set records for assists, rarely made an error, and averaged .345 at the plate. Their lives off the field were less heroic, though not necessarily less American than the majority of their Protestant contemporaries who regarded Catholics the same way many Americans today regard Muslims. Gay's essay also navigates the reader through the gambling culture of the times.

Honus Wagner and Jimmie Foxx had long, distinguished, and untarnished careers. They were both extraordinary fielders and hit equally well at the plate, averaging .327 and .325 respectively. Wagner was one of the greatest players of the game (often rated as the best shortstop) while Foxx (second to Lou Gehrig in defensive skills) may well have been the strongest at the plate. He nearly matched Babe Ruth's home run record five years after Ruth set the pace. He also performed well enough at first base for Ruth to choose him over Lou Gehrig for his 1929 All Star team. Their lives were so completely enmeshed in baseball that retirement left them at sea. In his treatment of these two quiet stars, "Honus Wagner and Jimmie Foxx: Baseball and the Lives After," A. Franklin Parks provides an illuminating analysis on their sad retirement lives that merits careful reading by fans who want to know more about their heroes than their baseball statistics and by players before they leave the field of play.

During Foxx's playing career radio broadcasters became almost as important as the players they described. They brought the game and the individual exploits of players like Foxx and Ruth to people's homes clearly and often imaginatively. Some broadcasters introduced a new lingo, even new words to our vocabulary. It is hard for generations raised on television to imagine their importance to an older nation that thrived on both baseball and the radio for their summer entertainment. Not even the advent of television killed the importance of the radio voices that fans depended on while they were on the road or could listen to while working or playing outdoors. In his essay "The Tenth Man: Baseball Radio Broadcasting," Ted Patterson, a sports announcer and a consummate historian of the subject, describes the history of baseball sportscasting. He reveals some of its tricks, introduces us to many of its greatest practitioners, and leaves many older baseball fans nostalgic for the summer afternoon rides where we could carry the game with us.

1
Becoming the National Pastime: The Crucible of Change
PETER MORRIS

Within a few years after the first great explosion of baseball enthusiasm swept the United States shortly after the Civil War many people confidently predicted that baseball was about to go the way of other fads. In particular, there was widespread belief that professionalism was ruining the game and would ensure its demise. A typical account noted in 1868: "Base ball has not made half the sensation this year that it did last, and probably next year will have fallen still more into the background ... base ball is being killed by the growing custom of employing professionals to do the hard work and play the matches."[1]

Despite such gloomy predictions, by the mid–1880s professional baseball was firmly established as a lucrative business and as a permanent part of American culture. The conventional explanation of what caused the transformation goes something like this: professional baseball struggled badly in the early 1870s until the National League was formed in 1876. This event, accordingly, proved to be the game's salvation by providing strong centralized leadership and making the tough decisions that enabled the game to get rid of gamblers and to establish a solid foundation for growth. There is some truth in this explanation, but it has some important limitations. The emphasis placed on this interpretation has led to neglect the far more intriguing processes that actually combined to shape baseball into the national pastime.

One major problem with the conventional interpretation is that it was first and most enthusiastically advanced by people who had a vested interest in the survival of the National League. Its two most notable proponents were Albert Goodwill Spalding, who became a multimillionaire by supplying the league's official baseballs and other equipment, and Henry Chadwick, who wrote the National League's official guide for many years. Obviously, historians need to be skeptical about a version of events that was advanced by the men responsible for the National League's official equipment and official guide. The view that strong centralized leadership provided by National League founder William Hulbert saved organized baseball from going to wrack and

The Boston Red Stockings and New York Giants on opening day at the Polo Grounds in 1886 (Prints and Photographs Division, Library of Congress).

ruin not only oversimplifies the story of the game's success, but neglects to sufficiently explain why baseball became a staple part of American culture.

A far more complex process took place, one that insured the game's national popularity. Baseball became the national pastime during the 1870s and early 1880s because many decisions were made — not by a central leadership — but by a fundamentally democratic and quintessentially American process during which everyone had their say. Americans have always been known as tinkerers who like to take things apart, figure out how they work, and then try to reassemble them. And that is what happened to baseball during these years: every element of it was taken apart and then put back together by fans, players, umpires, and others interested in the sport. Once this had been done, Americans accepted it as their national pastime because they had decided how it would be played.

The story of how this happened is by no means a brief one because it involves hundreds of changes. But a few examples should give some sense of how these changes occurred.[2] The batter's allotment of four balls and three strikes, for instance, is now taken for granted, but it actually came about after considerable trial-and-error. In 1879, it took nine balls for a walk and three strikes for a strikeout, but those figures were changed virtually every off-season for the next decade. After one year of nine balls and three strikes, it became eight balls and three strikes, then seven balls and three strikes. Next, the National League stuck with seven balls and three strikes while the other major league, the American Association, tried six balls and three strikes. The following year, the two leagues flip-flopped, with the American Association adopting seven balls and three strikes and the National League using six balls and three strikes. Then they both agreed on five balls and four strikes. Next they tried five balls and three strikes, and finally in 1889 they adopted four balls and three strikes. That arrangement has never since been changed.

Is four balls and three strikes the ideal balance? Although this compromise works well enough to have endured for nearly 120 years, that doesn't mean that three balls and two strikes wouldn't have worked just as well. It would be silly to argue that every outcome was perfect or inevitable, but what mattered was that the process ensured a resolution that would be workable. Thus, it was ultimately the process that mattered most because of all the tinkering that went on, all of the input that was made, and all of the resulting arguments combined to give everyone the sense that they had had a say in the decision.

This process of trial-and-error also played a critical role in baseball's emergence as America's national pastime. During the 1850s, cricket rivaled baseball in popularity and many expected that to continue. But what doomed cricket's ability to grow was the reality that it was already long established and had a firm set of rules. By contrast, baseball had a rulebook in name only, and many of the rules were little more than guidelines. There are numerous descriptions of early umpires searching for a rule that covered a particular situation, not finding one, and then making a common sense decision. More importantly, nobody saw anything wrong with that. Umpires consulted their idea of fair play, of gentlemanly conduct, of sportsmanship, and decided accordingly. Baseball was thus a game that invited input by its participants and experimentation. What could be more American than that?

During the 1870s and 1880s when hard-and-fast rules started to replace guidelines, what mattered most was that a democratic process determined how the game would be played. Sportswriters wrote long columns to offer their suggestions. Fans also had the sense that their opinions mattered, and weighed in. When sliding came into vogue, one wrote a letter to his local newspaper: "we should like to see the abolition of sliding. It is really a measure to dodge the baseman and not to gain time. It is not fair, manly, square work."[3] Spectators also had their say. After all, they could attend or not, based on whether they approved of the direction baseball was going. They could also cheer or hiss to show whether they approved of a new tactic. These responses were taken very seriously by game officials and sportswriters who tried to instruct fans on when they should cheer and whether they should hiss. Newspaper accounts offered many suggestions on how to play the game, many of which had strong moral undertones. "[Arthur Irwin] is evidently too weak physically to swing a bat and he therefore holds out the willow and 'bunts' the ball," read one early description of the bunt. "For this babyish performance he was roundly hissed by the spectators, and concluded to abandon it. Base ball is essentially a manly spirit, and its patrons object to such infantile tricks."[4] These many voices and much give-and-take determined the rules, thus giving the game a sense of public ownership in it.

All of this input resulted in fascinating debates that often mirrored a society in the midst of huge transitions: industrialization, the country being opened up by railroads, artisans changing to workers, rural folks moving to the cities — in short, a society undergoing dynamic change. The enormous changes facing Americans were often reflected in the simpler ones in baseball. They all fostered debates about basic values: fair play, equal opportunity, being tough and manly, being observant and resourceful, being a master of many skills or specializing in one. What made the creation of the rules of baseball such a fascinating process was that it often pitted those values against one another and forced people to decide which value was more important. What set baseball apart from the larger changes was that the public had greater control over the outcome of how baseball would be played than they did over where railroads would be built and the rates they would charge. Its formation was pure Americana.

And it was an ongoing phenomenon. When the question of allowing substitutes arose it forced people to take sides: is it more important for a ballplayer to have all the skills associated with baseball or should there be a place for the specialist? When players started to wear protective equipment such as masks, gloves and chest protectors, it made people ask which is more important: being tough or being resourceful? When the hidden ball trick started to be used, there were debates about that as well. Some said it was an ungentlemanly tactic to hide the ball and try to trick someone while others liked it because it demonstrated the value of paying attention at all times.

Hitting was also affected. In the early days, it was taken for granted that batters would try to knock the ball out of sight. But then in the 1860s new approaches began to emerge, including the bunt. Finally, a player named Tommy Barlow started walking up to the plate with a miniature bat.[5] This innovation led to a heated debate about whether the bunt was a clever play or the work of a sissy and indeed as late as 1894, many argued for banning the bunt. People argued passionately about these questions — so passionately indeed that there were times when it was clear that they were also arguing about some underlying philosophical questions.

Of all of the changes that these years saw, the most dramatic was the transformation of the pitcher's role. Pitchers were originally expected to toss the ball to batters with a simple underhand motion. They were called pitchers because the act was akin to pitching a horseshoe. All that the pitcher was really supposed to be doing was getting the action started. He was essentially just another fielder, and his ability to field his position and keep runners close to their bases often earned more comment than his deliveries to the plate. During the 1850s pitchers had tried to carve out a larger role for themselves, but at first this had a limited effect on the game because as long as someone is

1—Becoming the National Pastime 19

"pitching" the ball it's hard to subvert this basic intention. But throughout the 1860s, pitchers started making more and more overt efforts to throw the ball instead of pitching it. Raising their release points, twisting their wrists and elbows, they found ways to make it harder for batters to hit the ball.

This presented a huge problem. It changed the game fundamentally, and to many it seemed outrageous. Of course, most of those who were outraged were non-pitchers. From their perspective the pitchers had refused to accept the role they had been assigned and instead seized a far larger one. It was as if the actors playing Rosencrantz and Guildenstern in a production of Hamlet had decided that they didn't have enough lines and began to deliver their own soliloquies. Or as if a coach in a coach-pitch league had suddenly started hurling fastballs past the poor little tykes. In response, the rules-makers spent every off-season discussing new ideas for how they could limit the pitcher's role. Every winter they passed new rules to try to accomplish this—and every spring it became apparent that they had failed. Pitchers kept testing the limits and finding ways to get around every new set of rules. Pitching changes became yet another example of the game's experimentation and democratic involvement.

Finally, in 1884, rules-makers waved the white flag and told pitchers they could pitch overhand if they wanted. This decision, which might be called the great surrender of 1884, changed baseball in many dramatic ways: it made it impossible for pitchers to pitch everyday, it led to many arm injuries and shortened the careers of many pitchers. It also forced catchers to start wearing new equipment, it led pitchers to eventually be moved back to the current distance of sixty feet, six inches, it was one of the factors that led to the introduction of pitching mounds, and it played a large role in the changes in the number of balls and strikes that has been previously described.

But as important as all of these changes were, long before the great surrender of 1884, the various efforts that the rules-makers had made to thwart pitchers had had an even more important consequence. The purpose of all of the efforts of the rules-makers was to return baseball to being a simple conflict between batters and fielders as it had been before the pitchers had usurped a greater role for themselves. Instead, not only did they fail to limit the role of the pitcher, but they inadvertently forced a new figure to play a prominent role in the action: the umpire.

Umpires had always been part of baseball, but their role had traditionally been to enforce decorum. Typically, early umpires were distinguished citizens who didn't necessarily know the rules but could be counted on to make sure that the players acted like gentlemen by not swearing or arguing or otherwise behaving inappropriately. As one early ballplayer recalled: "The old time umpires were accorded the utmost courtesy by the players. They were given easy chairs, placed near the home plate, and provided with paper fans on hot days. Their absolute comfort was uppermost in the minds of the players. After each of our games in the early '60s, sandwiches, beer, cakes and other refreshments were served by the home team. The umpire always received the choicest bits of food and the largest glass of beer — in case he cared for such beverage. If he didn't, he simply expressed his desires in the thirst-quenching line before the game started — and he got it."[6] Another old-time player recalled: "The umpire's place was usually a point even with home plate and about twenty feet away. There an armchair was set for him and, on sunny days, he was entitled to an umbrella, either self-provided or a special one of vast circumference, fastened to the chair.... He had freedom of movement, but the prerogative was rarely used. In his pocket was a copy of 'Beadle's Dime Baseball Book,' then the hornbook of the game."[7] And, as previously mentioned, there were a lot of points that were not covered. The umpire would then do whatever seemed fair.

This leisurely role changed after pitchers started to carve out a larger role for themselves and the rules-makers began doing everything they could to prevent them. Suddenly, umpires were being expected to get out of their armchairs, take down the umbrella, put aside the large glass of beer and the cakes and make difficult judgment calls. Was that a ball or a strike? Was the base-runner out or safe? Did the outfielder catch the ball or trap it? If the umpire got one of these calls wrong, or even if some of the spectators thought he had got a call wrong, he would be subject to considerable grumbling and even verbal abuse. Before long, there was also the threat of physical abuse. By the 1880s, instead of being offered the largest glass of beer, umpires were instead having glasses of beer thrown at them. The earlier simple contest between batters and fielders now magnified the role of pitchers and umpire judgments, transforming a spare ritual into a murky mess.

This new reality in turn led to a barrage of new tactics that would previously have been deemed unsporting. Instead of gentlemanly accepting that a play had gone against them, players began to automatically appeal to the umpire to make a decision, prompting complaints about umpire judgment calls. In a more serious affront to gentleman standards, base-runners, instead of touching or rounding the bases, began to cut in front of them. The game had been changed fundamentally and forever, but not by the game's centralized leadership — indeed, in large part, it had changed in spite of them in a far more American entrepreneurial way.

One by one other key issues were hammered out and, piece by piece, the rules, customs, strategies, and tactics of baseball were assembled. The 1870s and 1880s were also years that saw the introduction of substitutes, a development that in turn gave prominent roles to coaches and non-playing managers. Also entering baseball were new strategies, including bunts, hit-and-run plays, every type of slide, and new positioning for fielders. New equipment emerged as well, including catchers' masks, chest protectors, mitts, and fielding gloves. And each of these changes had a ripple effect, leading to other changes both small and profound. Almost every one of the changes engendered a lively debate and a lot of practical experimenting and tinkering.

This raises the obvious question of how these issues were resolved. Once again, a lot of people have tried to take credit. Henry Chadwick was the most important sportswriter of the nineteenth century and took credit for many of the changes. He undoubtedly deserves some credit, but he also kept advocating ideas long after they had been shown to be impractical or unpopular. One of his long-running crusades was for baseball to add a tenth player and a tenth inning; another was that a 1–0 game was an ideal game; a third was for batters to switch to square bats. Chadwick was an Englishman by birth and this last idea, like many of his proposals, would have made baseball more like cricket at a time that most Americans were taking pride in the fact that baseball was becoming distinctively American insofar as how rules and regulations were adopted by many participants in the game. The final decision wasn't ultimately made by any individual or group, but instead was forged by the results that took place in front of everyone. The playing field itself functioned as a crucible, a testing ground for any prospective rule, tactic or strategy, and the players, umpires, fans and even the groundskeepers took part. It was democracy at work, and at work in a way in which everyone's participation mattered.

Catcher Harry Francis Vaughn in an 1889 Louisville, Kentucky, uniform holds a baseball with a logo advertising Old Judge cigarettes (Prints and Photographs Division, Library of Congress).

In this crucible, an idea that came from a high muckety-muck and that looked good on paper, would be rejected if it couldn't survive being tested on the field. While major league owners had the most prominent role, they didn't really have the final say because if they passed a bad rule, it wouldn't last. A perfect example is the bunt, which prompted a long-running campaign to abolish it. In 1894, at their annual meetings, the owners announced a compromise rule on bunting and immediately "they received such a jacketing from the newspaper men, players, enthusiasts, in fact from everybody that it made them fairly dance, and the first thing they did on convening the next morning was to reconsider their action of the previous day and amended the bunt question."[8] This was an extreme example, as most new rules lasted more than 24 hours, but the point should be clear: a bad idea couldn't survive no matter whose idea it was.

Henry Chadwick's proposal of square bats provides another perfect example. They were tried in an 1879 exhibition game which Chadwick himself reported: "Unluckily the Park groundkeeper had only provided three of the new four-sided bats and as these were all broken before two-thirds of the game were finished, the contest did not present a fair opportunity for testing the merits of the new sticks."[9] That was Chadwick's highly idiosyncratic interpretation of this experiment. Everyone else recognized the more mundane truth: that bats that break easily should not be adopted.

The flip side was that a good idea might become a permanent part of baseball no matter who first thought of it. There was value to soliciting ideas from as many people as possible—they could all be tried and the ones that worked could be kept. This meant that some unlikely heroes emerged, many of whom are forgotten because they were working-class Americans from humble backgrounds who weren't mentioned in the official guides.

Some of them were groundskeepers such as brothers Tom and John Murphy.[10] The Murphys and other hard-working late-nineteenth and early-twentieth century groundskeepers were given mud flats and abandoned garbage dumps and asked to turn them into functional baseball diamonds. The Murphys in particular redefined key field elements such as the base paths and the ground rules to the home team advantage, and by helping to introduce new elements such as the Baltimore chop based on the hardened infield which when the ball was hit downward produced a high hop that enabled the runner to reach first base ahead of the throw.

Perhaps their most noteworthy creation was the pitching mound. Some might assume that the mound entered baseball because baseball officials got together in a boardroom and wrote it into the rulebook. In fact, mounds began to appear on baseball diamonds a full fifteen years before they were ever mentioned in the rules. What happened was that on muddy days, groundskeepers would pile sawdust and straw on the pitcher's area so that the pitcher could have some traction. Eventually, pitchers started to see a benefit to standing on these little hillocks and groundskeepers started to create them whether or not it had been raining. We don't know for certain who first started doing this but, there's good reason to believe it was Tom Murphy. Even if some other groundskeeper thought of the idea first, the point remains that it was hard-working tinkerers who introduced the pitching mound to baseball and not a committee of rule-makers.

Just as important a role in baseball's development was played by umpires. As described earlier, the 1870s and 1880s saw umpires go from being offered glasses of beer to having the glasses of beer thrown at them. In subsequent years, the umpire's position only got harder and it often seemed that it took superhuman talents to fill the position. This was neatly illustrated when the

National League hired an umpire named Billy Stage in 1894. Stage brought two unique qualifications to the position. First of all, he was a law student, which was a very useful background for a man required to interpret the tangled thicket of rules. Just as important, Stage was the world record holder in the hundred-yard dash. This might seem an unnecessary qualification, but far from it since one lone umpire was still expected to cover the entire field and make calls all over it. Long gone were the days of umpires sitting in their armchairs under umbrellas and having "freedom of movement, ... but rarely used." Billy Stage used it frequently. Once the ball was put in play, he would dash from behind the plate and beat the batter to first base so as to make an accurate call. According to Hughey Jennings, sometimes he would even slide alongside the runner in order to get a closer look

As the Billy Stage saga suggests, and the unfolding game does even more so, it was truly an impossible task for one man to interpret a difficult and ever-changing set of rules, and to make difficult judgment calls all over the field, all the while knowing that he would get nothing but abuse for his efforts even if he somehow got every call right. Many men tried umpiring briefly and resigned.[11] Yet those who persevered gradually helped to shape vague rules into more readily enforceable ones and to slowly but surely earn greater respect for the profession. They too deserve great credit for their roles in shaping baseball.

Baseball thus became America's national pastime not because of financial decisions made in smoky boardrooms by businessmen. It became so because of decisions made collectively by a lot of Americans after carefully watching how the results played out on the field. And because those Americans knew that they had been part of that decision-making process, they believed that the game of baseball belonged to them. It became the *American national pastime* by being each of those things: American because of the contributions of so many Americans; national because those contributions came from all across the country, and a pastime because those contributions were made by people who wanted baseball to embody their hopes and dreams, and to be fun, not by people who sought to make money from it.

Some may argue that this revised outlook fails to give credit to the businessmen who founded the National League and made the tough financial decisions. Without doubt, these men made important decisions, such as introducing the reserve clause, limiting the number of franchises, placing restrictions on the size of cities, limiting cities to one franchise, introducing standard ticket prices and turnstiles, targeting a higher class of fans, and making an effort to eliminate gambling. But a strong case can be made that these decisions were less important in the game's increasing prosperity than a couple of factors that had nothing to do with the National League owners, but which created a far more favorable climate for professional baseball.

The first was the growing appeal of the sport and that was shaped by a cross-section of Americans whose decisions refined and improved the game.

The second was the railroads, which became cheaper and much more reliable during these years. This cut the costs of operating a professional baseball club dramatically and single-handedly turned baseball from a business proposition that was very shaky by any model to one that had the potential for profitability.

Let me illustrate this final point with a description of a baseball club's travels in 1877: "the next day it was decided to drive over, going by way of Ft. Snelling and Minnehaha Falls, ferrying the river, and returning by the prairie road, there being quite a number of miles of farming land between the two cities in those days."[12] That was an account of a trip from Minneapolis to St. Paul! Obviously, travel represented a huge obstacle to the profitability of early ball clubs and as transportation became easier and more affordable, baseball's economics were revolutionized.

Instead, when baseball began to prosper in the 1880s, credit was given to the owners. Similarly, they are still getting credit for the extraordinary developments of these years, even though they had little if anything to do with many of them. It is far more appropriate to apportion that credit among the many Americans who participated in the crucible of change that occurred on the playing field, on the sidelines, and in the stands. Collectively, they made the key decisions that made baseball the American national pastime.

2

The Science and Business of Baseball: The First Baltimore Orioles

Burt Solomon

The Baltimore Orioles of the 1890s were one of the great teams of any age, of any sport. They brought to perfection a style of baseball that was known then as scientific baseball, which is now called "inside baseball" or "small ball." It was the glorious age of science. Thomas Edison was king — there was a new invention every year. There were phonographs and telephones and incandescent bulbs and X-rays, so you could see inside of people without using a knife. You never knew what was coming next. Science was becoming America's new common faith. Progress was relentless. Success and riches were available to anyone who questioned an assumption or explored an unexamined possibility or noticed something that everyone else had missed. This was true in baseball, too.

Ned Hanlon, the manager and part-owner of the Orioles, was as smart in his way as an Edison, except that Edison was a showoff. Hanlon was a man of precision and logic. At home he had a clock in every room, and he had soup with every meal. He was the sort of man who saw the pattern in the details, then found a way to rearrange them. He could see things in other teams' ballplayers that their managers couldn't see, and so he made some very clever trades. Foxy Ned, he came to be called, and people eventually got scared to trade with him, and for good reason.

He got Hughey Jennings that way, a shortstop who was brilliant in the field but bailed out at every high and tight pitch. The coal miner's son from Scranton, Pennsylvania, had been a breaker boy — pulling the slate out of the coal going down the chutes, a dangerous job. Hanlon saw in him a desperation to succeed. Playing shortstop was better than working underground. Hanlon also traded for Joe Kelley, who was daring on the basepaths, aggressive at the bat, and had a compulsion to win, but needed to be taught the fundamentals. Already on his team was John McGraw — young, green, and intense. He had had a hardscrabble upbringing — diphtheria had killed his mother and some siblings — and he was an angry and competitive young man, with a face like a panther. Baseball to him was not a game.

Then before the 1894 season, Hanlon traded for the littlest guy in baseball, who claimed to be five foot four-and-a-half but would never consent to be measured, a left-handed third baseman — a rare species, and for good reason — named Willie Keeler. "Wee Willie" Keeler, as he came to be known, was a throw-in for a deal with the Brooklyn Trolley Dodgers, and he turned out to be even a better ballplayer than Hanlon had imagined. He was fearless in the field — he once caught a ball in right field in Washington by sticking his hand up through several strands of barbed wire that hemmed in the stands. At a time when most ballplayers preferred heavy bats that they held at the end and swung hard, he choked almost halfway up on the bat, so he could control it. He became the best place-hitter yet in the history of baseball — and probably, the greatest ever. His record for hits in consecutive games has been exceeded exactly once, by Joe DiMaggio in 1941.

All four of these Orioles — the Big Four, they came to be called — are in the Hall of Fame, and, since 1996, Ned Hanlon is too. And for good reason. Willie Keeler and the rest of the Orioles embodied a new style of play that reached its epitome in Ty Cobb and is still with us today.

Baseball at the time was a game of giants — the New York Giants, for instance, who *were*. It was a game of thick-bodied men who hit a soft, spongy ball as far as they could (which wasn't all that far) in sprawling ballparks that were shaped like city blocks — sometimes, trapezoids — with rough and rutted fields. Pitchers stood 55½ feet away, in a box, and tried to overpower the batters — notably, Denton True Young, a rawboned Ohio farmboy, whom we know as Cy Young, which was short for "Cyclone."[1] It was pitchers like that who sent batting averages skittering down and kept spectators away from the ballpark.

So in 1893, all but one of the owners — Cy Young's owner — were persuaded to move the pitcher back five feet, to 60 feet, six inches. The baseball experts pooh-poohed this at the time — it would matter a little for a few months at most, they said. But they were laughably wrong. Baseball would never be the same.

For the Baltimore Orioles, it made a world of difference, largely because Ned Hanlon figured out to take advantage of it. The differences were subtle, but Hanlon was subtle. A pitch took a tiny bit longer to get to the plate, so the batter had another instant to control what happened to it, so the speed and range of the fielders counted for more, and the pitcher took another moment to field a bunt, and a baserunner had another split second to steal a base. Raw power was giving way, at least a little bit, to speed and cunning.

It was after Hanlon traded for Wee Willie Keeler that the pieces fell into place. Hanlon kept a pad by his bed so could jot down ideas in the middle of the night. The Orioles had already invented the Baltimore chop, which was hacking down at the ball so it would bounce high, in hopes that the batter

Willie Keeler, "hitting them where they ain't," with the Baltimore Orioles in the 1890s (Prints and Photographs Division, Library of Congress).

could make it to first base before the ball came down and the infielder could throw it. The Orioles did not invent the double steal or the bunt or the hit-and-run, but they perfected them — and they used them. John McGraw leading off and Wee Willie Keeler batting second were just about unbeatable in the hit-and-run.

The players themselves invented the suicide squeeze. In 1894 nine or ten of the Orioles lived together in the same boardinghouse, and they went out on dates together and to church together. One night, they spent hours calibrating the chances of a runner on third base scoring on a sacrifice bunt if he left at the pitcher's first motion. The next morning they went out to the ballpark and tried it again and again, and they learned that if the bunt went anywhere between the foul lines and the runner left third base at the pitcher's first motion, he would score. They worked together and played together and praised one another when they excelled and roasted one another when they didn't, so everyone stayed on their toes.

"It is in some respects like checkers and chess," Hanlon said, "and must be played upon systematic plans. Modern baseball, as played by the Baltimores, is based upon the idea to keep opposing teams guessing. It is a case of dealing out uncertainties at all times. Against some teams the Baltimores adopt one style of play — against others they shift. They study the weak points of all teams and try to take advantage of those points accordingly."[2]

Willie Keeler probably said it best — and certainly more succinctly, and more famously. "Keep a clear eye," he said, "and hit 'em where they ain't."[3] In other words, be painstaking about what you're doing, so that you do it well, and figure out the gaps in your opponent's defense, the vulnerabilities, and put the ball there. This was, in its way, science.

The Orioles would try anything if there wasn't a rule against it, and sometimes if there was. McGraw in particular became known for running directly from first base to third base, if the only umpire's back was turned, and for holding the belt of an opposing baserunner at third base and for sharpening his spikes on the bench so that the other team could see. McGraw said later that they won a lot of games before the first pitch was thrown.

Tom Murphy, the groundskeeper, became an important man on the field. He built up the ground outside the third base line so that bunts would stay fair; and he mixed clay in the dirt in front of the plate and never watered it in the long hot Baltimore summer, to help the Baltimore chop. He also hid baseballs in the weeds by the outfield fence, because right field sloped down and couldn't be seen from the infield; and he mixed soap shavings in with the dirt around the pitching rubber. He would tell the Orioles' pitchers where the soap was, but not the other team's.

It all worked beautifully. The Baltimore Orioles won three pennants in a row, from 1894 to 1896, and then finished in second place the next two years. They were the most exciting and creative and successful team that baseball had ever seen. They were the supreme practitioners of the new dawning age of science.

They also mirrored the social practices of the time. The game of baseball had long functioned as a pure meritocracy; player selection reflected the national creed that performance mattered more than social background. In the 1880s the huge exception became baseball's adoption of the color line that at the time the nation was making a shameful addendum to the creed. The captain of the Chicago White Stockings—the big, blonde slugger, Adrian Anson—started the movement to bar black players from the major leagues when he refused to take the field against any ball club with a black player. Baltimore's southern customs would find this rule congenial. But it was the city's large German and Irish population who were especially pleased with the preponderance of their ethnic groups on the Orioles' team. Usually the sons of immigrants, they offset the discrimination they faced elsewhere with the success their talent and work ethic brought them on the playing field of baseball, keeping part of the American ethos alive. Another way in which baseball of the 1890s reflected its times was in its entrepreneurial nature. This was true, in part, on the field. That's how the Orioles played, responding to every opening, every man trying his utmost, contributing his share, the whole being greater than the sum of the parts. This was also true off the field. After the Orioles won their first pennant in 1894, the Big Four didn't send back their contracts for 1895. It was human nature to want a piece of such conspicuous success. They had been getting a salary of $1,500 a season and Hanlon gave them each a $500 raise. But the salary cap was $2,400 and they wanted more than a $500 raise. So Keeler wrote to Hanlon during the off-season and happened to mention how Kelley was making good money by starting a furniture-moving business and may or may not report to the team; McGraw and

2—The Science and Business of Baseball

The Orioles' 1896 championship team with Ned Hanlon in a suit (courtesy Babe Ruth Museum, Baltimore).

Jennings stayed out of contact. But Hanlon wasn't fooled. He didn't give an inch. He understood that baseball was a monopoly, that the ballplayers had no choice. And sure enough, right before the train was leaving Baltimore for spring training in Macon, Georgia, the ballplayers came to him, and he made them wait.

Indeed, it was the business of baseball that wound up destroying everything that this wonderful team had built up. And in this, too, baseball in the 1890s was quite a perfect reflection of America. After three straight pennants and two second-place finishes, in 1897 and 1898, the Orioles weren't drawing very well anymore. People in Baltimore had become bored with winning. The ballplayers got more and more selfish not only in terms of money but also in how they played. The team lost its edge. The Spanish-American War in 1898 also hurt. It was "a splendid little war," but it was a real war, where real people were dying. Fans were losing interest in the pretend war on the field.

The Spanish-American War had another effect. The financiers, flush with cash from their commissions on war loans, began using their money to create industrial trusts. This happened in Baltimore. During the fall and winter of 1898, the city's beer companies formed a trust, the trolley companies formed a trust, Baltimore's brickmakers formed a trust, the electric utilities and the gas companies did as well. But worse, the companies in Baltimore that produced things for a larger market were being gobbled up by the national trusts. This had already happened with the B&O Railroad, the most important company in Maryland; J.P. Morgan had taken control of the B&O as his price for

The Orioles' park in Baltimore, bulging at the seams in the 1890s (courtesy of Babe Ruth Museum, Baltimore).

bailing it out, when it went bankrupt after the depression of 1893. Now it was happening to the city's 14 can companies, to its eight fertilizer plants and to both of its tobacco companies, its sugar refinery, its copper refinery, its shipping lines, its biggest bakery, its whisky distillery, its piano manufacturer — and on and on. The proud and gracious city of Baltimore, long a major port and an important commercial and mercantile center, the sixth biggest city in the country at the time, was becoming a branch town. Baltimore was losing control over its own economy.[4]

Then in December 1898, it happened in baseball. The Orioles had started to lose money, and the majority owner, a brewer named Harry von der Horst, the son of a German immigrant, had put his own business into the local beer trust. About the same time, he started getting offers for the ballclub. The best offer, or maybe the most artfully timed, came from the Brooklyn Trolley Dodgers. They had an awful team — they had just finished tenth in the twelve-team National League, which was the only major league at the time. But they had a promising potential market. There was only one other team in all of Greater New York, which itself had just consolidated, by merging Brooklyn — which had been the fourth most populous city in the country on its own — to join Manhattan and the other boroughs. The Giants played at the northern end of Manhattan, which left a lot of potential fans for Brooklyn. So Brooklyn had a promising market and a lousy team, and Baltimore had a good team and a lousy market.

The deal they cut was called syndicate baseball. It was industrial trusts come to baseball. The Orioles owners took half-ownership in the Brooklyn club, and the Brooklyn owners took a half-interest in the Orioles, so that both teams had the same set of owners; they were commonly owned. They shipped most of the stars to Brooklyn, including Willie Keeler — who was from Brooklyn, and therefore a draw — and Hughey Jennings and Joe Kelley. The next season, in 1899, Brooklyn finished first in the National League, and again in 1900. When the ballplayers heard of the deal, the backup catcher, a long stringy fellow named Bill Clarke, was asked if he minded. No, he said very matter-of-factly, the owners are "out for money" just like the players are.[5]

This wasn't the only instance of syndicate baseball. St. Louis and Cleveland did the same thing the same season. St. Louis was the country's fourth biggest city, after Brooklyn was no longer a city, and it took the best of Cleveland's players. The 1899 Cleveland Spiders became the worst team in baseball history, ever, winning 20 games and losing 134. They spent the last two or three months playing entirely on the road, because the crowds in Cleveland were barely large enough to cover the visiting teams' hotel bills. This was the result of syndicate baseball.

The Orioles actually didn't do badly in 1899, on the field, because John McGraw stayed behind, as the player-manager — he was 26 years old — along with the team's captain and catcher, Wilbert Robinson. The two of them were in business together in Baltimore. They co-owned The Diamond, which may have been the first sports bar, located not far from where Camden Yards is now. Besides a saloon, it had bowling alleys — it is where duckpin bowling was invented — billiards, a reading room, a gymnasium with lockers, and an electric scoreboard that kept track, play by play, of games in progress. So McGraw and Robby were allowed to stay in Baltimore. With McGraw's intensity — there were no excuses with him, and he tried harder than anybody else — they played far above themselves, into fourth and even third place. Sportswriters called them The Leftovers, or the Orphans. But during the season McGraw's wife died suddenly, from complications of an appendectomy. He left for a while and the team flagged. Robinson tried to "jolly" them along, but it didn't work, though they still wound up in fourth place. Sentiment still had a place in baseball

But when it came to a choice between sentiment and business, business won after the 1899 season ended. The National League decided that having 12 teams was unwieldy and not very profitable — eight teams was better. Three of the teams perennially lost money — the ones in Cleveland, Louisville, and Washington — and there was a fight over which ballclub should be the fourth to die. The owner of the New York Giants, who was a bigwig in Tammany Hall, wanted to get rid of the Brooklyn team, to reduce the local competition. But Brooklyn had won the pennant, and the ballclub had some political smarts itself. Charley Ebbets, a part-owner, was a city councilman and a cog in Brooklyn's Democratic machine, a young gentleman on the rise, with the silky skills of a politician. So when the Tammany man couldn't touch Brooklyn, he went for the next best target, Brooklyn's partner in the syndicate, the Orioles. Suddenly, Baltimore had lost its National League franchise. It was no longer a major league city.

That was the first of three times in three years that New York whipped Baltimore in the business of baseball. In baseball, too, Baltimore was becoming a branch town. The next time was in 1902. The American League had begun in 1901 and placed franchises in three of the cities that the National League had abandoned, including Baltimore (and Washington and Cleveland). John McGraw, again, was the player-manager and a part-owner of this new team, which took the abandoned and market-tested name of the Baltimore Orioles. Joe Kelley was back as a player and also as a part-owner. Another part-owner was Joe Kelley's father-in-law, who was the Democratic political boss in Baltimore. Together they held 51 percent of the stock. One day in July of 1902, at the Stafford Hotel in Baltimore, which is now an apartment house for students at the University of Baltimore, McGraw and Kelley and Kelley's father-in-law sold their stock to the owners of the New York Giants of the National League. So for a day or two, the New York Giants of the National League owned a majority of the stock in the Baltimore Orioles of the American League. They released the best of the club's players and signed four of them themselves, including two who ended up in the Hall of Fame—Iron Joe McGinnity, the dominating and sturdy pitcher, who could pitch both ends of a doubleheader, and Roger Bresnahan, the great catcher. John McGraw became the manager of the Giants.

The third time that New York ruined Baltimore occurred after the end of the 1902 season. Ban Johnson, the ambitious president of the American League, had stepped in and assumed control of the Orioles. He refused to sell the ballclub to the minority owners, who wanted it, and at the end of the season it became evident why. The American League had eight teams, but none of them was in New York, and how could a league call itself a major league without a team in New York? So when the 1902 season ended, Ban Johnson moved the A.L. Orioles to New York City, to Manhattan, where they were named the Highlanders and later the Yankees. The Yankees, that is, used to *be* the Orioles. In the course of four years, Baltimore gave rise—life, really—to all three of the major league teams in New York. Baltimore lost its only major league team and didn't get another one for 52 years. This was the business of baseball a century ago.

The business of baseball also overtook Wee Willie Keeler. At the beginning of his career, he would tell his teammates how amazed he was that he was being paid to play baseball, that he would pay *them* if that's what it took to get onto the field. That didn't last long. He held out before the 1895 seasons and at other times too. Then in 1903, when he was playing for Brooklyn, the New York Highlanders offered him more money—$10,000—than a ballplayer had ever been paid before. Willie Keeler had just hurt his shoulder, tumbling out of a wagon in California. As a fielder and except for one season as a batter, he would never be the same. Surely he knew this, but was he going to say no to $10,000? Nobody would. Already the Highlanders, the future Yankees, had the biggest payroll, and for Willie Keeler, this was innocence lost. Nobody should think worse of him, for living in the real world, but it certainly changed him, and not for the better. So it goes.

Baseball has been a reflection of American life from its beginning, always incorporating the spirit of the times as the Orioles did in adopting scientific play, getting swept up in business shenanigans, and seizing the main chance — all common in the nation at the end of the nineteenth century. You could understand what was going on in the country by understanding what was going on in baseball. There was a semblance of democracy on the field and in the grandstands where working men sat next to titans of industry and women turned up too. There were ladies' days, and a ladies' section in the grandstand, without beer. It was a game for everyone.

Parts of it have changed, but not as much as one would think. Ballplayers jumped to new teams for more money and teams moved around too. Back then there was talk about not having the pitcher bat — the DH without the extra batter. The rules change occasionally, the stadiums come and go — and go retro — but the game doesn't change, not really. The number of zeroes has changed in the paychecks and in the size of the crowds. Players cheat with steroids instead of with slivers of soap in the dirt. But the owners still act like owners and the players like players. Consider part of a Baltimore *Morning Herald* editorial in 1901: "A quarter century ago this sport was simple, clean, easily enjoyed, free of selfishness and guile. Today, alas! it has fallen into evil ways, become the tool of greed, the victim of hucksters." 6 In the 1890s, just like the 1990s, the owners acted like owners and the players acted like players and the fans were basically an afterthought. It was no prettier then than today — and it was equally reflective of American life.

Learning about baseball a century ago can change how you feel about baseball now. It makes you more forgiving, for one thing, about all the bad things that go on now. You can hear about something awful and shake your head, but then you realize — hey, baseball survived it all before, and it will again.

3

The Birth of Modern Baseball

Frank Deford

Looking back on America twenty-five years after the turn of the last century the historian Mark Sullivan noted there were "minor distinctions" of that earlier period. There was "a national holiday known as Thanksgiving, rocking chairs, a greater fastidiousness about personal cleanliness as measured by the commonness of bathtubs, ice water, pie, New England boiled dinner, chewing gum" and two games. One was poker, "a diversion indigenous to this nation and containing definite elements of the interplay of psychology not found in ordinary cards." The other was baseball, "a game calling for unusually quick reactions intellectually, and prompt and easy co-operation muscularly."

There was a craze for two other sports at that time, too—croquet and ping-pong—but Sullivan didn't choose to mention them. It was very important to Americans that our games would not only be amusing, but also require inordinate intelligence. Listen to what a Baltimore newspaper at the time said about the heroes that played the game:

> The fin de siecle players must possess a high order of brains, must be of correct habits, have plenty of ambition and be possessed of a certain docility, an evenness of temper such as will insure proper discipline and the frictionless working together of the whole team.

Baseball had become what was called "the American national game" because it took brains to go with brawn, and teamwork. Often anything but docile and even-tempered as individual players, the game required that they play well together. American games were team games. And they were ours—all developed here in North America, just as the individual sports came from England.

Moreover, of all of our major institutions, sport has changed the least. Virtually all our major American sports came to flower in the last quarter of the nineteenth century, when industrialization, immigration, and the great move to cities took place. Baseball, football, basketball, boxing, tennis, golf, horse racing—all became popular then. The only major contemporary modern sports that weren't in place were ice hockey and automobile racing, both awaiting advancing technology. Why didn't soccer catch on in the United States when it was becoming the world game in almost every country. It's a shame de Tocqueville was no longer around to explain why. Perhaps our football developed out of the original football because it was more complicated. Perhaps soccer has too many unsatisfying ties. Americans have long disparaged ties in that famous phrase: a tie is like kissing your sister. Maybe Americans preferred baseball and football because they required more proficiency than soccer (and cricket)

It was baseball that became the number-one American sport, football number two. Both sports grew up at virtually the same time. They were on parallel tracks, and baseball surged ahead. Baseball was accepted as a professional enterprise as early as 1869, while football remained not only a school game, but an upper-class private school game. And while football could be mean and nasty even then, baseball was much more of what it came to be called: a national pastime. At a time when most Americans were working long hours six days a week, usually at hard strenuous labor, who had the spunk left to go out in their spare time to block and tackle other people. The other great American words that were often used in sport a century ago were ginger, pluck, and moxie. Baseball incorporated them all for the working man, farm and city alike.

There was another reason why baseball surged ahead of football. Only the rich college boys had the time and energy for football. This was a major reason why it failed to become a professional sport for so long. It was considered ungentlemanly for a college man to play a game for money. Walter Camp of Yale, who was the godfather of American football, explained it in a florid fashion:

> You don't need your boy "hired" by anyone. If he plays, he plays as a gentleman, and not as a professional. He plays for victory, not for money; and whatever bruises he may have in the flesh, his heart is right, and he can look you in the eye as a gentleman should.

Unfortunately, there are some things in the world that just don't work. Communism, for example. Giving a small child a goldfish to take care of. And amateurism, playing only for the love of the game-amo, amas, amateur. No matter how much somebody may love playing a sport, there is no logical reason why he can't also get paid playing it. People also love to sing and dance and act, but we don't expect singers, dancers, and actors to perform for free. Or writers, thank God. Only athletes.

The myth grew up that the ancient Greek Olympians competed as amateurs. Nonsense. They would have thought you goofy to ask them to practice for years and play just to win a laurel wreath. Greek athletes were rewarded with cash on the barrel, real estate, deferments, and women. The idea of amateurism — which the Frenchman, Baron de Coubertin, who revived the Olympics in the modern era latched onto, came from the British upper classes, who pretty much dreamed up the idea to keep sports to themselves. If you weren't paid to play, then only the rich could play. Amateurism was originally, and effectively, exclusionism. The American upper classes adapted it to some of their sports—notably football and tennis—while other sports, like golf and baseball, accepted professionals from the get-go.

This is not to say that college football players played in any half-hearted fashion. On the contrary, they went at it with so much passion they literally killed for old alma mater. In 1905, with a relatively small number of boys playing the game, eighteen were killed in the U.S. Teddy Roosevelt was so appalled that he called representatives from what was then the Big Three of athletics as well as academics—Harvard, Princeton, and Yale—down to the White House and essentially ordered them to either clean up the game or he would make sure it was abolished. Football was so manly and had so many noble qualities associated with its players that it survived to thrive as the great collegiate game.

Baseball, meanwhile, was played hard and was full of chicanery and devilment, but it was honest after its fashion. It was not embarrassed about being professional. The first openly pro team, the Cincinnati Red Stockings, were in business barely after the conclusion of the Civil War. Soon thereafter whole leagues began to bloom.

Its organizational principles and much of its heritage were quickly put in place. Trades of players, the reserve clause, no free agency, unions and strikes, major and minor leagues, large-market and small-market teams all came along early. So did beer at the ballpark, especially in cities with a large German population. Brewery barons caught on quickly that games played in the sunshine made the ideal place to sell their suds to the fans (then called "cranks"), sitting out in the bleachers (so-named because the hot sun whitened the wooden planks).

The Germans were so very important in baseball. Because they tended to meld easily into society, and intermarried with the Anglo-Saxons, their presence was not as obvious as other immigrants even though they were by far the largest ethnic group in nineteenth century America. Despite the modern Teutonic reputation for aggression, the Germans didn't care for the most violent sport—boxing. But they loved baseball. Many of its early players were called "Dutch," derived from deutsch. It was the German spirit of conviviality that drove their affection for certain sports.

But it was the Irish who came to dominate baseball, just as they did boxing. Sport is always the way up for every nationality and race at the bottom of the social ladder. The Irish were no different in the nineteenth century than would African-American and Hispanic-Americans be in the twentieth and twenty-first centuries. Their presence produced somewhat of a conflict, though. Just as the Irish players proved what a democratic sport our national game was, it also meant our national game was ruled by people who a great many Americans thought weren't truly American. At a time when the Catholic-

Protestant split was like the Sunni-Shite division today, the Irish were theologically and cultural suspicious. The sporting press more genteelly called them "The Sons of Erin."

The Sons of Erin first came to prominence in boxing and there was nothing genteel about the sport that was banned in most states, or its first great champion, the Boston Strongboy, John L. Sullivan. The Great John L. would quaff prodigious amounts of bourbon from beer steins, and upon entering any saloon would bellow out: "I can lick any sonuvabitch in the house." The Boston Irish loved him, gave him a great belt studded with diamonds, and cheered him in rhyme now lost to the sporting world:

> His colors are the Stars and Stripes.
> He also wears the green
> And he's the greatest slugger that
> The ring has ever seen
> No fighter in the world can beat
> Our true American.
> The champion of all champions,
> John L. Sullivan

Just as the Great John L. was the first national boxing superstar, another Irish hero, Mike Kelly, was probably the first true baseball icon. Some even say that he inspired *Casey at the Bat*, which was written in 1888 by a Harvard man named Ernest Thayer. Grandly subtitled, *A Ballad of the* Republic, it became the most popular poem ever written in the United States. Whether or not he was the basis for mighty Casey, Kelly was always called King Kelly. The Boston Beaneaters paid the princely sum of $10,000 to buy his contract from the Chicago White Stockings.

Unlike Sullivan, Kelly was a smoothy. He favored London-tailored suits, a tall silk hat, jeweled ascot and sharply-pointed patent leather shoes. His Boston fans gave him a carriage with two white horses so that he might go to the park in style. Once there, they would cry out in unison:

> Slide, Kelly, Slide
> Slide, Kelly on your belley
> Slide, Kelly, slide

And the King did. He also invented the hook slide and could be counted on for all sorts of bending of the rules. But he was a fine hitter, a true star. Unfortunately, for all his stylishness, King Kelly was as familiar with John Barleycorn as John L. Sullivan. He was dead at the age of thirty-six.

Meanwhile, in expansive New York, baseball languished. The owner of its team was a despised cheapskate, the team a laughingstock when institutional popularity counted so much to the nation's largest city. Once Brooklyn and the other boroughs were consolidated with Manhattan in 1898, the city's population soared to almost three and a half million. Only London in all the world was larger, but New York used four times the amount of electricity. The first subway opened for business in 1904 and in the following year there were seventy-eight thousand automobiles as well as an above-ground railroad that carried more passengers than all the other steam trains in North and South America combined. New York also had the world's largest hotel and Macy's opened in 1902 while new theatres were springing up. Longacre Square became Times Square in 1904, the first ball dropped in 1908.

Manhattan was also literally the most crowded and cosmopolitan place on the face of the earth at the end of the nineteenth century. Thirty-seven percent of New Yorkers were foreign-born, another 39 percent had at least one foreign-born parent. Something like eight hundred thousand Germans were in the city, almost three hundred thousand Irish and more than 200,000 Italians, sixty thousand blacks, and perhaps seven hundred thousand Jews from all nations. Most stage comedy was ethnic; so too were the humorous newspaper columns. Half a million people jammed together in one square mile on the Lower East Side, mostly crammed into six-story tenements called "dumbbells." It could be beastly hot, but somehow people laughed and played. And every mother's son took up the American national game of baseball, chucking whatever would pass for a ball over and around the two thousand pushcarts that filled the slum streets.

Two things happened then to make New York the center of the baseball universe, and thus to truly make baseball the lord of the sports realm. First, an ex-sports writer named Ban Johnson decided to create a competitor for the only major league—the National. What Johnson created was the American League, and soon he conspired to move the Baltimore Oriole franchise to New York, where the team was named the Highlanders because its stadium was built on a hill. The team subsequently became somewhat better known under a new nickname, the Yankees.

And two players—complete opposites—found their way to the New York National League team, the Giants. Together they made baseball the true national pastime. One was a tough little Irishman who had been one of the stars of the Orioles—John L. McGraw, who now managed as well as played, was known, to his disgust, as Muggsy. The other was a Presbyterian farm boy who had actually gone to Bucknell College, named Christy Mathewson. They—Muggsy and Matty—changed everything in New York, and by extension in American sport.

Muggsy was only 5-feet-7 ... maybe. His arms were so short his cuffs came down to his palms before he became wealthy enough to have custom made clothes made. He came from nothing, was virtually an orphan, the classic Horatio Alger American. Most of his family was wiped out by a diphtheria epidemic when he was a child. His education ended when he was about twelve, but he later went to college, at what is now St. Bonaventure in the off-season, becoming quite an educated man. When the Giants won twenty-six games in a row in 1914—still the major league record—the players decided

Christy Mathewson warms up at the Polo Grounds (Prints and Photographs Division, Library of Congress).

to give their manager a gift to celebrate the feat. They gave him the collected works of William Shakespeare. The Little Napoleon was a great leader and a world traveler. Once he had a *tête-à-tête* with George Bernard Shaw. A charmed Shaw remarked: "At last, I have met the one true American."

Off the field McGraw was a devout Catholic and the softest touch in the world. Any broke old ball player could count on Muggsy for a loan, walking around money. He was incredibly loyal. He named a succession of bull Terriers Truxton after a town he came from in upstate New York. Every morning when he was home, he would have the same breakfast of scrambled eggs, bacon, toast, coffee, and he would give a little to his dog, and, thereby to start the day, cry out: "It's Truxton against the world."

In the world of baseball Muggsy McGraw was profane, vindictive, vengeful, and downright cruel on the playing field or when he was in his cups. He was what was called a mucker in those days, a behavior that took a bad sport to another power. One umpire said: "McGraw starts each day by eating gunpowder and washing it down with warm blood." He would indeed sharpen his spikes before a game, the better to employ them as weapons.

At Baltimore, he started on the Orioles with four other great Irish players. Hughie Jennings was a coal miner's son who ended up with a law degree. Wee Willie Keeler was only 5-feet-4½, but he could do what he boasted: "Keep your eye clear & hit 'em where they ain't." Keeler, the right fielder, would hide extra baseballs in the tall grass so that he could pick up a spare if a hit got by him. Joe Kelley, the left fielder, was powerful for that time, and also, so hand-

Manager John McGraw in 1914 during a pregame warm-up at the Polo Grounds (Prints and Photographs Division, Library of Congress).

some the he would occasionally pull out a mirror to inspect his visage between pitches. Wilbert Robinson, known as Uncle Robbie, was a jovial catcher, ice to McGraw's fire. All made the Hall of Fame, and they revolutionized baseball by perfecting what Burt Solomon describes so well as the inside game.

As manager-player McGraw loved tough guys and quirky ones, thinking he could handle anybody. He kept bringing back a great ladies man named Turkey Mike Donlan — so called, because it was said, Turkey Mike could strut sitting down. His greater *bête noire* was one called Bugs Raymond, who once left the bullpen, went across the street to a saloon, traded the ball for booze, and arrived drunk on the mound. Once in the minors Bugs bragged he could drink two bottles of bourbon, eat an entire turkey and pitch and win a double-header, which he did.

McGraw also egged on opponents and fans. Fans would hurl everything from produce to rocks to umbrella spears at Muggsy and his players. He delighted in it all, and was constantly fighting, being thrown out of games and suspended. In 1909, the National League President shot himself to death — largely because of his disputes with the Giants' manager.

He was also a raconteur, good company, great manager, and was stubbornly spiteful. One off-season, he made $3000 a week in vaudeville, just telling stories. this was by far the highest amount paid anyone on the stage. Imagine Tiger Wood making a movie and getting paid more than Tom Cruise. Still, he was a better manager. Within two years after he took over the worst team in baseball at the turn of the century he made it the best. But he refused to play the champions of the American League in 1904 because

3—The Birth of Modern Baseball

John McGraw, second from right, and Christy Mathewson, right, in warm-up coats before a 1914 game (Prints and Photographs Division, Library of Congress).

he hated its President, Ben Johnson, so much. So, there was no World Series that year.

The Giants would play in one soon because McGraw had the best pitcher in baseball who also happened to be his antithesis as a human being, Christy Mathewson. As a baseball couple they were the classic embodiment of opposite attraction. Matty was a collegian in a sport which had few enough high school graduates and a time when only 6 percent had high school diplomas. He was our first All American boy, at least the first flesh-and-blood one. The first one in sports was the fictional Frank Merriwell of the dime novels, who was both a paragon and a great doer of daring deeds. The best you could call an American boy was "he's a regular Frank Merriwell."

And Christy Mathewson was a regular Frank Merriwell — or over time, maybe Frank Merriwell became a regular Christy Mathewson. On one occasion, when Matheson slid home in a cloud of dust, blinding the umpire, he asked Matty to call the play. He called himself out. Why would you do that? asked the catcher, dumbfounded. "Because I am a church elder," Matty replied.

Mathewson was not only a baseball star at Bucknell, but also the best field-goal kicker in the country, a basketball stalwart, an A student — 96 in Analytical Chemistry and German, 94 in Tactitus, 93 in Horace. He played in the school band, sang in the glee club, wrote poetry, participated in the Latin Philosophical Club, was class historian, and, of course, class president.

The Giant team that Mathewson joined was the worst in the major leagues in 1900, but as soon as McGraw arrived he blossomed — winning thirty games regularly, leading the league. In 1905, when the Giants won the National League again, and this time McGraw was forced to play the American League champions, Mathewson led the victory — New York's first world Championship — by pitching three shut-outs over the Philadelphia Athletics in only six days. It's a feat no one has or ever will duplicate.

But, more important, Mathewson was the first sports idol. He changed he way we think about professional athletics. As that first all-American boy, he was truly clean cut. Millions of American boys stopped wearing mustaches just because Matty didn't have one. He wrote books, even wrote a short-lived Broadway comedy, appeared on the vaudeville stage and in movie shorts. He was a checkers champion, an ace bridge player. He endorsed all sorts of products and was generally accepted as the fourth most famous man in America after two Presidents — Teddy Roosevelt and William Howard Taft, and William Jennings Bryan, who ran for the presidency three times. Perhaps most important, other college men followed Mathewson into the game. If baseball was honorable enough for Matty, it was fine for me too.

Even Muggsy adored Matty. McGraw and Mathewson became such good friends, that they, the mucker and the Merriwell, actually lived together, with their wives, for a year in the same apartment. Can you imagine any other manager living with their star player? And their wives? Mathewson's only child was born the next year. He named him John, after McGraw. John Christopher Mathewson.

It was also in 1908 that a song writer named Jack Norworth, famous for *Harvest Moon* and *Meet Me in Apple Blossom Time* looked out of the window of a train and saw a sign that said "Base Ball Today — Polo Grounds." Norworth had never seen a baseball game in his life, but he promptly dashed off a song that is, next to our patriotic hymns and "Happy Birthday," the best known song in America. Amazingly, even after this great success, Norworth still never bothered to go see a ball game for another thirty-three years. Wasn't he just a wee bit curious?

Sadly, Mathewson was gassed in World War One. He didn't have to go. He was thirty-eight years old. But he volunteered, and he was never well again. He had no chance to fight tuberculosis when that attacked him. He died at forty-five, during the 1925 World Series between the Pirates and Senators. The next day at Forbes Field, both teams, wearing black armbands, marched out to centerfield, where the flag was at half staff. The band played the national anthem, but muffled. And then, as the players started back to begin the game, many in the crowd began spontaneously to sing the old hymn, *Nearer My God to Thee.* A few days later, McGraw was a pallbearer when Matty was buried at Bucknell, and, then, when McGraw himself died a few years later, Mathewson's only son accompanied the casket to its final resting place, back in Baltimore.

It was the 1920s that is called the Golden Age of Sport, but, in fact, that was icing on the cake. The incubator of modern sports was the turn of the century, when American cities and American teams came together and contributed so much to what is American society today.

4

Tinker to Evers to Chance: Poetry in Motion

PAUL D. STAUDOHAR

Don't let anyone tell you the poet's pen isn't mightier than the official scorer's pencil.
— Warren Brown, Chicago sportswriter[1]

Chicago Cubs shortstop Joe Tinker, second baseman Johnny Evers, and first baseman Frank Chance formed the most famous double play combination in the history of baseball. They played on the finest Cub teams ever, and were elected to the Hall of Fame in 1946. Some historians believe that they do not belong there because their individual statistics were not remarkable. Others think the players deserve the honor because of the winning tradition and intangibles they brought to the game.

The names Tinker, Evers, and Chance first appeared in a box score in the September 16, 1902 *Chicago Tribune*.[2] The players remained together on the team until 1912, winning four pennants and two World Series. This essay examines the great Cub teams of that era and the careers of the three players, including the celebrated "Bonehead" Merkle incident. Also of interest is the famous poem, written in 1910 by a New York sportswriter, that immortalized "Tinker to Evers to Chance" and was important in getting them into Cooperstown as a trio.

The Times and the Team

The period of the greatest Cub glory took place in the midst of the dead-ball era. Until Spalding developed the cork-centered ball and Babe Ruth came along with his prodigious home run exploits, baseballs were rarely hit out of the park. Balls often remained in play for long periods, getting dirty and scuffed. The playing fields were not well manicured as they are today. The nature of the game emphasized manufacturing runs one at a time rather than playing for the big inning. Offensive strategies featured the sacrifice bunt, bunting for a hit, the squeeze play, base stealing, and the hit-and-run. Thus, Joe Tinker hit only 31 home runs in his regular-season career of 15 years, Frank Chance had only 20 in 17 years, and Johnny Evers a mere 12 over an 18-year span. Even Hall of Famer Frank "Home Run" Baker, one of the great sluggers of the day, hit only 96 round trippers during 13 years in the big-leagues.

Gloves were small by modern standards, which kept fielding percentages low. After 1900 a variety of trick pitches came into vogue, particularly the spitball. Application of saliva, tobacco juice, or slippery elm to a baseball or the pitcher's fingers caused the ball to twist and dip.[3] Some pitchers cut or scruffed balls with their belt buckles or sharp instruments concealed in their gloves, inducing the ball to perform unusual movements as it approached batters. Not surprisingly, pitchers dominated the game and batting averages were low.

The Cubs played all their home games during the Tinker-Evers-Chance years in the West Side Grounds, located at Polk and Lincoln (now Wolcott) streets. Opened in 1893, this 16,000-seat two-tiered wooden structure was also home to the city's black team, the Chicago American Giants. The ballpark was torn down in 1920, but by then the Cubs had already moved to what later became known as Wrigley Field, on the north side of town at Clark and Addition Streets. That ballpark was constructed in 1914 for Chicago's team in the rival Federal League. It was originally called Weeghman Park, for team owner Charles Weeghman, a Chicago restauranteur. After the Federal League folded in 1915, Weeghman purchased the Cubs and moved them to his ballpark.[4]

Chicago was an original member of the National League, which was founded in 1876 by William A. Hulbert, a successful grain and coal merchant, who became the team's president from 1876–82. Chicago won the league's first pennant behind the strong pitching of Albert Goodwill Spalding, who founded the prominent sporting goods company that made the league's baseballs. Under the leadership of the great player-manager Adrian "Cap" Anson the club won five more pennants, but by the dawn of the twentieth century it enjoyed little success on the field.

Until the Cubs began to win again, after Frank Chance became manager, attendance was not always high at the West Side Grounds. For the mid–September 1902 game in which Tinker, Evers, and Chance had their first 4–6–3 double play, only 260 fans were in attendance. But there is nothing like winning pennants to put customers in the seats, which the Cubs did in 1906, 1907, 1908, and 1910.

The Cubs' great rivals during these years were the New York Giants, managed by the redoubtable "Little Napoleon," John McGraw, and the Pittsburgh Pirates under player-manager Fred Clarke. Pitching was a big part of the Cubs' success against these formidable opponents. Mordecai "Three Finger" Brown was the ace of the staff. His nickname derives from an accident when he was a seven-year old farm boy. He mangled his hand in a feed chopper, losing his right index finger and damaging his pinkie. With just three usable fingers, one

Cubs first baseman Frank Chance warms up at the Polo Grounds (Prints and Photographs Division, Library of Congress).

of them crooked from a later mishap, Brown turned his disability into ability by developing a natural screwball that fooled batters. "Big Ed" Reulbach, Orval Overall, and Jack Pfiester were also outstanding pitchers for the Cubs during the pennant-winning years. Pfiester was known as "Jack the Giant Killer" because of his success against the New Yorkers.

There were other fine players on the team. Third baseman Harry Steinfeldt was an above average player who hit .268 over his career. The catcher was Johnny Kling, arguable the best in the league, who some say belongs in the Hall of Fame. A defensive specialist as well as a capable hitter, Kling had a lifetime batting average of .272. Of the Cub outfielders, the best was hard-hitting Frank "Wildfire" Schulte. He won the first ever National League Most Valuable Player Award in 1911 (then called the Chalmers Award, which was a car donated by automobile manufacturer Hugh Chalmers). Schulte led the league that year with 21 home runs, 21 triples, and 121 RBI's. Outfielders Jimmy Slagle and Jimmy Sheckard came over in trades and were solid players.

The owner and president of the Cubs from 1906–14 was Charles W. Murphy. A former newspaperman and baseball press agent, Murphy managed to get Charles P. Taft to bankroll his purchase of a majority interest in the team. Taft, the owner of the *Cincinnati Times-Star*, was the elder half-brother of future U.S. President William Howard Taft, himself a real baseball nut. Murphy was disliked by his players and fellow team owners. He was referred to as "freewheeling, impulsive, turbulent, contentious, and loud mouthed."[5] He was also considered cheap and of questionable integrity. These traits brought him into frequent conflict with Frank Chance, who especially resented Murphy's unwillingness to spend money to acquire talented players.

Frank Selee, the Cubs' manager before Chance, deserves credit for creating the famous trio and acquiring other key players. During the 1880s Selee had managed Boston to five National League pennants. Chance was a catcher initially. Tinker was a third baseman when he came up, and Evers a shortstop. It was Selee, a shrewd judge of talent, who converted Chance to a first baseman, assigned Evers to second, and put Tinker at short.[6] Thus, each of the players was at a new position. The adjustment was difficult, especially for Tinker who made 73 errors while Evers made 51 and Chance 37 in the first years at their new positions.

Johnny Evers turns a double play with Joe Tinker in the background (Prints and Photographs Division, Library of Congress).

The Cubs were known as the "brawl team," as they fought with opponents, umpires, fans, and among themselves. On September 13, 1905, the Cubs were playing an exhibition game in Bedford, Indiana. In the middle of the game Tinker and Evers began swinging at each other near second base. The team dressed at the hotel in the custom of the day. (It wasn't until the following year that Brooklyn Dodgers' owner Charlie Ebbets got the league to require that all parks stall dressing rooms.) The players were going to take horse-drawn taxis to the ballpark. Evers got into a cab by himself and drove off, leaving Tinker and others on the sidewalk. This irritated Tinker and when he reached the field he began remonstrating to Evers, which led to the fight.[7] After this incident the two agreed to not speak to each other, because it often made them angry when they did.

Although they didn't speak to each other for two years, Tinker and Evers never lacked ability to communicate on the field. Their on-field chemistry translated into knowing what each would do and was capable of doing. They had private signals for practically every move they made to outwit batters and base runners.⁸ They were well known for their ability to turn double plays at crucial times. They fielded well, threw the ball accurately, and had precision teamwork.

1906

The Cubs won the National League pennant for the first time in 20 years, setting records for total number of wins (116, with 36 losses), most consecutive wins (14), highest winning percentage (.763), shutouts (30), and fewest errors (194). The 1906 Cubs are considered one of the best teams ever. The Seattle Mariners won 116 games in 2001 to tie the record, but because they played more games the Cubs' winning percentage remains supreme. The club got stellar years from their pitchers. Mordecai Brown went 26–6 with an ERA of 1.04 and 10 shutouts. Carl Lundgren was 17–6 (2.21 ERA), Ed Reulbach 19–4 (1.65 ERA), Jack Pfiester 20–8 (1.56 ERA), and Orval Overall 12–3 (1.88 ERA). Harry Steinfeldt led the team in hitting at .327, Frank Chance batted .319, and Johnny Kling .312.

The World Series opponent was the plucky Chicago White Sox, who had won their last pennant in 1902. The Sox were led by manager and center fielder Fielder (his real name) Jones and pitcher Ed Walsh. Both teams had drawn large crowds during the season, which was the most financially successful in baseball history.⁹

The White Sox were 3–1 underdogs for the Series and were known as the "Hitless Wonders" because they batted only .230, lowest in the league, and hit just six home runs during the season. Nonetheless, the Sox won the first game 2–1, as 20-game winner Nick Altrock bested Brown. Reulbach won game two for the Cubs by a score of 7–1. Game three saw future Hall of Famer Walsh pitch a 3–0 shutout, giving the Sox the Series lead, but the Cubs evened it up on Brown's magnificent two-hit shutout. The sole Cubs' run was scored in the seventh inning when Chance singled, was bunted to third by Steinfeldt and Tinker, and scored on Evers' single. The White Sox regained the Series lead with an 8–6 victory and then won it all the following day by a score of 8–3, in one of the greatest upsets in baseball history. Tinker hit only .167, Evers .150, and Chance .238.

1907

In 1907 the Cubs won 107 games and captured the flag by a 17-game margin. The pitchers hurled 32 shutouts and had a collective ERA of 1.73. Brown was 20–6, Lundgren 18–7, Reulbach 17–4, Overall 23–8, and Pfiester 15–9. Johnny Kling was outstanding again at the plate. The great infield led the way as the team topped the league in fielding, with Evers surpassing all fielders with

500 assists. The Cubs were 8–5 favorites over the Detroit Tigers, who were led by a youthful Ty Cobb, a .350 batter during the regular season with 116 RBI's.[10] Complementing Cobb were future Hall of Famers, center fielder "Wahoo" Sam Crawford and manager Hughie Jennings.

The first game ended in a 3–3 tie, called at the end of the 12th inning because of darkness. The Cubs were lucky to get the tie, which came in the ninth inning when Tiger catcher Charlie "Butch" Schmidt failed to hold on to a third strike that would have ended the game. After that, the Cubs went on to sweep the Tigers by scores of 3–1, 5–1, 6–1, and 2–0 in the finale behind Brown. Cobb got only four hits and batted .200. Tinker hit just .154 and Chance .214, but Evers hit safely seven times and batted .350. Steinfeldt led Cub batters at .470. The Cubs stole a record 18 bases during the Series, six by center fielder Jimmy Slagle.

1908

The 1908 season was a close race between the Cubs, Giants, and Pirates, with the Cubs finishing first at 99–55. Brown and Reulbach had their greatest seasons with records of 29–9 and 24–7. The Cubs made it two in a row over the Tigers in the World Series, winning four games to one. In the second game of the Series Overall pitched a four-hitter, and he blanked the Tigers on a three-hitter in game five. Brown pitched a four-hit shutout in game four.

The Series was something of an anticlimax, following the fever pitch excitement of the Cubs' tie-breaking, pennant-winning victory over the Giants, set up by "Bonehead" Merkle's ruinous gaffe, discussed below.[11] Cobb redeemed himself, batting .368 for the Series. But it was Johnny Evers' year, as he led the club in hitting during the season with a .300 average and duplicated his 1907 performance in the Series, batting .350. Chance did even better in the Series, at .421, while Tinker hit .263. In game two, Tinker's homer in the eighth inning of a scoreless game drove in the first two Cub runs in a 6–1 victory. This was the first home run hit in a World Series game in five years.

The Cubs became the first team to win consecutive championships, but it would be the last time they would win it all. Following the season Kling retired because he won the world pocket billiard championship as a professional. He also had a salary dispute with the club but returned to play in 1910.

1910

In 1909 the Cubs went 104–49, pitching 32 shutouts, but the Pirates of player-manager Fred Clarke and shortstop Honus Wagner won 110 games and the pennant. The Pirates then defeated the Tigers in the World Series.

In 1910 the Cubs won the pennant at 104–50, with a 13-game lead over the Giants. Brown was 25–13 and rookie Len "King" Cole went 20–4. In the last big hurrah for Chance's Cubs, they were defeated in the World Series by the Philadelphia Athletics, four games to one. Evers did not play because of a broken leg. Despite having to play without the services of Eddie Plank, one of the all-time best left-handed pitchers, Connie Mack's Athletics still had the strong arms of Chief Bender and Jack Coombs. The Cubs countered with their own great staff of Brown, Reulbach, and Overall.

Chance hit .353 and Tinker .333 in the Series, but future Hall of Famers Eddie Collins and Frank Baker of the Athletics performed even more brilliantly, batting .429 and .409. Coombs out pitched Brown 7–2 in the final game. Not until 1918 would the Cubs have another distinguished season, and the superlative run of winning pennants for Tinker, Evers, and Chance was over. The club won 92 games in 1911, finishing second to McGraw's Giants, but seemed to have lost its confidence. In 1912 and 1913 the club slipped to third place.

The Merkle Incident

On September 23, 1908, what was been called "the most famous play in baseball history" occurred in a game between the Cubs and Giants.[12] Tinker had homered off the great Giants' pitcher Christy Mathewson in the fifth inning, but the Giants tied the game at 1–1 in the sixth. In the ninth inning it appeared that Giants had won the game. With runners on first and third, Al Bridwell slapped a single to center. The runner on third, Harry "Moose" McCormick, crossed the plate but the runner on first, Fred Merkle, ran halfway to second base, then turned and headed for the clubhouse. Although what Merkle did was the custom of the day, it was a fatal mistake because unless he touched second base Bridwell could not be credited with a hit and McCormick could not score.

Bridwell's single was fielded by Art "Solly" Hofman, who initially had no interest in the ball, thinking the game was over. Evers screamed at Hofman to throw him the ball. He threw the ball toward the infield but over the head of Evers, who was ready to do a force play on the absent Merkle. Joe "Iron Man" McGinnity, the future Hall of Famer pitcher, was coaching at third base for the Giants. He fielded the overthrow and was promptly jumped on by Tinker and Evers. McGinnity broke loose and threw the ball into the seats behind third base where it was caught by a spectator. The Cubs' Floyd "Kid" Kroh knocked the spectator off the ball and tossed it to Tinker who threw it to Evers at second base for the force out on Merkle. In the confusion it was uncertain whether the ball that wound up in Evers' hands was the one that Bridwell hit in the first place.

But Evers claimed it was the same ball, and described its retrieval as follows:

I can see the fellow who caught it yet ... a tall stringy middle-aged gent with a brown bowler hat on. Steinfeldt and Floyd Kroh, a young pitcher we'd added to our staff during the summer, raced after him. "Gimme the ball for just a minute," Steinfeldt begged him. "I'll bring it right back." The guy wouldn't let go and suddenly Kroh solved the problem. He hit the customer right on top of that stiff hat, drove it down over his eyes and as the gent folded up, the ball fell free and Kroh got it. I was yelling and waving my hands out by second base and Tinker relayed it over to me and I stepped on the bag and made sure O'Day saw me.[13]

Meanwhile, Mathewson and other Giants were trying to get Merkle back on the field from the clubhouse so he could touch second base. But the deed was done, as Merkle was called out by umpire Hank O'Day. Three weeks earlier, when the Cubs were playing at Pittsburgh, the same play had occurred, in which a Pirate had failed to touch second base after a winning hit.[14] Evers had stepped on second base to force the absent runner but empire O'Day declared the game over. O'Day, however, remembered the incident, which was appealed by Cub president Charles Murphy to National League president Harry Pulliam. O'Day knew that baseball rules required the runner to touch second base (a run cannot score when the third out is forced out). So O'Day made the correct ruling on Merkle and declared that the game ended in a 1–1 tie. Pulliam, who had witnessed the play, ruled on appeal that O'Day's decision of a tie game would stand.

The regular season ended in a tie between the Cubs and Giants, so the National League's board of directors ordered that the tie game be replayed in New York. Mathewson was fresh and ready to face the Cubs. His record going into the game was 37–10. Yet, the Cubs won 4–2 and captured the pennant.[15] The crowd at the game was the biggest ever to see baseball. An estimated 250,000 persons were outside the Polo Grounds, many of them on Coogan's Bluff overlooking the field. Pfiester started for the Cubs but was relieved by Brown in the first inning. Brown won the game over Mathewson. The key blows were a triple by Tinker and doubles by Schulte and Chance. With three of Chicago's eight hits, Chance was the offensive hero.

Merkle's name would be forever associated with a bonehead play. This is a pity because he was 19 years old at the time and neither McGraw nor the team blamed him for losing the pennant. There were other games in which the Giants had opportunities to make up the difference. Merkle developed into a steady ballplayer for 16 years on teams that won five pennants. But like the Giants Fred Snodgrass, another fine ballplayer, who muffed as easy fly ball in 1912 that enabled the Boston Red Sox to win the World Series, Merkle is remembered for little else.

Frank Chance

Born in Fresno, California in 1877, Frank Leroy Chance briefly attended Washington College in Irvington, California where he studied to become a dentist. At six feet and 190 pounds Chance was good sized for a ballplayer and joined the Cubs in 1898, one year after the departure of Cap Anson, as a 20-year old catcher. Interestingly, in his first game his battery mate was future Hall of Fame pitcher Clark Griffith, and his first at bat was against a pretty fair Cleveland pitcher named Cy Young.[16] As a young player Chance acquired the nickname "Husk," because of his rugged appearance.

By 1902 Chance had converted to first base and what was to become his great team was beginning to take shape. Tinker came to Chicago that year from Portland in the Pacific Northwest League and Evers from Troy in the New York State League. Steinfeldt, the fourth member of the infield that would achieve such distinction, came from Cincinnati in a 1906 trade. In 1902 the name of the team was changed to the Cubs because of the large number of young players who came to the ballclub.[17] Prior to that time the team had gone by various nicknames, such as the White Stockings (a name later adopted by Chicago's American League team and shortened to the White Sox), Orphans, Spuds, and Colts.

Chance was considered a tough guy. A good boxer, he supposedly once brawled with heavyweight "Gentleman Jim" Corbett in a Broadway café. As a player he would defiantly crowd the plate and was often hit with pitched balls. Frequently beanings led to severe headaches, hearing loss, and missed games in the field. As player-manager from 1905–1912 Chance was a strict disciplinarian. He treated his players as adults, but did not like to be crossed. His managerial philosophy has been aptly described as "Do it my way or see me after the game under the stands."[18] Chance took over as manager from Frank Selee who resigned during the season because of tuberculosis, and led the club to a third place finish in 1905.

Aside from his tough exterior, Chance was something of an intellectual. He could have made a good living outside of baseball as a professional in dentistry, business, or other fields. His father had been a successful bankers. Chance wrote occasional articles for the *Chicago Tribune* and even penned a baseball romance novel in the style of Frank Merriwell and Clair Bee, called *The Bride and the Pennant*.[19]

Chance's lifetime batting average was .297 and he was an accomplished fielder. Fleet-footed, he stole 67 bases in 1903, still a Cub record, and 57 in 1906, both times leading the league. His managerial record with the Cubs was outstanding, at 768–389 for a .664 percentage. Chance finished first in the league on four occasions, second twice, and once in third place (not counting the partial season in 1905). He won two World Series and owned a one-tenth interest in the Cubs. Chance purchased this share in 1906 for $10,000 and sold it in 1912 for $140,000.[20] His moniker of "The Peerless Leader" was well deserved.

In 1913, as a result of a break with club owner Charles Murphy, Chance became manager of the New York Yankees. He remained their manager until 1915 when he resigned. A year later Chance purchased the Los Angeles club in the Pacific Coast League, becoming its player-manager. He returned to the major leagues in 1923 to manage the Boston Red Sox, shortly before his death from tuberculosis the following year.

Johnny Evers

John Joseph Evers (pronounced Ee-vers, not Ev-vers) was born in Troy, New York in 1881. At five feet nine and 140 pounds, he was small for a big-leaguer, but he had the prominent jaw of a fighter and a feisty temperament. Renowned poet Ogden Nash wrote this:

> E is for Evers,
> His jaw in advance;
> Never afraid
> To Tinker with Chance.[21]

The moody, trigger-tongued Evers was quick to trade insults with teammates and opponents alike, including pugnacious Giants' manager John McGraw. Although his lifetime batting average is not spectacular at .270, his value to the team was far greater. Evers was a good base stealer, with 49 thefts in 1906 and 46 in 1907, and he was excellent defensively.[22]

Evers was a very smart player who spent a lot of time reading the baseball rulebook (it is said that he kept it under his pillow at night). He also wrote a book on baseball technique with sportswriter Hugh Fullerton.[23] His knowledge of the game would serve him especially well in the Merkle incident. Evers' nickname was "The Crab," because of the way he scrambled for ground balls. Later in his career he was called "The Human Crab," because of his combativeness. Bill Wambsganss called him "a maniac on the field," and in 1911 Evers had a nervous breakdown that caused him to miss over 100 games.[24] Fullerton described him as "a bundle of nerves with the best brain in baseball."[25] Hall of Fame umpire Bill Klem called Evers "the toughest and meanest man I ever saw on a ball field.[26] Evers was also nicknamed "The Trojan" because he hailed from Troy, New York.

After Chance left to manage the Yankees, Evers became the Cubs' player-manager in 1913. He guided the club to an 88–65 record, good for third best in the league. Thinking the club was better than it finished, cantankerous owner Charles Murphy fired Evers. Ironically, his successor as manager was Hank O'Day, former umpire who had called Merkle out, and had managed Cincinnati in 1912.

Evers was traded to the Boston Braves, where in 1914 he helped the team win the pennant. He continued his World Series mastery by hitting .438, as the Braves became the first team to win four straight games without a loss or tie, defeating the Philadelphia Athletics. Boston's team was known as the "Miracle Braves," because it rose from last place in July to finish first by 10-½ games. Evers went from the Braves to the Philadelphia Phillies in 1917 but played little after that season.

In 1921 Evers returned to the Cubs as manager but gave way during the season to Bill Killefer, as the club finished a dismal seventh. In another strange twist of fate, Evers was expected to become a coach for Frank Chance, who was planning to become the manager of the White Sox. Chance's death intervened, however, leaving Evers to manage the Sox during the 1924 season. He later returned to the Braves to serve as assistant manager from 1929–32. Evers suffered a stroke in 1942 and died of a cerebral hemorrhage in 1947.

Joe Tinker

In 1880 Joseph Bert Tinker was born in Muscotah, Kansas. He played ball at five foot nine and 175 pounds and had a lifetime batting average of .263. With an excellent eye at the late, he drew a lot of walks. Tinker was a slick fielder with good range who led National League shortstops in fielding five times. Swift on the base paths, he averaged 28 stolen bases as a Cub and was the first player to steal home twice in one game, at Cincinnati in 1910.

Tinker played some of the best games against the bitter-rival Giants and was especially effective against legendary pitcher Christy Mathewson. In a memorable game in 1911 Tinker had two singles, a double, and a triple against "Matty," scoring three times and stealing home in a 8–6 Cub win.

Tinker is thought to have been baseball's first holdout, when at the start of spring training in 1909 he arranged a meeting with owner Charles Murphy and said he would not play unless he got a $1,000 raise. After listening carefully to Tinker's thoughtful sales pitch, Murphy told him that while everything he said was true, "Where would you be without Evers?"[27] Tinker settled for a $200 raise and when he told Evers about it, Evers said that Murphy had asked him, "Where would you be without Tinker?"[28]

A natty dresser, Tinker was a great hero in Chicago, endorsing products such as Joe Tinker Cigars and Colgan's chewing gum. He was light-hearted and ordinarily easy going, but he had a hot temper. He didn't look for trouble but wouldn't hesitate to fight if provoked. To the amazement of the public, the entrepreneurial Tinker became a big hit on vaudeville. His clever skits led to rave reviews in the newspapers and in *Variety*, and he considerable augmented his income. As a result, he decided to quite baseball in 1913 to perform exclusively on the stage, but changed his mind to return to the game.[29]

Following the 1912 season the Cubs traded Tinker to Cincinnati, where he served a year as player-manager. He hit .317 for the Reds but was nonetheless sold to Brooklyn. When he demanded $2,000 of the purchase price, Reds' owner Garry Hermann offered instead a stein of beer and a cask of pickles.[30] This prompted Tinker to jump to the then-forming Federal League, where he became the player-manager of the Chicago Whales (the club was originally known as the Federals) in 1914. He hit .269 for the pennant-winning Whales the following year, bolstered by his old teammate Mordecai Brown.

When the Federal league folded after just two seasons Tinker returned to the Cubs as player-manager. The team finished fifth and Tinker was released. For several years thereafter he was the manager and part owner of the Columbus club in the American Association. He moved to Florida where he did some land speculation, operated a billiard parlor, and owned a successful sports bar in Orlando after Prohibition was repealed. Tinker suffered from diabetes for many years and died in 1948 on the 68th birthday.

The Poem

Franklin P. Adams was a columnist for newspapers in New York, including the *Evening Mail* and the *World*. The Cubs-Giants rivalry was the most intense in baseball and the Chicago infield had come up with numerous rally-killing double plays against the New Yorkers. This gave Adams the idea for the poem titled "Baseball's Sad Lexicon," which would become almost as familiar to fans as Ernest L. Thayer's poem "Casey at the Bat" and Jack Norworth's song "Take Me Out to the Ball Game."

Although Adams wrote the poem to elicit sympathy for the Giants among his New York readers, he was actually a native Chicagoan and a Cubs fan. Adams dashed off the rhyme because he wanted to attend a game that day and the foreman in the *Evening Mail* composing room said he needed eight more lines to fill his column space. Here is what he wrote:

> These are the saddest of possible words:
>   "Tinker to Evers to Chance"
> Trio of bear cubs and fleeter than birds,
>   Tinker and Evers and Chance
> Thoughtlessly pricking our gonfalon bubble,
> Making a Giant hit into a double—
> Words that are weighty with nothing but trouble:
>   "Tinker to Evers to Chance."

The poem has often appeared in print with slight variations in words, arrangement, and punctuation, as writers of stories about it take poetic license. For example, "Thoughtlessly" has been changed to "Ruthlessly." The word "gonfalon" is used by Adams to refer to a flag or banner, signifying the pennant. The word "double" refers to a double play, thus turning a hit into two outs. Adams never thought the poem was anything special, but history has determined otherwise. There is little doubt that his lyrical inspiration is what got the trio admitted to Cooperstown in 1946. Although the players' qualifications may be debatable, their high honor points up some fundamental truths: baseball is show business, the players are the stars, and the poetry of the game can be powerful.

Do They Belong in the Hall of Fame?

None of the trio was outstanding in terms of batting average, slugging percentage, home runs, or RBI's. On the other hand, they played in the dead-ball era when these statistics were less relevant and where intangibles more often led to success. Undeniably the players were all smart, tough, capable competitors who played on some of the greatest teams ever. That they knew how to win counts for much.

Their statistics are at or near the bottom when compared to other Hall of Famers. Among shortstops, for example, Tinker's batting average of .263 exceeds only that of Rabbit Maranville (.258), Luis Aparicio (.262), and Ozzie Smith (.262). Among second basemen, Evers' batting average of .270 beats only that of Bill Mazeroski (.260). Frank Chance's average of .297 compares somewhat better among first basemen, with Harmon Killebrew (.256), Willie McCovey (.270), and Tony Perez (.279) all hitting lower. But these power hitters far exceeded Chance's slugging percentage.

Although the trio is known as the most celebrated double play combination ever, former New York sportswriter Charlie Segar found that from 1906 to 1909, at the pinnacle of their success, they combined for only 56 double plays that were scored 4-6-3 or 6-4-3.[31] Double plays were not included in the game's statistics until 1919.

Tinker to Evers to Chance		Evers to Tinker to Chance	
1906	8	1906	9
1907	9	1907	6
1908	8	1908	8
1909	6	1909	2
Totals	31		25

In 1910 Tinkers, Evers and Chance made 16 double plays together.[32] These numbers are surprisingly low, yet they are typical of the dead-ball era. The loosely wound balls varied in quality and could not be hit hard enough to facilitate a lot of double plays. Also, there were fewer runners on base in a typical game.

While the trio did not complete that many conventional double plays as a unit, they made twin killings in other combinations, e.g. 3-6-3, 4-6, 6-4, or unassisted. Over their careers with the Cubs, Tinker was involved in 585 double plays and Evers 525.[33] Data from *The Baseball Encyclopedia* show their double plays from 1906–1910, as follows:

Year	Team DP's	Tinker DP's	Evers DP's	Chance DP's
1906	100	55	51	71
1907	110	45	58	64

Year	Team DP's	Tinker DP's	Evers UP's	Chance DP's
1908	76	48	39	56
1909	95	49	29	43
1910	110	54	55	48
Totals	491	251	232	282

Only Tinker led the league in double plays at his position which he did only once.[34] Still, they were all well above average defensively and played with a marvelous level of spirit and intensity, which surely was an inspiration to their teammates. From 1904–1909 the Cubs ranked no less than third in double plays in the league. Bill James, who is well known for his statistical analyses of baseball, calls Tinker, Evers, and Chance "The guts of a great team," and says that all three belong in Cooperstown.[35] James compares the trio favorably to players in later eras who competed with a much livelier baseball.

The dead ball, trick pitches, small gloves, and poorly maintained infields kept batting and fielding averages low. Tinker had the lowest batting average of the three, yet James says that as an offensive player Tinker "is in the same class as most of the other Hall of Fame shortstops and better than several of them."[36] In contrast to nearly all other historians, however, James considers Chance to be the "least qualified" of the three, because he did not play regularly as often and never batted 500 times in a season.[37] But James acknowledges that when Chance did play he was superlative. It is his success as a manager of well-disciplined teams that were among the best ever that also makes Chance special.

The trio's enmity towards each other is legendary and, it appears, a manifestation of their implacable will to win. As player-manager, Chance rode his team mercilessly. When something went wrong on the field Tinker and Evers would berate each other and fight in the clubhouse after games. Their acrimonious relationship finally had a happy ending, however. In 1938 Evers was in Chicago where the Cubs were playing the Yankees in the World Series. Unknown to either man, Tinker was there as well. The old combatants, who had not seen each other for years, were scheduled to appear on the same broadcast. When they met they embraced, fighting back the tears.[38] They remained friends after that.

All things considered, Tinker, Evers, and Chance each deserves to be in the Hall of Fame. The fact that they were enshrined as a trio, however, underscores the magic of Franklin Adams' whimsical rhyme.

5

The Adventures of Spoke and Smoky Joe

TIMOTHY M. GAY

When he unpacked his gear for good in the Boston clubhouse in 1908, Tris Speaker found a kindred spirit and pal for life in teammate Joe Wood. Speaker, a Texan, may have been raised on the periphery of the Wild West, not far from the Chisholm Trail, but Wood was the genuine article — a real cowpoke.

Born in Kansas City in 1889, Wood grew up in southwestern Colorado just a short stagecoach ride from such primitive outposts as Lizard Head Pass and Slumgullion Gulch. Wood's dad was a noted trial lawyer, representing such high-profile clients as the Western Federation of Miners and the Missouri Pacific and Santa Fe railroads. But at heart Wood *pere* was an adventurer; he sounds like a character straight out of a Bret Harte tale.

Wood's old man couldn't resist the siren song of a gold rush, racing up to the Klondike in 1897 and later panhandling in Nevada and California. As Joe told Lawrence Ritter, his father returned from Alaska "with his legs frozen, Yukon diarrhea, and lots of great stories, but no gold."[1]

When Joe was in his mid-teens, the Woods moved in a covered wagon to Ness City, a town on the Kansas prairie not far from Dodge City. There, young Joe began playing for the Ness City town nine against such frontier villages as High Point, Ransom, Ellis, Bazine, Wa Keeney, and Scott City.

"The ball game between two rival towns was a big event back then, with parades before the game and everything," Wood told Ritter. "The smaller the town the more important their ball club was. Boy if you beat a bigger town, they'd practically hand you the key to the city. And if you lost a game by making an error in the ninth inning or something like that — well, the best thing to do was just pack your 'grip' and hit the road, 'cause they'd never let you forget it."[2]

Young Wood was impossibly handsome. Photographers loved his dark choirboy features. He had brooding brown eyes, impeccably groomed black hair, and a sculpted chin and nose.

His good looks helped him earn his first dollars as a professional ballplayer.

5—The Adventures of Spoke and Smokey Joe

In September 1906, one of the "Bloomer Girl" outfits came barnstorming through Kansas and lost a game to Ness City's young pitching prodigy. Some of the Bloomer Girls actually were of the distaff persuasion, but about half the squad consisted of young men dressed up as women. The Bloomer Girls' manager approached Wood about joining the team, telling Joe that with his baby face, he wouldn't need to wear a wig like the other fellows. "So I asked Dad if I could go," Wood remembered to Ritter. "He thought it was sort of unusual, but he didn't raise any objections. I guess it must have appealed to his sense of the absurd."[3]

Young Joe spent that fall barnstorming with the Bloomer Girls, then was spotted by a scout for Cedar Rapids in the Three-I League and signed a $90 a month contract in January 1907. But before the Three-I season began, the Cedar Rapids owner transferred Wood's contract to the Hutchinson Salt Packers of the Western Association. He won 20 games for Hutchinson, unleashing the fastball that became his trademark. After the 1907 season, he was sold to the Kansas City Blues in the American Association. The Red Sox began bird-dogging Wood early in the 1908 season, finally signing him that August. There he first met Speaker, who once again had reported to the Huntington Avenue Grounds as a late-season call-up.

It's easy to see why Speaker and Wood became such fast friends. They were two Westerners caught in a town and a clubhouse a long way from the frontier. The roommates quickly developed such a close bond that some viewed the relationship as haughty; in the years to come, it caused teammates in two clubhouses to bristle. With their put-up-or-shut-up swagger, Wood and Speaker never let people forget that they hailed from a mythic part of the country. All the qualities traditionally associated with frontiersmen—orneriness, defiance, quick-trigger tempers—Speaker and Wood had in abundance, or at least pretended to. And they almost never hesitated to lord those qualities over people.

They also didn't hesitate to press their views on racial and religious superiority. Speaker and Wood were white Anglo Saxon Protestants who deeply distrusted the papists who had come to dominate Boston politics and culture. They never felt welcomed in the city's immigrant world, choosing to live miles away in a boarding home in the seaside village of Winthrop. It's instructive that given a choice between socializing in working class taverns where they'd never have to buy a beer or in stodgy gentlemen's clubs where black or white tie was *de rigueur*, they chose the latter. "My mental image of Speaker and Wood back then is two guys dressed to the 'nines' going out to play snooker or bridge in some fancy club," says baseball historian Richard Johnson, the head of the Sports Museum of New England.[4]

Speaker's booming baritone voice dominated a clubhouse the way his arm and feet dominated a game. The Texan won Boston's centerfield job in 1909 and soon began rivaling Detroit's Ty Cobb for all-around brilliance. The Cobb-Speaker rivalry didn't end for another 19 years.

Tris played so shallow and with such élan that he was virtually a fifth infielder. Year after year, he led the American League in chances, putouts, and assists. Record keeping was erratic back then, but at least six times in his career — and perhaps as many as nine — Speaker recorded unassisted double plays, spearing line drives in shallow center and beating the retreating runner to second base. Babe Ruth, a teammate on the great championship squad of 1915, always said Speaker made more spectacular plays than any centerfielder he'd ever seen.

Tris earned his nickname, "Spoke," when teammates hollered "Speaker spoke! Speaker spoke" whenever he got on base. Spoke to this day has more career doubles — 793 — than any player in history. His .345 lifetime batting average puts him among the top seven hitters of all time. When Spoke hit .386 in 1916, his first year as a member of the Cleveland Indians, he became the only hitter between 1907 and 1919 to wrest a batting title away from the redoubtable Cobb. Speaker's batting average in '16 was a full 100 points better than the next-best hitter in Cleveland's lineup.

Joe Wood, as an outfielder for the Cleveland Indians, demonstrates his all-around athleticism (Prints and Photographs Division, Library of Congress).

The Red Sox's sale of Speaker to the Indians on the eve of the 1916 season — for a then-record $55,000 — created more furor at the time than the sale of Babe Ruth to the Yankees three years later. Boston fans loved the scrappy way that Speaker patrolled centerfield and ran the bases. And Spoke was a winner. He had transformed a mediocre club into the best team in baseball, winning the World Series in 1912 against the New York Giants and again in 1915 against the Philadelphia Phillies.

As Cleveland's player-manager, he led the '20 Indians to a World Series crown (over the Brooklyn Dodgers) in his first full year at the helm. He's considered one of early baseball's most resourceful managers. Speaker is credited with pioneering the platoon system and developing a strategy to take advan-

Tris Speaker takes a practice swing (Prints and Photographs Division, Library of Congress).

tage of righty-lefty pitching and hitting match-ups. He was ultimately elected to the Hall of Fame in the second wave of inductees in the late '30s.

Young Tris never backed down from a fight; young Joe Wood was every bit as feisty as his pal. The two Rebels weren't subtle about letting Catholics know the disdain they felt toward them. Many a quarrel in the Sox clubhouse featured religious epithets being tossed back and forth between the Bill Carrigan-led Catholic contingent, nicknamed in press accounts the "K. C.s," or the Knights of Columbus, and the Speaker-Wood Protestant faction, which labeled themselves the "Masons." Speaker, especially, reveled in showing teammates and hangers-on just how tough he was. He and the aptly nicknamed "Rough" Carrigan were constantly at loggerheads. In 1911, Spoke and Rough supposedly fought the clubhouse brawl to end all clubhouse brawls.

Speaker and Wood also reveled in abusing people who had the misfortune of being born with a different skin color. A *Boston Globe* article from spring training one year related an episode where Speaker and Wood unmercifully hounded a young black bus boy, taking great delight in humiliating him in a restaurant full of teammates and fans.[5]

Wood's nickname derived from a remark Paul Shannon of the *Boston Post* made while watching Joe's fastball blaze to the plate during spring training in 1909: "That fellow really throws smoke."[6] Before Wood's shoulder and elbow were damaged, he threw as hard as anyone before or since. Only a handful of pitchers in big league history have had a fastball that hopped like Wood's. Like most hurlers of his day, he whipped the ball sidearm after an abrupt leg kick, a motion that put enormous strain on his right elbow and shoulder.

His great rival Walter Johnson was once asked to compare his own velocity to Wood's. "Can I throw harder than Joe Wood? Listen, my friend, there's no man alive who can throw harder than Smoky Joe Wood," the Big Train declared. But Johnson also observed early in Joe's career that Wood's "flick of the wrist motion might be troublesome over the years. He should protect himself and not wear himself out at a young age." Sadly, Johnson proved prophetic: Smoky Joe's last pitching victory came at the too-young age of 25. A succession of injuries had taken their toll. Grantland Rice saw Wood pitch near the end of the 1915 season and commented, "The smokeball appellation has been canned."[7]

The ache in Wood's right arm and shoulder never left him. Former Red Sox scout and historian Ed Walton, now deceased, befriended Smoky Joe in the 1970s and 1980s. In a 2004 interview, Walton said he witnessed numerous instances of the aging Wood grimacing in pain while simply shaking a hand or putting on a blazer. In his *Red Sox Triumphs and Tragedies*, Walton writes that during Wood's epochal 1912 season, when he went 34–5, Smoky Joe often volunteered for extra duty. "If the game was close and a relief pitcher might be needed, his teammates would come and say, 'How about it, Woodie?' And usually manager Stahl would say, 'Okay, go down to the corner (as they called the bullpen in those days).' Joe would start throwing just in case he was needed."[8]

It's testament to Wood's character and natural athletic skills that once his arm soured, he turned himself into a creditable outfielder and batter. In 1921, he hit .366 in some 200 at bats for the Indians. The next year, with more than 500 at bats, he hit .297. His bullpen mate Charley Hall once said: "Show me anything athletically that involved working with the hands and body and ask me who I'd single out as the best, and I'd say without hesitation that I'd pit Joe Wood against the world. He was the most natural and talented of them all."[9]

After the Sox purchased him from Kansas City, Wood appeared in six games at the end of the 1908 season. Like Speaker, he showed a glimmer of greatness to come that fall, going 1–1 with an earned run average of 2.38. In 1909, he started 19 games, appeared in five others, and compiled a record of 11–7, lowering his ERA to 2.21. In addition to his meteoric fastball, he developed a repertoire that included what the *Boston Globe's* Tim Murnane once described as "slow drops and dreamy curves."[10] In short order, he became one of the most feared right-handers in the American League.

He also became one of the more controversial figures in the dead-ball epoch — no mean accomplishment given the competition. Among his pals in baseball was the execrable Hal Chase, who hung out with the wrong element and was never beneath fixing a game. Chase's modus operandi wasn't subtle: "Hey, Hal, what are the odds?" fans used to holler at him as he took the field.

Wood and Chase played a lot of poker together, Wood told historian Larry Ritter in 1963. When Hal winked at Joe as Chase was shuffling the cards, it meant Wood could expect to be dealt four "4s"—and presumably split the pot with Chase when the smoke cleared.[11]

Nearly a century after the 1912 World Series, Wood's collapse in its next-to-last game (the '12 Series was a best-of-seven games contest, but the second game had been called on account of darkness and declared a non-game) still triggers considerable head scratching.

The Red Sox were leading the New York Giants of John McGraw and Christy Mathewson that October three games-to-two. A Boston clinch looked assured that afternoon because Wood had been so stout in the post-season.

Smoky Joe had dominated opponents during the '12 campaign, winning 34 games and hurling 10 shutouts.[12] Wood had acquitted himself well in the Series, winning games one and four while striking out a total of 19 Giants. In game one, Wood had snuffed out a Giant rally in the ninth to preserve a 4–3 win. "I threw so hard I thought my arm would fly right off my body," Joe supposedly declared in the clubhouse afterward.[13]

For game six at the Polo Grounds, with the Sox leading at that point three-games-to-one, Wood was primed and ready to go. But Boston owner James McAleer doubtless wanted the Series to move back to Boston for one more day of big box office. Over the protestations of Red Sox player-manager Jake Stahl, McAleer insisted that second year man Buck O'Brien start the sixth game. O'Brien was cuffed up for five runs in the first inning. The Sox went on to lose 5–2.

As explored in Glenn Stout and Richard Johnson's *Red Sox Century*, the post-game innuendo floating around Boston was that O'Brien didn't know he was scheduled to pitch until he arrived at the Polo Grounds just before the game started. Supposedly nursing a hangover from too much revelry in Manhattan the night before, Buck was in no condition to take the slab.

Joe Wood's brother Paul, under the misconception that his un-hittable sibling would start, had bet a hundred bucks—a tidy sum in those days—on the Sox in game six. On the train ride back to Boston following the game, Paul Wood was so bent on revenge that he reportedly baited O'Brien into a fight, inflicting a black eye.[14]

It wasn't the first time that Boston's American League franchise had been suspected of post-season shenanigans to hype the gate. In 1903, the first modern World Series, the great pitcher Cy Young and his Pilgrim (as the team was then called) teammates allegedly "threw" game one against the Pittsburgh Pirates to protest the meager financial incentives—and manipulate more favorable odds for the Boston club for the remainder of the post-season. Young got scuffed up in the top of the first inning, his fielders made several embarrassing gaffes behind him, and the Pirates managed to pull off not one but two double-steals—all before a peeved overflow crowd in the South End. Boston's players and the club's owner, the story went, had taken full advantage of those more lucrative stakes once the odds evened out following Pittsburgh's victory. Boston fans knew that story all too well—and they thought history was repeating itself.[15]

As the seventh game of the '12 Series approached, the tension on the field and in the stands at Fenway got even uglier. There was no rest day between the sixth and seventh contests; the players got off the train and—bleary-eyed—were back at Fenway after a short night's rest.

Brand-new that year, the ballpark was packed to the rafters as it had been throughout the Series, so crowded that standing-room-only sections had been cordoned off on the field itself. Thousands of people were craning their necks behind roped off areas in the outfield, barely 300 feet from home plate. Many of them were bellowing the chants for which Red Sox fans had become infamous. One of them, sung to the tune of a popular ballad called "Tammany," went:

> *Carrigan, Carrigan*
> *Speaker, Lewis, Wood and Stahl.*
> *Bradley, Engle, Pape and Hall*
> *Wagner, Gardner, Hooper, too.*
> *Hit them! Hit them! Hit them! Hit them!*
> *Do, boys, do!*

But with the first pitch of the seventh game just minutes away, Boston's biggest cheerleaders were conspicuously absent. They were the self-anointed "Royal Rooters," a group of several hundred super-fans led by Mayor "Honey Fitz" Fitzgerald and Ned "Nuf Ced" McGreevey, the proprietor of the Third Base saloon.

McGreevey earned his nickname by thundering "Enough said!" when his customers' arguments over sports or politics grew too loud or long. Either nervous that the Royal Rooters wouldn't show or acting out of spite—or perhaps both—McAleer's green eyeshade deputy, club treasurer Robert McRoy, sold the Rooters' usual seats to fans queued up outside the ballpark. Since the club had sold Series' tickets in strips of three games—and three games had already been played at Fenway—in management's view, tickets to a fourth home game could only be secured on a first-come, first served basis. It was a pesky little detail that was never communicated to the Rooters, nor anyone else, for that matter.

A few moments later, waving pennants and accompanied by a brass band, Fitz, McGreevey and company marched through the then-opening in the centerfield bleachers, only to discover that their usual seats had been bartered out from under them. McAleer and McRoy had relegated the Royal Rooters, whose allegiance went back, literally, to day one in the franchise's history, to standing-room-only in left field.

Outraged, Mayor Fitz demanded a huddle with team officials, which took place in front of the pitcher's mound. No soap, His Honor was told: the Rooters were stuck in standing room. After their leader's appeal was denied, many of the Rooters went berserk, knocking over a temporary restraining fence and refusing to leave the playing field. Adding insult to injury, fans seated along the third base line began pelting the Rooters with peanuts, crackerjack, scorecards, and anything else on which they could get their hands. The situation became so frenzied that mounted police were called in to restore order, galloping headlong into the throng from the open area in centerfield, billy clubs in hand.[16]

Amid this chaos, Smoky Joe was trying to warm up. In forbidding conditions, the start of the game was delayed for more than a half hour as the police and coaches and players from both teams herded the Rooters behind the restraint in left field. Wood's unsettled warm-up and the mayhem all around him could not have helped his frame of mind. Like his brother, Joe, too, reportedly had a confrontation with the hapless Buck O'Brien. The two supposedly had to be separated outside the clubhouse a couple of hours before the ballgame started; a bat allegedly had to be wrung out of Wood's hands.[17] O'Brien not only had the misfortune of losing game six, he was guilty of another sin in Wood's eyes. Buck was an immigrant kid and a practicing Roman Catholic, a background and a religion deplored by Wood and Speaker.

When the game finally started, Smoky Joe Wood was awful. For the only time all season, he got knocked out of the box early. Before being replaced in the top of the second, he threw barely a dozen pitches, giving up seven hits and six runs. Tim Murnane of the *Boston Globe*, whose observations commanded universal respect (Murnane's pronouncements were considered "pretty much *ex cathedra*," in the words of modern *Globe* sportswriter Bob Ryan), volunteered that Wood appeared to be "cutting the ball over the heart of the plate." With runners at first and second and nobody out, Wood curiously chose to pitch from a full wind-up instead of the stretch, allowing the Giants to dash off an easy double-steal.[17]

Wood's teammates dragged the Sox further into the mire; one of the finest fielding teams in history made a peck of mental and physical errors behind him. The hi-jinks didn't stop after Wood left the game. As reported in the next day's *New York Times*, in the top of the second, relief pitcher Charley Hall tried to pick a Giant runner off of second base. Hall's throw eluded both the Sox shortstop and Speaker, its all-world centerfielder. It eventually had to be tracked down by Boston's right fielder as the Giant runners sauntered around the bases.[18]

When the game mercifully ended in the cold and mist, it was 11–4, Giants. The Series was now even at three games each. "When he (Wood) walked to the pitching mound.... Wood wore a halo," the *Times* asserted. "But before three hours had gone, fickle fandom was looking about for someone else to put on the pedestal."[19]

To "fickle fandom," the Red Sox faithful, the whole episode stunk to high heaven. It wasn't just the Royal Rooters who suspected the fix was in; Murnane and other reporters, among them Hugh Fullerton of the *Chicago Daily Tribune*, hinted that game seven wasn't on the level. Many people feared the worst: that the Red Sox had deliberately thrown the game to recover their losses from the "tied" contest. With Wood pitching, the conspiracy theory went, the Giants had been heavy underdogs. If the Sox players had laid money on the Giants, they would have made a killing.

The Royal Rooters felt so betrayed they gathered *en masse* on Jersey Street after the game, singing sarcastic songs of praise to the Giants. Cries of "The hell with the Red Sox!" and "Who gives a damn whether they win or lose!" rang through the Fens. The Rooters' cause was taken up by an editorial in the next day's *Globe*, which likened the club's use of mounted police to Cossacks putting down a Russian peasant revolt.[20]

A coin was tossed to determine the location of the eighth and final game. The Giants' surrogate called "heads"; it came up "tails." The clincher would be at Fenway the next day, October 16, 1912.

Red Sox fans were in a tizzy. With many of them convinced that the team's owner had compromised game six and that their beloved players had thrown game seven, they stayed away from game eight in droves. The Rooters angrily boycotted, with Mayor Fitz leading the catcalls.

Sadly, then, only a half-capacity crowd was on hand to witness the final match-up of the 1912 World Series—one of the best baseball games ever played.

Game eight was everything the previous two contests weren't: beautifully pitched, taut, gut-wrenching baseball. Joe Wood had thrown only a handful of pitches the day before and could easily have been sent to the mound again. But given Wood's mercurial behavior the past 48 hours, manager Jake Stahl couldn't trust him. He turned to rookie Hugh Bedient, who pitched brilliantly for seven innings, but was removed for a pinch-hitter.

Taking Bedient out of the game left Stahl with the toughest decision of his managerial career. He weighed his options—then signaled for Joe Wood to begin warming up. Wood, perhaps not miraculously, rediscovered his touch. Smoky Joe mowed the Giants down in the eighth and again in the ninth.

Ironically, the goat of the previous game became one of Boston's heroes. Wood ended up winning the game when the Red Sox rallied for two runs against Matty in the bottom of the tenth, aided by two bizarre New York miscues: center fielder Fred Snodgrass' infamous muff of a fly ball; and the confusion among Matty, first baseman Fred Snodgrass, and catch Chief Meyers that allowed Speaker's foul pop-up to fall untouched.[21]

Sadly, Wood would never come close to matching his brilliance in the '12 season. The pain in his shoulder and elbow wouldn't allow it. Today he's almost as well known for his role in the unsavory cheating allegations that were leveled against Speaker and Ty Cobb by a former teammate of all three men.

Dutch Leonard, the former Red Sox and Tiger, claimed in 1926 that on the last weekend of the 1919 regular season, Speaker and Wood, by then of the Cleveland Indians, and Cobb and Leonard of the Tigers met under the stands in Detroit to plot the fixing of the next day's game so that Detroit could win third-place money outright. Sure enough, the Tigers won handily the next day in a suspiciously fast and loose game.[22]

When Leonard presented evidence of the fix to American League president Ban Johnson, the AL czar quietly confronted Cobb and Speaker and arranged for them to quit the game in the late fall of '26. In the weeks that followed, however, Commissioner Kenesaw Mountain Landis got involved—and Cobb and Speaker hired high-priced legal counsel.

If Joe Wood's 1963 recollections to Ritter are accurate, the two icons and their attorneys played hardball with the commissioner. "See, they got together with an attorney in Detroit, my friend Spoke, and they got a bunch of stuff together and typewritten and deposited it in a bank vault in Cleveland, and if they would have chased Cobb and Speaker out of baseball, it would have all come out."[23]

Smoky Joe later regretted having been so candid with Ritter and asked him to destroy the tape and transcript of the interview. Professor Ritter kept Wood's incriminating comments out of *The Glory of Their Times*, but never excised the transcript. Along with Ritter's subsequent interview of Wood two years later, the 1963 transcript is on file in the Ritter archives at the University of Notre Dame.

Wood revealed that Speaker and Ty Cobb, in effect, played a game of "chicken" with Landis in 1926–27. Smoky Joe told Ritter that Cobb and Speaker hired high-priced attorneys who advised them to put together a sworn statement listing every nasty cheating episode they'd ever heard of. The Cobb-Speaker legal team, Wood claimed, then told Landis that if he didn't back down and reinstate the two stars, they would "go public" with the charges. Landis acquiesced, but insisted that the stars leave their respective teams. Cobb went to Connie Mack's Philadelphia Athletics for two seasons. Speaker signed with the Washington Senators for one year, then joined Ty in Philadelphia for a final season that proved futile for both of them.

Smoky Joe also raised doubts in that original interview about the integrity of Cleveland's 1920 pennant. Wood claimed that Chicago pitcher Eddie Cicotte told him early in the '20 season that the White Sox were worried that another appearance in the post-season would cast additional scrutiny on their 1919 shenanigans. So the White Sox rolled over and allowed the Indians to win the '20 pennant. The 1920 campaign was "not on the up and up," Wood told Ritter.[24] The Wood interview with Ritter is the closest thing baseball historians will ever have to a "smoking gun" on the pervasiveness of cheating in the old days.

Spoke and Smoky Joe stayed friends and hunting and fishing buddies until the day Speaker died in 1958. The two cowboys brought to baseball more than a taste of the rough-and-tumble frontier they'd known as children.

6

Honus Wagner and Jimmie Foxx: Baseball and the Lives After

A. Franklin Parks

Relatively few sports national commentators and columnists know enough about Honus Wagner and Jimmie Foxx to talk about them — despite the fact that the Flying Dutchman and ol' Double X constantly show up in authoritative lists of the greatest baseball players of all time. In addition, there is no abundance of developed biographical information on the two. Brief surveys on line and in anthologies appear, but they have not attracted the slew of biographers that more visible players like Cobb, Ruth, Gehrig, and the like have. Memories of their lives and achievements, however, are held most vigilantly in the communities where they were raised and in the homes of the teams where they played loyally. Two biographies stand out as providing the best glimpses of the lives and careers of these two remarkable players: Arthur D. Hittner's *Honus Wagner: The Life of Baseball's "Flying Dutchman"*[1] and Mark R. Millikin's *Jimmie Foxx: The Pride of Sudlersville.*[2]

At first blush, these two great players appear to be somewhat of an odd couple. But the histories of Honus Wagner and Jimmie Foxx are, in many respects, complementary histories of the development and maturation of the American pastime. Wagner played during the turn of the century in what is called the "dead-ball" era, and Foxx rose to fame in the twenties and thirties, a time of great change in the sport often referred to as the "Ruth Era." Their careers spanned the period that saw everything from the creation of the American League to the establishment of a World Series to the institution of the Baseball Hall of Fame. They were responsible, along with the Sultan of Swat and others such as Shoeless Joe Jackson, Ty Cobb, Tris Speaker, Cy Young, Walter Johnson, Christy Mathewson, Grover Cleveland Alexander, Connie Mack, Lefty Grove, Lou Gehrig, Satchel Paige, Josh Gibson, Rogers Hornsby, the colorful and cunning John McGraw and countless others for bringing the sport into the mainstream of American life and culture.

Wagner and Foxx saw baseball become big business, at which many entrepreneurs failed. They also saw the sport of country and city boys from Irish and German origins become legitimatized as a career choice and in a sense internationalized, eventually attracting men of southern and eastern European origin as well as players from the other Americas. Then, after retirement, they would see the brief addition of women to the sport as World War II drew men from their ranks to fight in Europe and ultimately the open inclusion of Jews and the integration of African Americans into the mainstream of the national pastime.

Why are they not as often cited by sports announcers and recalled by sports historians when comparisons are made and when greatness is evaluated? It's possible that, in Foxx's case, he was simply out publicized by the host of mythical players from his period. It also may be that his post-career life casted a shadow over his career. In Wagner's case, it's a bit more difficult to say. One reason is perhaps his loyalty to Pittsburgh and the National League eventually moved him into the background as the American Leaguers of the Twenties took over the spotlight. It also may be that he was, by comparison to others of his generation and later, colorful on the field but somewhat lackluster in his private life.

Honus Wagner swats a ball at Forbes Field (Prints and Photographs Division, Library of Congress).

Honus Wagner has been described as one of the best all-around players ever to grace the diamond and a contender for the distinction of being one of the greatest shortstops of all time.[3] Wagner's playing career spanned 21 years, from 1897 through 1917, during which time he won eight batting crowns—he earned number eight at age 37—and led the National League in RBI five times, in slugging percentage six times, and in stolen bases five times. Among the homerun leaders of his era, he remains among the top performers of all time in the categories of hits, doubles, and triples. A consummate infielder, Wagner had a .947 fielding average. Having hit over .300 for seventeen consecutive seasons, assembled a lifetime batting average of .329, led the Pirates to the pennant four times, and played in the first World Series against the Boston

Americans in 1903, Honus Wagner was voted into the inaugural class of the Hall of Fame in 1936.

Jimmie Foxx, prior to Mark McGwire, was considered the most prolific right hand batter to ever play the game. He still remains as one of the greatest power hitters ever. Foxx, who had some difficulty establishing his position on the diamond before settling into the role of first baseman, was the American League's Most Valuable Player three times—in 1932, 1933, and 1938—and was selected to the All-Star Team nine times, between 1933 and 1941. During the years from 1929 to 1941, with the Philadelphia Athletics and later the Boston Red Sox, Foxx led the League in homeruns four times, in batting average five times, in RBI three times—with 100 RBI or greater each during the period—and in slugging percentage five times. His statistical accomplishments go on and on. The winner of the A.L. Triple Crown in 1933, Foxx played in two World Series with the Athletics, in 1929 and 1930, and was elected to Baseball's Hall of Fame in 1951.

This photograph of Jimmie Foxx features his massive arm (Prints and Photographs Division, Library of Congress).

Though separated by a generation of major league ball players, Wagner and Foxx had a number of comparable personal and professional characteristics that contributed to the developing stereotype of the hero of American pastime. Like a good number of their generation, neither completed high school. And, like Ruth, both seemed unsuited physically for a sport that requires agility as well as strength. Both were about 5'11", above average in height then, and at best between 180 and 200 lbs. Foxx, handsome with a weightlifter's build, liked to show off his biceps by cutting off his shirt sleeves. He was competent as a target behind the plate and on first, but his body was not flexible nor his reactions quick; he had trouble making accurate throws. Wagner, bow-legged and described as "amplitudinous and triangular," did not have the Derek Jeter build for a shortstop. Wagner, one can tell from the pictures, was not as handsome as

Foxx, but the Pittsburgh shortstop was still active and effective into his 40s, whereas Foxx, troubled by health problems, sinus and otherwise, was a wreck at age 36. During their careers, both had trouble settling into a position. Both pitched. Foxx ended up on first and third, having been bumped from catching for the A's by Mickey Cochrane. Wagner ended up on short after being in the outfield and pitching.

In their personal lives, both had a love affair with the American automobile. Foxx regularly and flamboyantly sported the latest status symbol at the height of his career. Wagner, of course, lived in the age of the automobile's first appearance and subsequently gave the Pittsburgh police a good number of headaches with his erratic driving. Wagner actually owned a garage and tinkered with cars during a period after his retirement. What is more, both Wagner and Foxx enjoyed the outdoors and hunting in the off-season. In fact, Wagner, in 1910, journeyed to Georgia to hunt with Ty Cobb. Foxx, on the other hand, went to Western Maryland to hunt with his teammate, Lefty Grove, and subsequently invited Grove to the Eastern Shore of Maryland — his home area — for some goose hunting.

Despite their similarities, Wagner and Foxx played baseball under decidedly different circumstances. While Wagner spent his career in the "dead-ball" era, Foxx played in the "Ruth" or "quick ball" era. Prior to 1920, baseballs were not frequently replaced during a game as they are today. Often, to save costs, the balls were kept in play despite their condition through as many as 100 pitches. Also, if a ball was hit into the crowd, often it was thrown back and re-used. Of course, as the game progressed, the ball became softer. However, baseballs were already softer to begin with, due to the way in which they were manufactured. New regulations instituted in 1919 required them to be wound tighter. Also, during the dead-ball era, spitballs were permitted. The game ball would be in sorry condition after even one inning of being plied with foreign substances and scruffed by pitchers to make it more active. One wonders what would have happened had Wagner faced the un-doctored quick ball.

Another dissimilarity between Foxx and Wagner was that Wagner was a well-rounded player, outstanding on offense as well as defense, a crafty baserunner, inclined to tricks on the basepaths in an age of tricksterism; whereas Foxx will be remembered primarily as a power hitter and, though no slouch, not as big an asset in the field. Their field personas, in turn, contrasted with their personalities off the field. Wagner was a shy, non-assuming son of a coal miner off the field, but a fierce competitor on the field; Foxx, though the son of a farmer, was out-going, Ruthesque, and extravagant, but basically mild mannered during the game. Wagner took his fishing gear with him on the road, played basketball, hunted and bowled off-season; and was conservative with his money. Wagner is not described as a womanizer, though he did have serious friendships with women in various places at various times; he eventually married a woman 15 years younger at age 42. Foxx, on the other hand, was a partier and did appear to have a number of liaisons while married twice. When receiving a paycheck, Foxx was generous to a fault.

Honus Wagner with rod and reel in Dawson Springs, Kentucky. An avid fisherman, the shortstop traveled everywhere with his tackle (courtesy Hearst News American Photographic Collection in the University of Maryland Special Collections Library, College Park).

Despite their dissimilarities, the careers of Wagner and Foxx demonstrate the oddities of newly developing pastime: the emergence and decline of semipro teams, the growth and demise of leagues—for example, the Atlantic and the Federal Leagues and countless minor leagues—the financial problems associated with owning and managing a team, and the shifting circumstances surrounding owner/player relations. Further, both Wagner and Foxx had interesting lives and would these days gain the attention of the tabloids—perhaps, though, for different reasons.

As a teenager, Wagner worked in the coal mines and in a steel mill briefly. He was then unsuccessfully apprenticed to his brother as a barber. He would, however, sneak away from the barber shop to play sandlot ball. Later, as a semipro and professional ballplayer, he would give his fellow players free haircuts on Sundays. During his early career he played with a number of semipro teams in Ohio and Pennsylvania, occasionally under an alias. As Hittner states,

> Aliases were commonly employed by ballplayers of the era to evade contracts and maximize playing opportunities. For example, it was not unusual for Al Wagner [Honus's older brother] to secure playing engagements with a variety of local semipro clubs under his own or another name. He would select the most appealing, leaving his brother to choose among the balance (compelling him to use whatever moniker was appropriate to the circumstances). "The thought of doing anything wrong never entered our heads," Wagner admitted. "They did all kinds of things like that then."[4]

Another interesting point for sports fans in the age of agents and contract negotiations, Wagner actually reneged on the first contract he received from the Pirates because they were going to farm him out to Kansas City of the Western League. He opted instead to join the Paterson, New Jersey, team of the Atlantic League. Pittsburgh management let him go, but with the proviso that should he develop, they would have first dibs. His first professional team, though, was the ill-fated Louisville Colonels, which were eventually in such financial straits that in 1899 they had sell off 14 of their players to Pittsburgh, and Wagner was among the 14. So Wagner came home and began his 18-year career with the Pirates.

Wagner experienced a number of suspensions and expulsions for his flairs of temper on the field. One such incident occurred in St. Louis in 1902. After angrily challenging a call made by the umpire over a foul ball, Wagner was ejected. But instead of leaving the ball field, he spent the rest of the game in the bleachers with the fans, alternately hooting the umpire and arguing his case. On another occasion, in 1912, in a game against the Reds, he sicced his dog, which he often brought to games, on an umpire. Despite his aggressive behavior on the field, Wagner was loved by the fans, particularly those of German descent. When he hit well or pulled off one of his spectacular fielding feats, they would serenade him in their native language.

At his peak, Wagner earned $10,000 a year. Had he jumped ship and joined newly formed leagues whose owners were forever raiding the established leagues for talent and who made a number of overtures to the Pittsburgh shortstop, he could have doubled that figure. But he remained loyal to the Pirates and to his hometown.

After retirement, Wagner evaded a number of financial opportunities, one of which was an offer made by the Piedmont Tobacco Company to use his picture on a baseball card to be included in cigarette packs sold nationally. Wagner declined the offer, stating that he didn't want his picture in cigarette packs. Later, his daughter clarified his response by adding that the great shortstop, who smoked cigars and chewed tobacco, did not want kids to have to buy cigarettes to get his card. The company had, however, already started to distribute the packs with his card inside. Despite attempts to recall the packs, a few still remained at large, and their worth today is the greatest of any baseball cards in history.

Jimmie Foxx's life affords even more grist for the journalist's mill. The "Sudlersville Slugger" got his start in the Eastern Shore [of Maryland] League. He was "discovered" by John Franklin "Homerun" Baker, who retired to Trappe, Maryland, from a distinguished career playing third base for the Athletics and the Yankees. Baker recruited Foxx from the Shore town of Sudlersville and from high school to catch for the Easton Farmers, a newly formed team in the Eastern Shore Baseball League. The Eastern Shore League had begun in 1922 with six teams from Maryland and Virginia communities; in 1923, it started with eight, but three dropped out. The Farmers were admitted in 1924, and it was in that year that Baker, impressed with Foxx, brought the young player to the attention of Connie Mack. Foxx completed the 1924 season with Easton, playing against such teams as the Crisfield Crabbers and the Parksley Spuds. The Spuds of Parksley, Virginia, won the pennant, however. And when they entered into a five-state series at the end of the season, they were allowed to take on two additional players, one of whom was Foxx. The Spuds, needless to say, won the series.

Gentleman Jimmie Foxx signs a ball for a young fan in the dugout (Prints and Photographs Division, Library of Congress).

In February of 1925, at 17 years of age, Foxx caught the train for Ft. Myers and spring training with the Philadelphia Athletics. On board with him was Walter Moses "Lefty" Grove, who at that point was 25 years of age and who had had more seasoning as a professional than Foxx. This encounter would begin a lifelong friendship that saw them through their years at Philadelphia and later when both ended up on Boston. As members of the Philadelphia Athletics team in 1928, they traveled to Grove's home area to play against the Cumberland [Md.] Colts of the Middle Atlantic League, before a packed house. Grove made an appearance in the 8th inning to the delight of the crowd. This 1928 team, interestingly enough, included the aging Tris Speaker, who, along with Ty Cobb in 1927—two bridges to the era of Honus Wagner—had been taken on by Philadelphia owner Connie Mack after they were released by their respective teams due to a belated accusation that they fixed a game in 1919. During this relatively brief period of association, Foxx and fellow A's slugger, Al Simmons, had ample opportunities to talk with the veterans and to learn from them.

The 1929 Athletics are considered by many to be one of best teams ever assembled. The talented team included Foxx, Grove, catcher Mickey Cochrane, and Simmons. Foxx never slipped below .350 the whole season, and the A's beat the Cubs in the World Series. Meanwhile, Foxx was getting Ruth's attention. Ruth chose Foxx over Gehrig in 1929 for his All Star Big League Baseball Team. In 1932, Foxx challenged Ruth's 1927 record of 60 homeruns in a season by hitting 58. Plus, Foxx's stories sounded a lot like Ruth's. An anecdote was spread about how a game-winning homerun hit by Foxx inspired a boy suffering from tuberculosis in a New Jersey hospital. As the story goes, when the boy's idol heard about the boy's condition and his devotion to the Athletics, Foxx paid him an uplifting visit. Finally, prior to contests between the Athletics and the Yankees, Foxx and the Babe posed for pictures and sometimes even trading bats. They were on the first American League All-Star Team in 1933. And in 1934, Ruth included Foxx with his All-Stars to tour Canada, Hawaii, and Japan.

Foxx ended his professional career with Boston, where he rejoined the aging Grove, who, in 1941, got his 300th career win. Foxx also inspired a young rookie who joined the team in 1939 and who in 1941 hit .406. This rookie was, of course, Ted Williams. Williams always revered the older player, stating, "I never discussed hitting with Jimmie Foxx. All I did was look in awe of what he could do at 190 pounds and how hard he could hit 'em. The sound of the ball against the bat when he swung it — there's only one other player that had the same sound to me when he hit the ball, and that was Mickey Mantle."[5]

Baseball owner and promoter Bill Veeck is often quoted as saying, "Baseball is almost the only orderly thing in a very disorderly world. If you get three strikes, even the best lawyer in the world can't get you off."[6] In many ways, it was and is the order of the game — the lineup, the positions on the field, the sequence of bases, the allowance of three strikes to every batter, the unexpected sprinkled among the expected — that makes baseball a refuge in a world that tends to be chaotic. In its promise of order, it provided hope and respite for the beleaguered fans and players of the times in which The Flying Dutchman performed an seemingly impossible feat in the infield or Ol' Double X squared around and connected with a pitch sending it out of the park. This order — as well as the fan adulation, the money, and love of the game — was also essential to the lives of Wagner and Foxx, for they, like many players before them and countless ones after them, clung to the game past their prime, past their effectiveness. The writing was on the wall for the aging and injured 42-year-old Wagner in 1916 as he struggled to play one more season. Returning in 1917, he surged briefly in the early season but ended up leaving the game after flirting with player/manager status. Plagued with health problems, a 34-year-old Foxx struggled with the Red Sox during the 1941 season only to be sold to the Cubs the next year, during which his batting average plummeted. In and out of retirement the next three years, Foxx, besieged by personal problems as well, attempted comebacks with little success and ultimately retired from active playing to relative obscurity.

Thomas Boswell, in a now famous *Washington Post* column from September of 1980, metaphorically describes the phenomenon that Wagner and Foxx, and indeed other aging baseball players, experienced, stating,

> To a ballplayer, the game is a seed he planted as a child, a kind of beautiful creeping ivy that he was delighted to have entwine him. As an adult, he felt supported in every sense — financial, emotional, psychic — by his green, rich, growing game,

just as ivy can strengthen a brick wall. But ivy, given time, can overpower and tear down a house.

So, in a way, the aging player, whose life seems to be a mansion, knows that he is in a strong and even dangerous grip. In the end, he may not know how much of his strength, how much of his ability to stand alone, comes from the brick and mortar of his own identity and how much is borrowed from the vine that engulfs him more each year, even as it props him up. No wonder he is so fearful when the time arrives to hew through the root and pull free.[7]

This phenomenon, Boswell adds, is unique to baseball:

In baseball, you see, no one ever believes he's really lost it. No American team sport is half so fascinated with the process of aging as baseball, perhaps because none of our games is so based on skill and timing rather than brute force. Nor does any sport offer prospects for an athletic old age that is so rich in possibilities for either humiliation or the greatest fame.

Every athlete in every sport deteriorates. But in baseball that battle against time — where a standoff means temporary victory — can be attended for as much as a decade by a dogged will and an analytical mind. Perhaps no sport encourages its men to rage so nobly against the erosion of their youth.[8]

The problem is, of course, when the moment of separation necessarily occurs and the rage subsides. Paul White, in a 2005 *USA Today* column, explores the "what next?" question in an interview with former White Sox outfielder Lyle Mouton at the winter meetings. In essence, White asks Mouton why he is there, looking for another chance at the majors, why he is hanging on instead of creating a new life for himself outside baseball.

"Because you've done it for so long," Mouton says. "You miss the people involved in the game. It's a case of being familiar with it. Remember, you get out of the game and you haven't built experience outside of baseball. Most people at this age are done feeling their way through the 'this job's not for me' part of their lives."[9]

But, as White points out, the real world awaits. "And for all but the select few and their millions, the growth process begins all over again when the games are over."

Both Wagner and Foxx had difficulties with the growth process once playing baseball was no longer an option. Wagner, after retirement, demonstrated a restlessness, an inability to focus on one line of work, repairing cars, pumping gasoline, launching a half-hearted campaign for sheriff, coaching football and basketball at a local high school, managing unsuccessfully an Eastern Ohio league team, failing at a sporting goods venture, and ultimately serving in a low-paying role as sergeant at arms in the state legislature in Harrisburg. Eventually, his fortunes had fallen so low when he was in his late fifties that Pirate management created a coaching job for Wagner, which he kept until he retired at age 77.

Foxx's life after baseball was perhaps even more tragic. Frank Fitzpatrick, in a 1999 *Philadelphia Inquirer* piece, chronicles Foxx's decline, following Double X's lackluster attempt at comeback with the Athletics and subsequent retirement in 1945: minor league coach or player, bar leader, women's baseball team manager, university baseball coach, and other jobs.

Mack called him one of the "most likable guys" he had ever managed, but he couldn't handle his money. He had earned $270,000 as a player, but by the late 1950s he and his wife were relying on their children and friends for support.

"I guess I was born to be broke," Foxx said in 1958.

He suffered a heart attack in 1963. The drinking continued, and his premature death surprised no one.[10]

The ordered disorder of baseball serves the sports fan of today in a similar fashion to the way it served Wagner and Foxx, isolating us temporarily from a world that seems out of control at times, providing an arena in which human conflict and adversity is confined to nine innings. However, for most of us, that momentary suspension of reality gives way to reality as the last pitch is thrown and we leave the stands for the parking lot. For Wagner and Foxx—as it has for many others in baseball—the artificial harmony that re-forms elements of the threatening world outside of "game"—along with other perquisites—made exit from sport difficult if not impossible. Neither of these legendary players managed well afterwards on his own; both evidently needed the imposed regimen of baseball to make the most of their lives. Babe Ruth once said, "If it wasn't for baseball, I'd be in either the penitentiary or the cemetery."[11] Perhaps the same could be said for a number of our outstanding athletes, including Honus and Jimmie.

7

The Tenth Man: Baseball and Radio Broadcasting

TED PATTERSON

"When I get lonesome and homesick, the most wonderful remedy is to pick up the baseball game on short-wave and to know that I am listening to the same game, the same announcers, the same words that my dad is hearing back home."
— a G.I. letter to Armed Forces Radio, World War II

The Roaring 1920s, with the likes of Babe Ruth, Jack Dempsey, Red Grange, the Four Horsemen of Notre Dame, Bobby Jones and Bill Tilden, were deemed the "Golden Age of American Sports." Fortuitously, just in time for "Million Dollar Gates" in boxing and Babe Ruth's home run barrage, came radio. The marriage of baseball and radio was officially consummated on the afternoon of August 5, 1921, when KDKA in Pittsburgh broadcast the Pirates 8–5 win over the Phillies. Harold Arlin, a Westinghouse foreman who had gone up to the factory roof to check out the experimental station, suddenly found himself as the nation's first full-time radio broadcaster. Arlin became the jack-of-all-trades behind the microphone, interviewing such well-known celebrities as Will Rogers and Babe Ruth

Radio stations soon began sprouting like weeds across the nation's landscape to meet the demand for this new kind of home entertainment. If people couldn't afford a radio, they made their own, combining Mothers Oats boxes, galena wire and some good old-fashioned ingenuity. The all New York 1921 World Series followed Arlin's foray into baseball. The Yankees played the Giants at the Polo Grounds and instead of just KDKA, the other two Westinghouse stations, one in Newark, New Jersey, and the other in Springfield, Massachusetts, hooked up lines at the Polo Grounds to form a mini-network.

Since there were no such thing as experienced play-by-play sportscasters, the station managers selected famous sportswriters to describe the action. In 1921, it was the legendary sports writer, Grantland Rice. In 1922, Rice was joined by fellow scribe W.O. "Bill" McGheehan as the Giants and Yankees met again. Player boards were set up in several large cities, and the progress of the game was marked on a giant chart. For years the public had been accustomed to the remarkable speed shown by the newspapers in providing mechanical and electric boards, but the radio boards would beat the newspaper boards by about half a minute. Near City Hall in New York, one street with radio boards showed the Giants scoring a run and a huge cheer erupted. Thirty seconds later, on another street, came a similar roar as the newspaper board posted the same run.

The immediacy of radio was undeniable. Wrote Glenn Scott in *Wireless Age* magazine: "We radio listeners lived the series as did they who were actually in the stands. And we did it in the comfort of our homes, or in our offices, leaning back in a chair, with our feet on the boss's desk." Rice's voice was heard not only by ships at sea, but by lighthouse keepers, the sick, the shut-ins, the farmers and the factory workers. "We heard the ovation for Jack Dempsey as he entered the stands," wrote Scott. "We heard the cheering for Christy Mathewson who came to see and write about the game after his two-year successful battle against tuberculosis. Several times we even heard the crack of the bat on the nose of the ball—or was it just our imagination? We all but saw."

Not everyone was equipped to make the transition from writing about sporting events to talking about them as they happened. In 1923, the well-known sports writer Graham McNamee broadcast his first World Series when the Yankees again met the Giants. It was the new Yankee Stadium's inaugural series. McNamee was there to assist Bill McGheehan, who suddenly walked off the assignment in the fourth game, disgusted with trying to do something he was ill equipped to do—broadcast a baseball game. New York *Evening Telegram* baseball writer Fred Lieb said McGheehan was an odd choice to be picked in the first place. "Bill was not a loquacious man, and he was quite moody. You could be with him for half an hour without him uttering a word."

Some simply lacked knowledge of baseball. For all of his descriptive ability, McNamee wasn't very knowledgeable about the game itself. His lack of expertise first became apparent in his broadcast of the 1923 World Series. At the 1927 World Series between the Yankees and Pirates, writer Ring Lardner sat in an adjoining seat to the NBC radio booth where McNamee was broadcasting. "It was like attending a doubleheader," wrote Lardner. "You saw one game and heard another." Realizing that inept broadcasting might jeopardize public enthusiasm for the sport, Commissioner Kenesaw Landis eventually had him removed from broadcasting. Landis became insistent that owners employ baseball savvy play-by-play broadcasters

Writers who knew the game well and owners who put players on the field had their own special concerns about radio broadcasting. The Baseball Writers Association of America initially objected to World Series broadcasts on the grounds that they would hinder the sale of papers that carried stories on the games. Instead, radio broadcasts dramatically increased newspaper sales as listeners wanted to read more detail about what happened at the game. In the 1920s the public had an insatiable appetite for sports, a phenomenon increasingly understood by radio stations. Major league owners were not as farsighted as radio pioneers. Many of them were afraid that fans would stay away from the parks if free description of them were available on the radio. One of the longest holdouts was Barney Dreyfus, the owner of the Pittsburgh Pirates. It wasn't until the mid-1930s that the Pirates finally relented and let radio officially air their games. Until then, announcers such as Johnny Boyer and Al Helfer "pirated" the games. Station personnel would climb trees, telephone poles and use any other means to relay the happenings at Forbes Field into Pirate fans living rooms.

Owner intransigence lasted longer in New York City where the owners of the three teams had agreed to bar live broadcasts from their parks for years. It wasn't until 1939 when Larry MacPhail brought Red Barber to Brooklyn from Cincinnati that the New York ban was lifted. These were the years before clubs realized that they could charge rights fees for the privilege of broadcasting their games. It also took several years for stations to realize they could sell advertising time to beer, cigarette and car companies that would defray the cost of using telephone lines, and pay other expenses. Slowly but surely the financial gain derived from taking the game as it was it was played was evident to both station and team owners. People who never before took an interest in sports became avid fans. They listened to an event one day and found themselves wanting to be there in person the next. Attendance and gate receipts soared.

Unlike Pittsburgh and New York, Chicago was not hesitant about jumping into the broadcasting of home games of the Cubs and White Sox. In 1924, WMAQ, owned by the Chicago *Daily News*, began regular broadcasts of the Cubs. A young rewrite man at the paper, Hal Totten, volunteered to broadcast the games, thinking it an excellent way to view the games for free. Cubs owner William Wrigley, Jr., however, desired a former player to handle the announcing and called on former Cub, Solly Hoffman. Hoffman lasted exactly one day, completely overwhelmed by the job. Totten was back on the air the following day with his familiar "G'bye now" signoff, remaining for 19 years through the 1943 season.

Chicago soon became the mecca of baseball broadcasting as five more stations began airing the same game at the same time. Joining Totten were Quin Ryan and Bob Elson on WGN, Pat Flanagan on WBBM, Johnny O'Hara and later Russ Hodges over at WJJD, Jimmy Dudley and Jack Drees on WIND, and baseball legend Tris Speaker on WENR. One station even hired the unlikely trio of Charley Grimm, Lew Fonseca and Joe E. Brown to call the action. It was possible for a youngster leaving school to walk home and never miss a play of the game because every single radio along the way had the ballgame tuned in, booming out of windows and screened in porches.

Chicago listeners had six stations to pick from. Of that group of Chicago announcers, Elson had by far the longest tenure. "The Commander" began broadcasting on WGN in 1928, and was still describing White Sox games in

1970. "For well over a decade I worked all the games myself," Elson told this author in 1967. "Doubleheaders, the show before the game, the show between games, post game, 48 commercials and the play-by-play. All without a partner." Elson was also the first to do player interviews before games from the field. "Judge Landis gave me permission to run a microphone down to the field. At first the players were nervous and hesitant, but once they got the hang of it they made snappy, intelligent comments." One Chicago writer, in talking about the Old Commander's longevity, said, "He's been in radio since the Kingfish of *Amos 'n' Andy* was a minnow and since Sox great Luke Appling was a little leaguer."

In St. Louis, no one was more beloved in the 1930s and 1940s than France Laux. He began his radio career in Tulsa, recreating the 1927 World Series on 90 seconds notice. He joined KMOX in St. Louis in 1929 and was still there 40 years later. He began broadcasting Cardinal and Browns games in 1929 and continued for 26 years. "In those early days at Sportsman's Park, there was no radio booth," said Laux in 1967. "The first two years I sat downstairs in the stands behind the screen, and then, to escape inquisitive fans, moved to the edge of the upper deck." France didn't have a partner in those pioneer early years. During one Sunday doubleheader, Laux was on the air for six straight hours. No other voice was heard on KMOX during that entire stretch. Nationally, Laux became the CBS voice of the World Series. He began this role in 1932 and two years later was part of the first sponsored World Series as the Ford Motor Company paid NBC and CBS $50,000 each for the commercial rights. Laux's omission from the list of broadcasters in the Hall of Fame is a glaring error.

Baseball's authoritative commissioner saw to it that both quality and objectivity were observed in broadcasting the game that he regulated. In 1933, Commissioner Landis relegated the networks' two aces, Graham McNamee and Ted Husing, to secondary roles because of their lack of baseball knowledge. Landis also insisted that announcers avoid subjectivity in their description of the game, telling them that no degree of injustice, not even a hanging of someone in centerfield, called for a judgment. Report the construction of the gallows "but not the justice of the hanging" was his command. Landis handed down other rules that rankled both announcers and fans. One of them forbade announcers connected with World Series teams to broadcast series games because he felt they would be biased. In 1934, the Detroit Tigers won the American League pennant after a 25-year dry spell. The Tiger fans rebelled when it was announced Ty Tyson couldn't broadcast the games. Over 600,000 signatures were amassed by Tiger fans and mailed to Landis and the networks. A compromise was reached when Landis allowed him to air the games on WWJ in Detroit, independent of the CBS and NBC networks.

As the 1930s wore on, every team except the three New York teams was airing its games on radio. The announcers were held in high regard, almost as beloved as the players they talked about. In Boston there was Fred Hoey.

In Philadelphia, By Saam did both the A's and Phillies. Cleveland sported Tom "Red" Manning and the first player-turned-announcer in Jack Graney. Ty Tyson was the voice of the Tigers on WWJ while Waite Hoyt, following a twenty year pitching career, was telling stories about the old Yankees in between describing the exploits of the Reds in Cincinnati. In Pittsburgh, a wisp of a man named Rosey Rosewell was describing the fortunes of his beloved Pirates.

Nowhere was a broadcaster more revered than Rosey during his eighteen year stint as the voice of the Pirates. He was more popular than the players he talked about. He weighed all of 115 pounds, yet was a giant figure in western Pennsylvania, proudly calling himself "America's most partial baseball broadcaster." He was the Pirates MVP, "the blithe spirit who brought fans into the park despite mediocre performances," wrote Harry Keck in the Pittsburgh *Sun-Telegraph*. "His patter over the airwaves meant more to the box office than Ralph Kiner's big bat. With colorful phrases such as "Raise the window Aunt Minnie, here she comes," describing a home run, Rosey had proven former owner Barney Dreyfuss wrong about radio broadcasting hurting gate receipts. He introduced baseball to the housewives who fell in love with the game and with Rosey. There were many a burnt roast or a late dinner blamed on the attention they paid to Rosewell's broadcasts. Once he invited female listeners to come and see him recreate a road game from the KDKA studios. Worried that nobody would come, he had his wife call a few friends. To Rosey's amazement, nearly 5,000 women showed up, spilling out of the studio and down several blocks. Attendance at Pirate games jumped from 600,000 to over a million. With Rosewell broadcasting the Pirates games, it didn't matter whether they finished first or last. "They were my Buccos," he boasted. So it was with the fans who listened to him religiously.

Rosey's successor in Pittsburgh in the 1950s was one of the most flamboyant baseball broadcaster of the golden age of radio. Nicknamed "The Gunner," Bob Prince spent 10 years in Rosey's shadow before taking over, relegated to doing commercials and handling sound effects, such as the glass breaking in Aunt Minnie's window. In his second year he was allowed to do one inning. As the years went on, Prince did more and more, sometimes five innings if Rosey wanted to take a little nap. Like his mentor, Prince coined some colorful phrases, such as "How sweet it is" when describing a "Bobby" Clemente homer, and "We had them all the way" when the Pirates would rally for a victory. Prince was so esteemed by the Pirate organization that he was included in their annual team pictures, a rare honor for a broadcaster. Bob Prince was only 65 when he died on June 10, 1985.

In St. Louis, fans who included most of the Missouri Valley of the country, fell equally in love with a colorful pitcher who left none of his flair for unique colloquial language on the mound. Dizzy Dean's butchery of grammar and syntax drew the wrath of the Missouri English Teachers Association, who wanted him off the air because of his grammatical indiscretions that set a poor example for young students. The year was 1947, and the teachers complained to the Federal Communications Commission that Dean's descriptions of games were replete with errors and malaprops. When Dean, whose four grades in school exceeded his father's formal education, mentioned the matter during a broadcast, business immediately picked up for the telegraph company and Post Office department. Scores of letters and telegrams poured into station WIL, almost without exception taking Dizzy's side and condemning the teachers. "We would rather listen to you than the teachers any day, so don't change your style," was a typical message. "You and your listeners at least know what you are talking about, which is more than can be said of some teachers," read another. Dizzy took the barrage of publicity calmly, yet defiantly continued his ungrammatical descriptions. "Slaughter slud safe into second," "Marion throwed Reiser out at first," "The runners held their respectable bases," and "Musial stands confidentially at the plate" replaced the King's English in Dean's radio classroom. His more endearing descriptions of the play he described spoke volumes about his own rural roots in the cotton fields of Arkansas and his appeal to his rustic audience in rural America where everyone instantly understood that "there goes a tall can o' corn to right field" meant a high fly ball.

Rosey Rosewell, left, describes the action of a re-created Pirates game with help from assistant Bob Prince (with horn) and an unidentified engineer (courtesy Ted Patterson).

Another southern-born broadcaster, Red Barber, testified to the power of vivid description that radio contained for listeners who yearned for a visual display of the game that unfolded in their mind through the eyes of the narrator with a gift for dramatic phrases. Urbane New Yorkers soon relished it as much as rural Southerners. He was the foremost exemplar of this poetic potential of radio. Barber was unique and captivating because he blended clear reporting of action on the field and meticulous command of language with signature catchphrases that relayed to his listeners the dynamics of the moment. Most of them were metaphors drawn from the rural South where many players originated. Yet, it didn't take long for urban city slickers to warm up to them. When Barber started a Dodger game with "They're tearing up the pea patch," listeners knew the Dodgers were on a hot streak. A Mississippian by birth, Barber dropped out of the University of Florida when an opportunity to fill in for a professor to read a scientific paper on the campus radio station hooked him on using his superb diction to report sports. His college radio career led him to Cincinnati when Powell Crosley, Jr. who bought the team in 1934, hoping to sell the radios he manufactured between innings of games, told his general manager, Larry McPhail, to hire the sports announcer that had impressed him on his sojourns to Florida.

Neither MacPhail nor his young announcer were adverse to challenges. Barber broadcast the first major league game he had seen on Opening Day and the first major league night game that anyone saw in May 1935. The innovative MacPhail spearheaded the idea of night baseball, which had been tried with success in several minor league ballparks. The Reds' general manager was so enamored with radio that he had a special hookup installed from station WSAI to his office at Crosley Field. At the flip of a switch MacPhail could be heard on the air promoting an event or informing the fans of a trade. When he "traded" himself to the Dodgers in 1939 he brought Barber with him and refused to extend a five year contract that had banned big league broadcasting in New York.

The irony of an announcer with a southern drawl broadcasting games to ethnic, blue collar workers in Brooklyn went unnoticed as Barber's folksy style of play-by-play description soon made him an institution. His mixture of meticulously reporting play on the wit colorful catchphrases kept listeners riveted to the game. In just one word, "rhubarb," they knew there was a heated argument on the field. He saw the action from the "catbird seat," his mythical roost so-named when he saw a player or the team perform well, thus "sitting pretty." His fairness also became renown. No one ever doubted his loyalty to the Dodgers. Neither did they doubt his objective reporting of the game he saw from his elevated seat. When the Dodgers' general manager, Branch Rickey told him of his decision to put Jackie Robinson on the field in 1947, Barber put aside his southern racial orthodoxy to report his performance and thereafter became an ardent supporter of Robinson and the stream of black players whom followed him. *Sporting News* recognized him as the top play-by-play broadcaster in the major leagues.

Barber tallied another historic first by broadcasting the first major league game ever televised when the Dodgers hosted the Reds in a doubleheader at Ebbets field on NBC on August 26, 1939. The rights fee consisted of placing a television set in the press box so that the writers could check it out. Barber sat in an open booth in the upper deck behind third base, without a monitor. There was one camera along both baselines. Barber interviewed Dodger manager Leo Durocher and several players before the game asking Dolph Camilli of the Dodgers to hold up his gigantic hands to the camera. Innocently enough, the new medium of live events being viewed as they happened in one's living

7—The Tenth Man

Dodger announcers Red Barber, left, and Connie Desmond, right, with Dodger owner Branch Rickey in the announcer's box at Ebbets Field circa 1947 (courtesy Ted Patterson).

room would, in the span of a decade or so, change the face of American sports forever. The public received the experiment enthusiastically, with the TV building at the nearby World's Fair in Flushing, bursting at the seams with curious fans. Barber televised the opening game of the 1940 season, and at least one game a week until the war came. In 1946, MacPhail, now with the Yankees, sold the first commercial TV broadcast rights to the Dumont network for $75,000.

In 1948, when Red was sidelined with an ulcer, another southern announcer made the leap from minor league baseball to launch one of the most distinguished careers in baseball broadcasting history. The Dodgers were in desperate need of a broadcaster to share duties with Connie Desmond. The young voice of the Atlanta Crackers, Ernie Harwell, was their top choice, but Cracker owner Earl Mann drove a hard bargain. He asked for a player in return at season's end. The player was catcher Cliff Dapper, who became the Atlanta field manager the following year. Harwell remained through the 1949 season before teaming with Russ Hodges on the Giant broadcasts. "I felt that announcing Cracker baseball would be the zenith of my career," remembers Harwell, who would remarkably broadcast baseball in seven different decades. He would

A television camera is aimed at Ebbets Field during the first televised baseball game in 1939 (courtesy Ted Patterson).

join the Baltimore Orioles as their first broadcaster in 1954 and then in 1960 begin a relationship as the voice of the Detroit Tigers that lasted over 40 years.

Only one other broadcaster can rival Ernie's longevity streak. Vin Scully started in Brooklyn with the Dodgers of "Boys of Summer" fame, fresh off the Fordham University campus and into Red's "Catbird" seat at Ebbets Field. Barber first heard Scully doing a college football game on the CBS Football Roundup. He liked the youngster's voice and delivery, and knew he was too young to demand a high asking price. "The agreement reached was that I would go to spring training on a one-month option," remembers Vin. "Either I make it or they could lose me in the Everglades." That was 58 seasons ago and Scully is still broadcasting Dodger baseball.

What is so amazing is that he still has enthusiasm for the game, in spite all the other demands that a broadcaster covering a team has to endure. First and foremost are the road trips, the packing and unpacking, the long plane rides, and the changes in time zones that cost valuable sleep time. Throughout all this and more travel hassles now produced by terrorism, Scully says he has" never grown tired of broadcasting major league baseball," Nor has he tried to "pawn myself off as a baseball brain or the sport's foremost authority. I'm not interested in a golden microphone on my tombstone. On the contrary, I'm just a fellow doing a job, and if I get stuck or make a mistake, I'll be the first to make it known."

Over in the Bronx, in the Yankees broadcast booth, sat Mel Allen, another Southerner who assimilated himself not just to the northern metropolis, but to a team whose name signified the historic enemy. The national game had a way of breaking down sectional barriers as well as racial ones. Allen began broadcasting Yankees and Giants home games in 1939, switching to the Yankees exclusively in 1946, before being fired after the 1964 season, the last season of the team's long championship dynasty. Entering the University of Alabama at the tender age of 15, intent on becoming a lawyer, Mel spent eight years at Alabama, graduating with a law degree in 1936. His first announcing job was doing the PA at Alabama home football games in 1934. Impressed with Mel's expertise on the microphone, Crimson Tide coach Frank Thomas recommended Mel to a Birmingham radio station, where, in 1935, he was hired to broadcast Alabama and Auburn games for $5 a game.

After two seasons he took a vacation to New York and out of curiosity, asked to audition at the CBS building. To his surprise he was offered a part-time job that he thought would last six months. He became the understudy to sports announcing legend Ted Husing and news stalwart Robert Trout. In 1938, he helped France Laux and Bill Dyer announce the 1938 World Series despite never having seen a major league game. Then came the 1939 Yankee-Giant schedule, which he worked with Arch McDonald, Connie Desmond and actor J.C. Flippen. In 1946, he joined the Yankees exclusively, working with a series of partners that ranged from Al Helfer, Russ Hodges, Curt Gowdy, Jim Woods and Phil Rizzuto, not to mention Red Barber, who left the Dodgers in 1953, and joined Mel and the Yankees. Mel Allen and Red Barber, two Southerners in the Yankee broadcast booth, demonstrated that the tenth man in baseball again transcended sectional division. Fittingly, they were the first inductees to the broadcasters wing at the Hall of Fame in 1978.

Allen could be a tough taskmaster to announcers who served their tutelage under this master of the art. "I thought I was pretty good in Oklahoma but found out the big leagues were just that — the big leagues, and that I wasn't so hot" recalled Wyoming native, Curt Gowdy, who in 1949 found his way to the nation's media capitol, "I was in awe of Mel and the big city overwhelmed me. Mel sharpened me up on the game of baseball and the art of delivering commercial pitches without interrupting the flow of the game." Another pupil, Jim Woods, joined Mel and the Yankee broadcasts in 1953. "In an early exhibition, Mantle was the hitter and I was at the mike. Mel, sitting next to me, had a habit of snapping his fingers when he heard something that displeased him, and after I described Mickey fouling a pitch off back on top, the fingers began to snap. I looked at Mel and said, 'What's wrong?' He looked at me and said, 'On top of what?' 'The roof,' I answered. 'Well, then say the roof and complete your sentence.' Little things like that made better announcers out of all of us who ever worked with Mel Allen." Fired after the 1964 season when CBS purchased the Yankees, Mel did studio work and televised games in Cleveland in 1967, but didn't have his heart in it. He enjoyed a rebirth with the highly successful "This Week in Baseball" weekly show that returned him to prominence in the 1970's and 1980's before he died in 1996.

While Barber and Allen were broadcasting the fortunes of the Dodgers and Yankees, Russ Hodges was airing the exploits of the New York Giants at the Polo Grounds. In 1949, Giants owner Horace Stoneham needed a replacement for Frankie Frisch the former player turned broadcaster who returned to the field as one of Leo Durocher's coaches. Durocher traded his heavy hitters like Johnny Mize, Sid Gordon and Willard Marshall, and acquired fiery players like Alvin Dark and Eddie Stanky, players cut from the Durocher mold. By 1951, the Giants were contending and when Willie Mays arrived from Minneapolis in May. "I remember they began to climb in the standings." Years later Hodges recalled Willie's first at bat in the Polo Grounds. "He homered on the first pitch Warren Spahn served up." That was the first of hundreds of times that Russ uttered his famous home run call "Bye-Bye Baby" on a Mays home run. He saw and described them all until his premature passing in April of 1971 at the age of 60.

Even with Willie's heroics in 1951, the Giants still trailed the Dodgers by 13½ games on August 11, 16 in the loss column. Russ settled into his groove to begin describing one of the monumental stretch drives in baseball history that began with a 16 game winning streak and culminated with Bobby Thomson's "Shot Heard 'Round the World" home run at the Polo Grounds on the afternoon of October 3. Hodges's memorable broadcast of the final inning, culminating with "There's a long drive, I believe, THE GIANTS WIN THE PENNANT THE GIANTS WIN THE PENNANT THE GIANTS WIN THE PENNANT THE GIANTS WIN THE PENNANT ... Thomson hit it into the lower deck of the left field stands, and they're going crazy. I don't believe it, I will not believe it!" has gone down as perhaps the most listened to description in baseball history. Fortunately, the memorable description was saved for future audiences and preserved in history by a common Brooklyn fan, Lawrence Goldberg. Fiddling with a new tape recorder that he had just received for his birthday, he captured the moment for the rest of us, since the Giant flagship station failed to record the game.

After the dramatic events at the Polo Grounds ended and the broadcast concluded, Goldberg turned off his new tape machine, not realizing that he was the only person who recorded that legendary moment. For reasons unknown, Goldberg, so enraptured by Hodges' riveting broadcast, decided to call Russ and inform him that he had taped the game. "I thought it was just some fan wanting World Series tickets," Russ told me many years later. "When Mr. Goldberg told me he had taped the final few innings I was ecstatic. If you notice when listening, the broadcast sounds a bit tinny and muffled. That's because the microphone was sitting probably a foot from the radio. Plus there was the customary static from listening to a radio. It was definitely an amateur production but it's gone down as my signature trademark."

As radio became a basic staple of baseball, only half of the season schedule was covered live and at the ballpark. Road games for over two decades were aired at the station in recreated form. In fact, originating games on the road didn't become a reality until after World War II. In the case of the Pirates, it didn't happen until after the Korean War in 1955. Costs were just too prohibitive to install phone lines and to pay expenses for traveling broadcasters. So, rather than have no road game broadcasts, the stations would recreate the games from an air studio with the announcers receiving coded updates off the Western Union ticker. Some broadcasters used piped in crowd noise and other gimmicks to make the game sound real. Others just sat waiting for the ticker to then describe what was happening.

Perhaps the most famous "recreator" of them all was Ronald, "Dutch" Reagan. The future President of the United States recreated the Cubs and White Sox games, sponsored by General Mills, on WHO in Des Moines, Iowa, in the mid–1930s. Reagan had never witnessed a big league game in person, but with the help of Chicago baseball announcer Pat Flanagan, he quickly mastered the art of telegraphic reconstruction. "Pat was a good teacher, and before too long I was spinning out games for all the world as if I were not 400 miles from the ballpark." In 1937, Reagan talked his station bosses into letting him cover the Cubs in spring training on Catalina Island off the coast of southern California. On a tour of Hollywood, he took his now celebrated screen test that landed him a contract with Warner Brothers and an eventual political career that culminated in the White House.

In Washington, Arch McDonald became a household name, not from his broadcasts from Griffith Stadium, but rather his recreations of Senator road games. In Arch's first year in Washington in 1934, he handled only the telegraphic recreations of the road games, except for opening day, because team owner Clark Griffith thought attendance would suffer with the home games on radio. Singing his familiar theme song, "The Old Pine Tree," Arch soon won over the Senator faithful with his brand of hillbilly humor and down-home philosophy. In 1935, McDonald began recreating games from a portable studio in the window of the downtown Peoples drug store, and using a tiny hammer making a ping sound to signify a hit, he soon had an average of 300 onlookers as he recreated the road games. In 1937, General Mills and station WJSV in Washington sent McDonald to the Senator's spring camp in Orlando, Florida, and with the use of a 1,000 mile direct line, the longest yet used for daily programming, he became the only announcer in spring training to broadcast on a live, daily basis.

In Cleveland, former Indians player Jack Graney perfected recreations into a highly precise art form. Possessing a crisp, stirring delivery, Graney was a master at setting a scene and his enthusiasm packed a sense of built-in drama. His ability to recreate a game from a telegraphic code on a small piece of paper was beyond reproach. He said he had an advantage over broadcasters in other cities because he had played in every American League park. When the telegrapher handed him a note saying the ball had just caromed off the scoreboard at Navin Field in Detroit, Graney knew exactly where the spot was located because he had bounced off the same wall numerous times. "I disliked recreations," Graney told the author in our 1968 interview. "It was a dizzy job and more than once I'd wake up in a cold sweat and nervous fright over what I said in the studio, hundreds of miles from the actual sight of the game. If I mistakenly positioned a runner on third instead of second or, or had two runners inadvertently switched around in the order they had scored, I'd get letters."

Depending on an announcer's demeanor and zest for flirting with danger, the announcer would either stay right with the action, or stay an inning or so behind to allow for Western Union misadventures. In 1937, Jim Britt began recreating Buffalo Bison games on station WBEN. Britt was a devil-may-care type who liked living on the edge. His counterpart, Roger Baker, on a rival station, owned the town and had a huge listenership. "The first time I did a recreation in competition with Roger, I finished the Buffalo-Syracuse game 20 minutes before he did." The first two no-hit, no-run games Britt ever broadcast he didn't see. They were recreations of Johnny Vander Meer's no-hitters against Boston and Brooklyn. He was seated in the Statler hotel in Buffalo, recreating major league games on days the Bison weren't playing. Britt moved next to Boston where he did the play-by-play of both the Braves and the Red Sox.

The most prolific and realistic sounding recreations were a product of the Liberty Broadcasting System, a creation of sportscaster Gordon McLendon, nicknamed the old Scotchman. Based in Dallas, Texas, the Liberty Network flourished in the early 1950s. Rights fees were fairly non-existent, which enabled the network to broadcast just about any game it chose to. Several broadcasters gained network exposure at Liberty with its biggest star, Lindsey Nelson. Liberty broadcast two baseball games a day and six football games a weekend in the fall, beginning with the Miami Hurricanes on Friday night and ending with the Los Angeles Rams on Sunday afternoon. "We had baseball running out of our ears," said Nelson. "It seems like every waking moment I was saying, 'Play ball with the Liberty Broadcasting System.' It was utter heaven for a sports announcer because we did sports. I once did 60 games in 30 days."

While baseball, save for some important games such as the 1951 Giants-Dodgers playoff series, was recreated, football was done live. "Our re-creations were better than our live broadcasts, and this was one of our problems," remembered Nelson. "We could control all of the factors surrounding a game when we recreated, which we couldn't do when we were at the park live." A crew was sent to record the playing of the National Anthem and the public address announcer at each park for the sake of realism. "So when we said, 'And now ladies and gentlemen, at Ebbets Field in Brooklyn, our National Anthem,' it was really that anthem, just not one sung that particular day. During a game we had four turntables going simultaneously, two with normal crowd noise and two with more excitement, depending on the happenings in the game. We even used our men's room as an echo chamber to make public address announcements. A Monday afternoon game at Wrigley Field in front of 4,000 fans would sound kind of dull, but when we piped in the sound of 30,000 fans from a recording, excitement was at a fever pitch."

Referring to the Liberty Network and his boyhood in Mississippi, Willie Morris later noted in *The New Yorker* that "The Old Scotchman's games were rare and remarkable entities, things of beauty. Later when I came across the writings of Thomas Wolfe, I felt I had heard him before, from Shibe Park, Crosley Field and Yankee Stadium. On those summer afternoons, almost every radio in Yazoo City was tuned to the Old Scotchman, and his rhetoric dominated the place. It hovered in the branches of the trees, bounced off the hills and came out of car exhausts. It touched our need for a simple and unmitigated eloquence. In Mississippi, I sometimes think now, it was the final flowering of a poetic age."

Baseball's golden age of radio, beginning in the early 1920s, waned in the early 1950s as television became the new king on the mass media stage. Making its debut in the backdrop of the New York World's Fair in 1939, TV covered baseball as early as 1946 when the Yankees became the first team to sell TV rights to games to the Dumont Network for $75,000. In 1947, NBC televised the Yankee games, CBS had the Dodgers and Dumont covered the Yankees. Also in 1947 NBC, CBS and Dumont shared the rights for the first World Series telecast at a cost of $65,000. It was aired on a regional network in the East. The announcers were Bob Edge, Bob Stanton and Bill Slater. They received less than $100 each for their efforts, but they blazed the trail. By 1951, the World Series was seen coast to coast. Bars and taverns were the first to seize the importance of television sports, especially baseball and boxing. In 1948, the "Gillette Cavalcade of Sports" debuted on NBC with sportswriters Jimmy Powers and Bill Corum behind the mikes. Television sets were leaving stores as fast as they came in.

The popularity of television took its toll not on the major league teams, but in the minor leagues. The minors reached their peak right after World War II, but the advent of television almost killed the minors. It was a logical proposition. Why would a fan go to support a minor league game when he could watch a big league game of the week in the comfort of his living room on TV? The coverage was primitive and basic with a camera anchored in the second deck behind home plate, and cameras down each line. There was no center field camera, no instant replay, no close-ups, no color — just the game without gimmicks. When 1949 rolled around, one million Americans were bragging about being TV owners. Just one year later, the figure quadrupled. Milton Berle was already dubbed "Mr. Television" and "Mr. Tuesday Night."

New York was the pacesetter of TV baseball. While most of the teams were televising a handful of games, the Yankees, Giants and Dodgers were airing upwards of half their schedule. But even in the mass media capitol, TV was a challenge for the broadcasters, This was especially true when the games were simulcast on both radio and television. They were either talking too much on one medium or not enough on the other. Moreover, with television, the broadcasters no longer could soar into wild flights of imagination, painting word pictures however they liked. They were trapped by the TV tube and what it revealed. Greater emphasis had to be placed on accuracy because the fan watching could see what was happening.

Yet, baseball provided television with an experimental stage for broadcasting sports. In 1957, NBC joined CBS with "Game of the Week" telecasts with NBC debuting the first center field camera, giving viewers a head-on shot of the batter from behind the pitcher for the World Series, won by the Braves over the Yankees in seven games. The first color baseball telecast occurred at Ebbets Field on August 11, 1951, years ahead of its use for other venues. Red Barber and Connie Desmond were the broadcasters for the double header with the Braves. The 1955 World Series, known mostly for the heroic Dodger victory over the rival Yankees, was the first series to be telecast in color, on WRCA-TV in New York.

The first team to televise a sizable schedule of games in color on a local and regional basis was the Cincinnati Reds in 1959. Owned by pace setting television tycoon Powell Crosley, the Reds home colorcasts produced marked increases in set sales, park attendance and number of viewers. It began modestly on a regional network, including Columbus, Dayton, and Indianapolis, with a total of 12 Saturday and Sunday home games. Television set sales zoomed over the 30,000 mark. The colorcast of each game was promoted on taxi-cabs, buses and tavern windows, not to mention TV Guides and newspapers. Yet for every cause there is an effect and as television became a basic staple of American life, nightly activities ground to a halt. Night baseball had bought the minor leagues some time, but television in many instances served as the death knell of baseball in small towns.

Minor league baseball wasn't all that suffered. Nightclubs, restaurants, movie theatres, drive-ins and neighborhood fight clubs all began losing money and eventually closing. And as each year went by, more improvements were added for the delight of the fans: instant replays, stop action, slow-motion, centerfield cameras, and more. The technological advances made baseball two games, not one. There was the game the fan paid to see in the ballpark. The second was free, on TV, and showed the fan infinitely more. The growth of baseball on TV, however, wasn't without problems. A resentful newspaper press corps took exception to the higher paid "Golden Voices" who had easier access to the players and managers.

Then there was the internal conflict within the broadcasting fraternity itself. It arose with the mushrooming influx of former players turned announcers, who began at the top at the expense of the broadcasters who started at the bottom rungs and tried to work their way up the ladder through their versatility-never meeting an event they couldn't describe. The player's game expertise was meant to add an additional dimension to telecasts and frequently did in the form of fractured syntax. The broadcasters who spent a lifetime in the industry resented these "upstarts" much as the print media that was shrinking throughout the nation resented the broadcasters themselves. Many of these "upstarts," though, became popular, and often beloved in their respective locales; among them, Phil Rizzuto, Pee Wee Reese, Bob Uecker, George Kell, Joe Nuxhall, Mike Shannon, Nellie King, Ken Harrelson, Herb Score, Jerry Coleman and Richie Ashburn, to name a few.

Yet, the bond between announcer and fan was never as it once was. Broadcasters today, save for a rare gem such as John Miller, lack the requisite command of language, baseball knowledge, and gusto that has always distinguished great baseball broadcasting. Television has made the announcer a prisoner of the camera, a reactor and a labeler, rather than a wordsmith and scene painter such as Red Barber in his radio days when his description of a far away game to an unseen audience was played out in the theatre of their minds.

The personal experience that announcers shared with the players enriched the drama they shared with the fans. Former Brooklyn Dodger announcer, Connie Desmond, said it best, when talking about his own life with a team:

> When spring training gets underway, the itch becomes almost unbearable. It brings back memories of the breezes in Havana and the Caribbean. I think of the thrills of the World Series and All-Star games and the sorrows such as the hours on trains and on airplanes. The packing, the unpacking, the farewells to your families. Your reception as you walk into the dugout. The faces of men and their ability to rise to the occasion when the odds are against them. It was my job to help report it all to the unseen audience. Broadcasting was a demanding occupation, both mentally and physically. Just being away from home so long can be heartbreaking. Yet I had to go to the scene; the scene could not come to me.... What really is the purpose of a play-by-play sportscaster? Very simple: We are there because they are not.

For their listeners they were the tenth man on the team.

Part II

BEYOND THE MAJORS

The lure of playing in the major leagues was irresistible to millions of young men who had baseballs skills, but getting to "the bigs" was out of reach for almost all of them. Even those who did required apprenticeship on minor league teams. Others settled in for a longer sojourn, waiting for a call from above, or simply played out their career entertaining the local fans in the leagues that proliferated in the early twentieth century. In southern West Virginia baseball teams multiplied between the two world wars. Sometimes whole towns turned out to watch their favorites play the game and to join in the social life that followed it, according to William E. Akin in his essay, "West Virginia Coalfield Baseball, 1921–1941." Akin, who has written a fuller study of this subject, also explains how these teams sometimes became pawns in the war between capital and labor. In West Virginia, baseball was clearly intertwined with the life of the state.

African American men loved the game, too, and many of them would have found their way to the major leagues had it not been for the shame of racial prejudice that kept them out. Until 1947, and a few years beyond that, they played in what were called the Negro Leagues. It was their majors. Many of them matched the prodigious feats of their white counterparts, and some exceeded them. Like the other big leagues, the "colored" teams were also a business for those who owned them or controlled their schedules. Only a few had parks of their own. This disadvantage, and other financial obstacles described in the essay by Robert V. Leffler Jr., "Boom and Bust: The Elite Giants and Black Baseball in Baltimore, 1936–1951," was hard on everyone involved. Fortunately, the players loved the game, their fans loved the way they played, and white major leaguers who played against them in exhibition game knew how good many of them were. Leffler's essay focuses on the complexities of the team's business arrangements, the owners' relationship with the local black communities, and the parks they played in.

8

West Virginia Coalfield Baseball, 1921–1941

WILLIAM E. AKIN

Bitter industrial warfare broke out in the bituminous coalfields following the Armistice ending the Great War. The United Mine Workers union wished to consolidate its wartime gains and extend its sway over the low-wage southern coalfields while miners struggled against post-war wage cuts and coal operators launched a violent campaign to destroy the hated union and drive it from the coal camps forever.

The coal establishment, backed as it was by Baldwin-Felts guards, private armies, local law enforcement, state police, National Guard and eventually the U. S. army, wielded overwhelming power. Against all odds, coal miners in southern West Virginia carried on a two-year struggle. This industrial warfare came to a head in the mountains south of the state capital in Charleston and north of the county seat town of Logan. Historian David Corbin characterized the struggle as "an uprising of the southern West Virginia miners against the coal establishment." In a frenzied two-week long fight known as the Battle of Blair Mountain in August 1921 upwards to 20,000 miners fought the forces of American capitalism. When President Warren Harding sent in regular army troops and planes the operators gained a complete victory.[1] The reality was that miners could strike, fight strikebreakers, burn tipples, and fire the mines, but they could not win.

With their union squashed and class solidarity destroyed, miners, as historian Corbin writes, turned to alcohol to wash away their cares and fatalism to carry them back into the mines. Coal operators, for their part, still faced the necessity of getting coal out of the ground and on its way to markets. For this they needed a steady, reliable, and productive workforce. Some owners and operators concluded that undisguised power had reached a point of diminishing returns. After the mine wars these operators began to implement more subtle means of keeping workers peaceful and wages low. Welfare capitalism offered a method of creating a "satisfied, stable and productive labor force."[2]

Baseball proved to be a strategic vehicle for implementing the owners' more subtle approach to controlling their workers. In the two decades between the Battle of Blair Mountain and Pearl Harbor baseball flourished as never before or since in the southern West Virginia coalfields. Nearly all West Virginia natives who reached the major leagues in the interwar years did their apprenticeship in coalfield ball. Hundreds of good players, some young kids, some grizzled veterans of pro baseball made their way to the mines looking for a chance to play ball. For some of those the mine teams offered a way to test their skills and launch a pro career. For others, it just offered a chance to keep playing. Mine operators made coalfield ball possible. They sponsored teams, build fields, paid for uniforms, recruited and hired players, found cushy jobs for them, and gave them time off from work to play ball.

Several companies saw benefits to baseball even before the twenties. In Gary, a company town in McDowell County owned by U. S. Steel, engineers and railroad workers from the North had formed teams as early as 1902. By 1906 the company provided its employees with a baseball field and small wooden grandstand. Walter P. Tams, one of the few operators who lived in his company-owned town, boasted of the best recreation facilities in the region, including a company baseball team named for him, the Tams Majors. However, the real model for welfare capitalism in southern West Virginia was the Raleigh Coal and Coke Company, just outside of Beckley, the seat of Raleigh County. In 1919 the company formed the Raleigh Mining Institute (RMI) to orchestrate a recreation program for its employees. The RMI Park would eventually become the center of baseball in the entire region.[3] In 1919, however, most coal operators were too busy fighting miners to follow the RMI model.

The spark that ignited coalfield baseball came in 1924. After that date baseball became the centerpiece of welfare capitalism in the southern West Virginia coalfields. Early in the summer 1924 several influential Bluefield businessmen, including newspaper owner Ike Shott, formed a baseball team. Bluefield, on the eastern edge of the southern West Virginia coalfields, was the largest city in the region with 20,000 people. The Norfolk and Western Railroad hub, and the center of legal, banking, and wholesale activities for the southern part of the state, Bluefield had a sizable and well-to-do middle class. For these people, a baseball team appealed to their civic pride. They named the team the Blue-Grays in recognition of the city's location on the West Virginia-Virginia border.[4]

The Blue-Grays prospered on the field and at the gate. Playing at the Fairgrounds, the team charged admission to its games. Manager Dick Neberger hired a former major league pitcher, John "Chick" Smith, and several hotshot youngsters from out of state. The Blue-Grays played in the semi-pro Blue Ridge League against teams from Virginia and North Carolina until the league folded in late-July.

Bluefield's new team generated a virtual explosion of baseball that quickly spread the game to the Pocahontas coalfield to the west. In Bramwell, a town of company offices and mansions for coal operators, wealthy residents happily donated land for a diamond and money for uniforms. From there teams sprung up all along the Norfolk and Western Railroad in Mercer and McDowell counties. Teams formed in places named Pocahontas, McComas, Maybeury, Elkhorn, Powhatan, Northfork, Coalwood, Berwind, and in the McDowell county seat of Welch. In Gary, mine superintendent Colonel Edward O'Toole expanded and upgraded the little ballpark until he had finest ballpark in the region, including a horseshoe shaped covered grandstand running from first to third base.

As soon as these teams formed, the competitive juices of coal operators drove them to up the ante. Not content with pride in their teams' successes, operators began betting their counterparts large sums of money on the outcome of games. With money as well as bragging rights at stake, quality players quickly became in great demand. Following the example of the Blue-Grays, company teams began recruiting players from outside the coal camps. Pitchers, especially, were in demand. Future major leaguers Vic Sorrell, Bob Smith, Harry "Hoge" Workman, John Woods, Guy Morrison, and Paul Derringer pitched on coalfield teams in 1924–1925. The money was good enough to attract former big league pitchers Chick Smith, Phil Douglass, and Nick Cullop. John "Stud" Stuart hurried home after his major league season ended to pick up extra cash. Ethan Allen, then a student at the University of Cincinnati, established himself as the best coalfield batter of 1924 and 1925. He went on to play thirteen major league seasons after which he coached at Yale University for twenty-two years.

An October 1924 barnstorming trip through the area by the Cincinnati Reds generated even more baseball fever. Touring along the Norfolk and Western line, the Reds stopped for games against local stars in Williamson, Welch, Gary, and Bluefield. Heavy advanced publicity assured that record crowds turned out to see the major leaguers.[5]

For the 1925 season, the town of Coalwood, later made famous by Homer Hickam and his Rocket Boys, boasted the region's most famous player when it brought in "Shufflin'" Phil Douglas. Thirty-five and with a serious drinking problem, he had spent nine seasons pitching in the majors. In his last season with the New York Giants, Douglas won eleven games, lost only four, and posted the best earned run average in the National League. Unfortunately, his drinking and anger at manager John McGraw led to Douglas' threat to throw a game, and that caused his lifetime suspension from Organized Baseball. Douglas had little education and few skills except pitching. If he could no longer pitch in New York, he would pitch in Coalwood.[6] There the powers-that-be appreciated him, as well as the fans. Also, in Coalwood he would have no problem finding alcohol.

In 1925 Frank M. Archer took over the Blue-Grays and quickly formed the first organized league in the region, named simply the Coalfield League. Bluefield, Gary, Coalwood and Pocahontas-Bramwell made up the four-team circuit. Teams played each other weekly from Memorial Day into August, arranging games with other teams during the week. Bluefield jumped out to an early lead behind Vic Sorrell's dominant pitching only to lose the lead when Sorrell left to play in Organized Ball, and then come back to win the league title after Sorrell returned. In addition to the four league teams, dozens of mines fielded teams. Most played three days a week through the summer.

The fast times quickly ended after 1925. Operators retreated from the excesses of the past two summers. Gone was the oversized betting by the coal operators. Without that the need to recruit high priced players vanished. Operators, however, seeing the advantages to baseball continued to underwrite the costs of hundreds of teams. Baseball, however, had spread to virtually every coal patch, camp and town throughout the mountains of Southern West Virginia. Teams represented coal towns named Stone Coal, Coalwood, Coaldale, and Hot Coal, Loup Creek, Dry Creek, Rock Creek and Camp Creek, Sophia and Helen, Crab Orchard and Cranberry, War and Pax, East Gulf and Winding Gulf, Glen White, Glen Rodgers, Glen Morgan, Glen Jean, and Glen Daniel, Raleigh, Lester and Stotesbury, Redstar and Bluefield, Slabrock and Slabfork, Hiawatha and Pocahontas.[7]

Coalfield baseball settled into a routine after 1925. Games were played only on Sundays and holidays. Mines occasionally hired a man because of his baseball skills, but most players now came from the ranks of mine families. Baseball was no longer a toy for rich coal operators; it had become a tool for creating a satisfied labor force.

Even without high priced players, games remained highly competitive, hard-fought affairs. Play was rough and brawls not uncommon. Every town had a heckler with a booming voice who jeered and taunted opposing players. Former Gary manager A.N. Harris recalled: "The enthusiasm for a particular team often caused fights, individual and mob." Harris and Bob Bowman, who went to the majors from the coalfield, remembered guns being fired at games, although in enthusiasm rather than anger.[8] There is no evidence of any one being killed.

Although coal operators ceased their excessive wagering, at least in public, betting remained a pervasive part of coalfield ball. Knowing this put pressure on the pitchers. Bowman recalled feeling greater pressure to win in coalfield ball than he did in the majors because at mine games "the boys were betting their shirts.... I had to win or else."[9]

Miners worked six days a week, so Sundays were "precious time," to use a term Robert and Helen Lynd coined in *Middletown*. They reserved their precious time for church and baseball. Harris remembered: "All week long the citizens of McDowell County looked forward to the baseball game to be played on Sunday afternoons." A Berwind native recalled: "Sunday in Berwind was baseball." Historian Crandall Shifflett's understated summary rings true: "Baseball was the miners' sport!"[10]

Games took on a social significance. In the Twenties, visiting teams typically arrived by train. The Norfolk &Western ran special trains for games between teams from the larger towns. Later, after 1934 when the union came in and wages increased, fans and players traveled to away games in Model T Fords. The home team could expect to see virtually the entire town turn out for games. Of course, most town populations numbered in the hundreds not the thousands. Okey Mills, a star pitcher before becoming sheriff of Raleigh County, remembered: "Baseball was the center of entertainment."[11] It was not uncommon to have as many women and children spectators as men. Fans commonly overflowed the small stands, lining the foul lines and at times even stood in the deep outfield or watched from hillsides or slag heaps outside the grounds. Children chased foul balls.

After the games, a festive atmosphere replaced the enthusiasm of the competition. Today tailgating precedes sporting events; then the food and drink came after the game. Players, families, and fans gathered on the field or under nearby trees to socialize. Often, visiting players, as well as the home team, joined the picnic on the grounds. Women broke out baskets of food. Men broke out a bottle; miners always seemed to know where they could obtain a bottle of homebrew. After Prohibition ended, beer became the preferred drink. The socializing might last until darkness.[12]

Coal companies willingly committed large chunks of scarce flat land to the baseball field. The mine tipple and entrance often dominated one hillside, with residences on a hill across the way. The flatland between provided the site of the ball diamond. None of the fields resemble the manicured parks of today. All had dirt infields. A smooth, skinned field could play fast and true, much like Astroturf fields fifty years later. Almost none reached that level of quality. Ruts and stones were more common. Fielding became an adventure. Bad bounces were common. "If the ball took a bad hop and hit you in the face," coalfield veteran Cecil Lacy recalled, "well, that was too bad."[13] Men who worked in coal had to be tough.

The small cities of Bluefield, Welch, Williamson, and Beckley had enclosed parks with roofed grandstands. By 1938 they also had lights. Gary, Raleigh and a handful of other towns also had enclosed parks. In smaller coal camps diamonds had uncovered wooden stands, open bleachers actually, typically four to seven rows deep. At those fields, dugouts and outfield fences were uncommon. So home runs, generally, came from long hits between outfielders and speed on the base paths.[14]

Ballplayers had a special status in the coal camps. Sebert Toney, Jr. remembered: "They were given a real cushy job topside." Players often worked as clerks in the company store, doing repairs on company buildings, or stringing utility lines. One former player described the status he felt as a player: "Your wife would wash your uniform and hang it out on the line. You could see that uniform while walking back home from the mines and you'd feel that pride all over again."[15]

While coal operators could see baseball as a form of social control, baseball created strong community bonds. The game connected people in a shared experience and raised the spirit of the entire community. At baseball

This West Virginia coal town setting has space in the valley for a ball field (courtesy William E. Akin).

games, residents bonded into a community. The game obliterated distinctions. Miners, who five years earlier burned the coal tipple and fought mine guards, now sat side by side with the owners and cheered for the company team. At games, Catholics and Protestants, Hungarians and Scotch-Irish shared a common cause, and broke bread together after the game. Of course there were limits to baseball's ability to create community; blacks and whites remained largely separate on the playing field as they did in other areas of their lives.

Strong African-American teams began to appear in the late-twenties. Southern West Virginia had a sizable black population; mostly derived from men who originally came to the area as strikebreakers. Initially, operators did not bother creating baseball opportunities for African-American employees, but for the same reasons that companies sponsored white teams—to create loyalty to the company, as a barrier against unions, and as a means of social control—they saw fit to form black teams. The African-American teams played on the same fields as the white locals, but black and white teams from the same town never played each other. Black citizenry greeted their baseball teams with enthusiasm that often surpassed their white counterparts. Some African-American teams even had uniformed cheerleaders.

Beginning in the Twenties, the famous Homestead Grays barnstormed through the region playing African-American teams in the few enclosed parks. By the Thirties, white teams as well as blacks happily scheduled barnstorming Negro League teams, including the Memphis Red Sox, Birmingham Black Barons, Kansas City Monarchs, and Pittsburgh Crawfords. These teams always brought out big crowds. The Crawfords were the favorites of white as well as black fans, and the Crawford star Oscar Charleston was a bigger draw than Satchel Paige.

Two new leagues organized in 1927. In Mercer and McDowell counties, the Coalfield Association replaced the initial league of 1925. The Association included the Bramwell Indians, Coalwood Robins, Gary Coal Diggers, and Welch Senators. In Welch, the seat of McDowell County, John Blakely, who was rapidly amassing a fortune in insurance, built Blakely Park for his Senators. An enclosed park with covered grandstand, it rivaled Gary's field. Coalwood, having replaced Phil Douglas with young Paul Derringer as its pitching ace, copped the first league title.[16]

The second league formed to the north in Raleigh County. Needy McQuade, sports editor of the *Raleigh Register* in Beckley, was the energizing force behind the creation of the Raleigh County Baseball League. The center of coalfield baseball quickly moved from the southern tier of counties of Mercer, McDowell, Mingo and Logan, to the Beckley area. The demand for membership was so great that Needy formed two divisions of eight teams each. Division winners met in a playoff at the conclusion of the season for the county championship, a format that lasted until the 1950s.[17]

The organization of coalfield baseball took a further leap in 1929 with the creation of the semi-pro Tri-State League. This league consisted of teams from three of West Virginia's four largest cities—Huntington, Charleston, and Parkersburg—plus coalfield cities of Beckley and Williamson, and a team from Ashland, Kentucky. Logan replaced Parkersburg in 1930. As mine teams had done in 1924, owners loaded up with outside talent. Some were former major league players such as Wayland Dean; others were college prospects, a group that included Duke's Bill Weber. Two former minor league players proved to be the big stars: Holt "Cat" Milner was the most feared hitter, and Kelsey Jennings the top pitcher. The majority of players were veterans of coalfield ball happy to move from coal camps into town.[18]

Despite the Depression, Tri-State League cities showed a profit in 1930. The experience so buoyed the teams' owners that Huntington, Charleston, and Beckley jumped at the opportunity to enter Organized Baseball. In 1931 they gained membership in the Middle Atlantic League, the fastest Class C league in the country. Charleston and Huntington made the transition to professional ball, but in the Beckley area, several coal mine teams outdrew the professional Black Knights.

In the early Thirties, the growing economic depression affected coalfield baseball, as it did the entire coal industry. As the bituminous industry teetered on the verge of bankruptcy by 1930, coal companies cut their expenses. Many no longer felt they could no longer afford the luxury of a baseball team. By 1932, the Raleigh League fielded less than half the number of teams it had before the Wall Street Crash. Other counties experienced similar losses.[19]

The unionization of the coal mining industry in 1933 presented more problems for coalfield baseball. As the UMW organized the southern coalfields in, coal companies whose primary goal in sponsoring baseball teams had been to keep workers happy and the union out, lost their reason to put resources into baseball. Even so, many teams somehow managed to survive. By the mid–Thirties the Raleigh League again operated with a full compliment of teams. The United Mine Workers created its own league in 1933. The WMW League continued through the 1930s, but the quality of play did not match that of the Raleigh County League.

Without company sponsorship mine teams had to finance their own operation. Those with access to enclosed parks could charge admission, at least for games against barnstorming teams. Donkey baseball games were good once a summer. All teams commonly passed the hat at games. The unofficial check-off on paydays offered another technique for supporting teams. When miners picked up their pay, the local team stood next in line next to the pay master, asking miners for a fifty-cent donation each payday. Miners seldom refused. Some few charged admission. Most made do by postponing the purchase of new uniforms, so team photos show players sporting a variety of uniforms.[20] After 1934 most teams managed to survive the remainder of the decade.

By the mid–Thirties the leagues reestablished a rhythm that carried until World War II. The Raleigh County A and B leagues operated with eighteen teams and the UMW league had eight more. A Tri-County League in Logan, McDowell, and Mercer counties lasted through the depression years. Elkhorn, a tiny Mercer County coal patch, dominated because or Bob Bowman's pitching until he left for pro ball in 1936.

Fred "Sheriff" Blake, an Anstead, West Virginia native and former Chicago Cub ace, became a legend in the coalfields in the Thirties. Blake had pitched in the National League throughout the twenties, posting double-digit wins for six seasons. In 1932 he returned to Glen White, a coal town of 700 near Beckley, owned by the Kopers Coal Company. In the major leagues Blake's wildness prevented him from becoming a dominant pitcher, but in the coalfields that wildness served him well; batters feared for their lives when they faced him. Blake convinced former Cub teammate Earl Webb, a lifetime .300 hitter, to join him in Glen White. The Koppers captured four Raleigh League titles before Blake returned to the major league for a brief stint in 1937. He returned to the hills where he pitched and managed into the Fifties.

Blake and Webb competed against younger players who would go from the coalfields to the majors. The pitchers dominated the list: Vern Bickford, Harry Perkowski, Bob Bowman, Arnold Carter, Max Butcher, and Charlie "Major" Bowles. Others were catchers Sig Broskie and Frank Reiber; infielder John Bero; and outfielders Hal Rice and Tom Cafego. None became stars. Most just stayed for the proverbial cup of coffee in the big leagues, but they made it.

African-American teams also flourished in the Thirties. The best of the group were the Holden Bearcats in Logan County, the Kyle Cardinals in

McDowell County, and the Raleigh Clippers from the mining camp outside Beckley. The Clippers Grover Lewis was to black fans what Sheriff Blake was to whites. He had played for the Homestead Grays, 1925–1929, before returning to Raleigh as player-manager for the Clippers from 1931 into the 1950s. Second baseman Tommy "Toots" Sampson, a magician in the field, left to play for the Chicago American Giants, Birmingham Black Barons and other black teams between 1938 and 1949. Outfielder S. G. "Garson" Totten went on to play for the New York Cubans in the 1940s. The Clippers regularly attracted 500 fans to their games, but they sold out RMI park with over 3,000 white, as well as black, fans for games against the Homestead Grays, Pittsburgh Crawfords, and House of David.[21]

Occasionally African-American teams played white squads. In 1940 the Slab Fork Indians, winner of the newly formed Tri-County Negro League, took on Raleigh League winner Stotesbury, losing 19–9. The same year, black and white all-star teams from Raleigh County played a three game series. Grover Lewis organized a team of "colored all-stars," and Blake put together the white squad. Lewis' team took only one game, a 6–3 decision. With former major league pitchers Blake and John Gorska starting, the whites won two games, each by just one run. Earl "Red" Martin, just three years away from being the top hitter in all of Organized Baseball, was the batting star for the white all-stars. Clipper outfielder Angus Evans remembered "no racial tensions on the diamond. We played ball."[22]

The formation of the Class D Mountain State League in 1937 reduced the appeal of the coal mine teams. The league placed teams in Bluefield, Beckley, Welch, Williamson, and Logan, the largest towns of the region. Having won the right to a shorter work week, miners from surrounding coal towns flocked to the small cities on Saturdays and often stayed to see the pros play on Saturday night.

As war approached, the culture of the mine communities and the towns themselves began to change. New Deal highway dollars had paved roads, and union wages allowed more miners to own their own automobiles. Cars made it possible for some miners to live away from their work place. The Works Projects Administration and Civilian Conservation Corps funded the development of parks and recreation facilities. As miners became more mobile, mine families found other recreation opportunities for a Sunday afternoon.

Other cracks began to appear in the tight coal patch communities. Companies began to sell off their houses to the miners. With Prohibition a thing of the past, beer joints cropped up to provide a place for miners to drink away from the ball field, and often away from family. As defense industries began to create a demand for labor in the industrial cities of Ohio, mountain families began leaving the dangerous struggle to mine coal for safer manufacturing jobs.

Baseball had brought people together in the Twenties and Thirties. The game had connected communities in a shared experience. By 1940, as war clouds gathered, baseball had little chance of holding the communities together in the face of massive social and demographic changes. The days of the coal camps and coalfield baseball were not yet over, but the heyday of coal and coalfield baseball had passed.

9

Boom and Bust: The Elite Giants and Black Baseball in Baltimore, 1936–1951

ROBERT V. LEFFLER, JR.

Owners of Negro baseball franchises in Baltimore were not notoriously involved in black community affairs. They owned teams for a combination of reasons—financial, philanthropic, and avocational. Late in 1934, when white sportsmen deserted the Baltimore Black Sox, the local situation looked grim.

Compared to other cities, Baltimore—a minor league town since 1902— languished in ballpark poverty. Maryland Park, for many years a favorite among African-American fans, became a junk lot. Oriole Park at 29th and Greenmount was segregated for International League games and, though possibly available to black teams on a rental basis, seated only 10,495 persons. Municipal Stadium—constructed of earth, cement, and wood in 1922 to compete with Philadelphia for the yearly staging of the Army-Navy game—accommodated 70,000 football fans; it did not have a baseball diamond. Various other fields were just that—fields, with a few rows of simple wooden bleachers behind each bench. Then there was Bugle Field, a 6,000-seat wooden park in East Baltimore owned by Joe Cambria of the Bugle Coat, Tie and Apron Company.

Though Bugle Park offered the logical place for fielding a "colored" team, it was ridiculous in size next to the rentable ballparks in East Coast cities that claimed major-league franchises. Yankee Stadium seated 67,000 fans. Brooklyn's Ebbets Field 32,000, Philadelphia's Shibe Park 33,000, and Washington's Griffith Stadium 37,000. The black leagues in Brooklyn and Philadelphia benefited similarly from the large populations and lucrative gates; they were stadium rich. In Brooklyn Dexter Park held 15,000, and in Philadelphia Parkside Field 20,000.[1] Being able, if need be, to rent larger fields enhanced ownership of a black franchise outside of Baltimore.

Black teams elsewhere also had successful white booking agents. Eddie

Gottlieb of Philadelphia acquired control of the Philly Stars from Ed Bolden in 1935. Before long Negro teams of top professional caliber had to hire him if they wanted to play in Philadelphia, Baltimore, or any place in-between.[2] White booking agents served as middlemen for black teams; many white park owners would not negotiate with black team owners like Nat Strong, Cum Posey, and Gus Greenlee. Gottlieb's hold on such cities as Baltimore, Philadelphia, Harrisburg, Wilmington, and Washington (where he operated with Douglas Smith) cost black and white team owners alike a percentage of the gate if they could not promote the games themselves. In cities with a locally owned black franchise, team owners did not feel the same pinch unless they needed the use of the white ballpark and happened to be black. A city without a team was at the mercy of the booking agents in terms of black baseball promotions. If in June, for example, the Homestead Grays and Philly Stars played a game in Oriole Park before only one thousand fans, Gottlieb likely would drop the city from "major league" promotions for a long time. In 1936 and 1937 Gottlieb and Smith controlled the baseball season, arranging games for Bugle Field and Oriole Park according to local fan interest. This straight business approach left baseball fans to the whims of finance. They needed a local sponsoring group — of either race — either to recreate the Black Sox of old or attract a new team.

The Nashville Elite Giants, founded in 1918 by Nashville gambling casino owner Tom Wilson, had been a vagabond team since 1935, first claiming Griffith Stadium and then in 1936–37, without changing their name, scheduling a number of games in Baltimore.[3] There they were at the mercy of booking agents. Only a permanent, bona fide tie to the city would permit Wilson, a black owner, to establish a business edge. As always fan interest and the involvement of community-oriented persons were important factors in luring a franchise. Since there was no black financial support for resurrecting the Black Sox, a local individual had to step forward and lead a civic effort to bring the Elite Giants to Baltimore. Such a leader appeared in a young black Social Security Administration employee, Richard D. Powell.

In 1936 Powell began to rally black Baltimoreans like members of the Frontiers Club behind the Nashville team and open a search for a Baltimore park it could call home. First Powell measured black philanthropic potential and community spirit; he had no desire to set up a chancy business arrangement with another white-owned team, especially given Baltimore's ballpark poverty. He and other backers aimed to woo a prospective franchise mover with promises of loyalty and consistent community support.

Powell spent the 1936 and 1937 seasons courting Wilson's Elites by having them invited to home-cooked meals and overnight stays with local fans (ballplayers usually stayed at the humble York Hotel on Madison Avenue and ate their meals at segregated restaurants). Powell also convinced Wilson and his business manager, Vernon Green, to establish Maryland residency — despite the fact that Wilson's income derived from his secretive gambling base in Nashville. Finally Wilson announced that the team would move to Baltimore for the 1938 season.[4] Smith, meanwhile, attempted to rent Oriole Park for the team's home games. The prospect of a black team playing a number of night games in their neighborhood riled white residents of Waverly, however; they petitioned the Oriole management to deny the Elites' request.[5] Though black teams had rented parks in Baltimore since 1874, the Orioles went along with the wishes of their neighbors and put the Elites out. Wilson and Smith naturally turned to Bugle Field. Cambria's business managers agreed to lease the field through the Elites' first season.

The year went smoothly for the Elites, and by play-off time the Orioles invited them to use Oriole Park after all. All major competition from Washington ended early when the Washington Black Senators of the National Negro League collapsed. The Elites were then able to make up for the tiny capacity of Bugle Field by occasionally being the home team at Griffith Stadium. They enjoyed that role on 10 August, when the Baltimore team hosted the Pittsburgh Crawfords before eleven thousand fans. Local semi-pro teams—the Monumental Elks, who played at Bugle when the Elites were away, or Dr. Joseph Thomas's "Original Baltimore Black Sox," a local nine from Turners Station—provided little financial worry for Wilson, Powell, and Smith. Only touring interracial softball teams like Joe Louis's Brown Bombers and a white team known as the Dr. Peppers provided the Elites notable competition. They played exhibition games, mostly in Washington.[6]

In 1938 baseball in Baltimore varied, but there were fans enough to support all of it. Black baseball was just beginning a boom that would last until around 1944, and signs of this upturn were much in evidence. Semi-pro teams in the Baltimore-Washington area then included the Elks, Original Black Sox, Maryland Black Sox, Anacostia Athletics, and Oxon Hill Aztecs. Such interest predicted a bright and burgeoning future for black baseball in Maryland.

The 1939 season, however, began in controversy. Wilson won re-election as NNL president, but black newspaper columnists like Sam Lacy of the *Baltimore Afro-American* and Art Carter decried the sport's lack of community interest under Wilson as well as the league's general inefficiency. Newark's Abe Manley wanted Wilson's job and was disgruntled when he did not get it. Gus Greenlee decided to disband his Pittsburgh Crawfords, a team that had been a backbone of the league. Plans for a dramatic season opener at Yankee Stadium on 14 May went sour because the Crawfords were supposed to have played. Alex Pompez, a well known Harlem gambling lord, and his New York Cubans tried to force entry into the NNL, and Manley's wife Effa opposed admission bitterly. A Toledo man named John Grigsby bought the Crawford's contracts and moved them to Ohio, the league finally let Pompez in, and league affairs settled down. Columnists began writing about baseball as a game again.[7]

Meanwhile, the Elites had obtained use of Oriole Park for Sunday games the entire season (otherwise they continued to play at Bugle Field) while their rivals—in the form of newly created "major leagues" from old semi-pro circuits—gained on them. Washington planned to field a new team, the Royal Giants, in a Middle Atlantic League. John H. Griner, a local white insurance man, established a league he called the Negro American Baseball Association; Dr. Joseph Thomas helped conceive the Negro International League. Although Griner's league and the Royal Giants lasted only for a month, Thomas's team and league did better, providing the Elites stiff competition the entire season.[8]

As the 1939 season got underway, fans of the Negro National League and its competitors may well have noticed interesting events beyond the parks. In Germany Hitler blustered with talk about the "master race." The Daughters of the American Revolution denied African-American singer Marian Anderson permission to hold a concert in Constitution Hall, basing their decision on the District of Columbia segregation statutes. On the other hand, state senator Charles Perry, a New York City Democrat, sponsored a resolution in the New York legislature calling for the admittance of blacks to major-league baseball. The resolution passed and went to the baseball commissioner, Judge Kenesaw Mountain Landis, who side-stepped it with non-committal verbiage.[9]

Maybe hints that the majors might soon be integrated accounted for the Elites' dramatic increase in attendance that year. In early June the Elites drew 12,500 fans at Yankee Stadium. The splinter league faltered. Dr. Thomas deserted the International League because of cheating on gate shares. The Belleville (Virginia) Grays' owner Bishop H.Z. Plummer charged the Royal Giants with expense padding in order to cheat on the gate split. The Elites continued to draw good crowds in Baltimore, and the climax came in September when 7,500 enthusiasts went to Oriole Park for the first games of the playoff series with Newark. Later that month when Baltimore defeated Pittsburgh's Homestead Grays for the NNL title 15,000 people showed up for the game at Yankee Stadium.[10]

The season was a turning point. It ushered in a dramatic rise in black-baseball interest, yet it also marked the beginning of the end for the sport. During the war years, blacks were called upon to work together with whites in many efforts. President Roosevelt had involved blacks in his administration to a degree earlier unheard of. Urban blacks (who increased in numbers during the war) were fascinated by the prospect of any upward mobility, and they viewed baseball as possibly the lowest attainable rung on the ladder of integration. In the short run, however, black baseball exhibited tremendous vitality, and Baltimore offered a splendid example.

The 1940 Negro National League season began with the usual controversy over the loop presidency. Tom Wilson won again, but the black owners showed new militancy by removing the hold of Gottlieb and Saperstein. Effa Manley's politicking moved Saperstein out of the picture and greatly limited Gottlieb's authority to book games on the league's behalf.[11] Fresh competition from other leagues threatened to cut into the NNL gate if fan interest declined at all.

Dr. Thomas renewed his efforts at league organizing. This time, the circuit was the Interstate League, and the team was called the Edgewater Giants for Edgewater Park in Turners Station. Thomas made plans to enlarge Edgewater Park to seat two thousand people under roof and tried to build the legitimacy of his team by attracting civic leaders to the home opener. A bi-racial cast of dignitaries—including Baltimore Mayor Howard Jackson, who threw out the first ball—came to the Giants' first game. Two thousand others also attended the interracial affair as the Giants defeated the Heurich Brewers, the white, national semi-pro champions. Other competition for the Elites came from Washington in the form of a franchise move. The Homestead Grays left Pittsburgh permanently at the beginning of the 1940 season and stayed in Washington until they disbanded in 1948.[12]

Not to be outdone, however, the Elites in June 1940 promoted a game to benefit the Chick Webb Memorial Recreation Center (the National prominent jazz drummer had died in his native Baltimore a year earlier). Sponsored by Dr. Ralph Young and billed as "Baltimore's Biggest Baseball Day," the game with the Black Yanks drew five thousand fans to Oriole Park and raised $6,000 for the building of the center. Theater celebrities and jazz stars helped highlight the promotion.[13]

Despite the Edgewater and Washington teams, the Elites' crowds at Oriole Park were consistently good throughout the rest of the 1940 season. A Sunday double-header drew four thousand fans in mid–July; five thousand people came in mid–August for a four-team doubleheader. Even on the road, the Elites drew enviable attention. In late July New York Mayor Fiorello LaGuardia and twenty-five thousand others saw the Elites and Grays at Yankee Stadium. Baltimore could support both its major black teams at the same time. On a Sunday in July when the Elites were battling the Philly Stars before four thousand at Oriole Park, the Edgewater club filled its park to its two-thousand capacity for a game with the Oxon Hill Aztecs.[14]

Crowds and promotional efforts increased in 1941. The Newark Eagles opened their season before fifteen thousand fans at Ruppert Stadium, and the same number saw the Black Yanks' opener at Yankee Stadium, with LaGuardia throwing out the first ball. After opening at Oriole Park before six thousand cheering partisans, the Elites and Grays took their show to Harrisburg the next day and drew another thousand to Island Stadium (where Mayor Russell T. Tuckey threw out the first ball). At Edgewater, Dr. Thomas had gone completely "big-time," hiring the veteran NNL manager Ben Taylor to run his team and booking the Brooklyn Royal Giants for his home opener. In late May he brought the world-famous Ethiopian Clowns to Baltimore for a date at Edgewater. Again, overflow crowds of two thousand showed up at each event. The climactic draw came at Comiskey Park in Chicago, where more than fifty thousand people came to watch the annual East-West all-Star game. The Elites stretched enthusiasm into October before heading south for the winter. In the final of a series of exhibition games, they beat the Oriole All-Stars (white members of the minor-league Orioles) before five thousand fans at Oriole Park.

The fact that black team owners squabbled little that year gave some indication of their financial success.

Sadly, it was short-lived. In the spring of 1942 a throng of fifty-five hundred saw the Elites' opening game at Oriole Park as "Baltimore Sportsman" Willie Adams threw out the first ball.[15] A fight at the end of the game resulted in minor damage to the park, however, and that one act, more than any other, eventually spelled the Elites' doom. Bugle Field, where they had to go, rested on land of considerable commercial value — more than what the team paid for a ten-year lease agreement. At Edgewater Dr. Thomas overreached himself, changing the name of his team to the Baltimore Grays and booking a game with the Chicago American Giants, the soundest, longest-running franchise in black baseball history. The Grays' victory over Chicago was at once their zenith and the beginning of their decline, for they had lost much of their local appeal by going "big-time."

Throughout the remainder of 1942 and continuing into 1943, Baltimore continued to support its NNL and NAL teams. Crowds of thousands commonly jammed into Bugle Field. Mayor Theodore McKeldin, always late, became a fixture as a first-ball tossed at Elites' openers. Even the practice of players jumping to Mexico (as did Baltimore's Tom Butts and Roy Campanella) seemed not to hurt the game's popularity. When in 1943 the wartime office of defense transport prohibited special bus travel for black teams, they rode trains and temporarily discontinued the practice of barnstorming. (The end of barnstorming may have added stability to the game; training at home, players and fans were more likely to develop a pre-season identity.)[16]

Attendance of 8,000 at the opening-day game between the Elites and Grays at Griffith Stadium bespoke the black league's continuing popularity. When the same two clubs played at Bugle Field next day, the crowd of 3,000 included Mayor McKeldin, late as usually. During the season teams from the East (NAL) and West (NNL) began raiding each other's rosters, and astute owners like Cum Posey advocated a single league for the survival of black baseball. But a mid-season attempt at this solution by way of inter-league play proved ineffective; teams were doing too well. With crowds as high as 20,000 at Griffith Stadium, the Grays, for example, showed a figure of 125,000 total attendance at the mid-way point of the 1943 season. The annual East-West All-Star game in Chicago's Comiskey Park had a record turnout of 51,000 paid attendance.[17] In truth, wartime fuel shortages and forced use of public transportation favored professional baseball clubs. Wartime conditions forced semi-pro and marginal professional leagues out of business, for trolley cars and bus lines simply did not go to out of the way parks in small Negro enclaves. Owners in the organized black leagues had a golden opportunity to build for the future.

The 1944 season began with no sign of decline in black sport. Before seven thousand people at Bugle Field, the Elites celebrated the return of drawing cards Roy Campanella and Pee Wee Butts from Latin America. McKeldin took the mound for the inaugural toss to Police Commissioner H. R. Atkinson (Atkinson promptly hit the ball into right field). The next night eight thousand more came to watch a game with the Homestead Grays. In cities with major-league stadiums, the throngs were even greater: fifty-eight thousand saw a Black Yanks game at Yankee Stadium and twenty-six thousand paid to see the Elites and Cubans at Briggs Stadium in Detroit. Ironically enough, the biggest problem for the Elites in 1944 was the burning of Oriole Park, home of their chief rivals in Baltimore, the International League Orioles. Elites general manager Vernon Green expected the white club to try to force the black team out of Bugle Field (Green had no binding agreement for the park's rental). The savior in the situation proved to be McKeldin, who offered the Birds use of the Municipal Stadium on 34th Street. Ill-suited for baseball, the stadium was still more attractive to the Orioles than seven-thousand-seat Bugle park.[18]

League squabbling and player jumping continued to plague both of the major Negro leagues throughout the season. There was no collapse this time, as in 1929–30, but institutionalized troubles only got worse. In June 1946 Bill Wright of the Elites jumped to the Mexican League, claiming that he gained a $6,000 raise over his Elite salary of $3,000.[19] Three Puerto Rican players quit the Elites after fighting with second-baseman Jim Gilliam. Green fined Gilliam $50. In its deal governing the use of Bugle Field, the club remained at the mercy of the Joe Cambria interests.

Then there was the effort to integrate professional baseball. In 1941 Doc Prothro, manager of the Philadelphia Phillies, had said publicly that the team signing the best blacks would dominate baseball for a decade. Such sentiments, whatever their motivation, only fueled the movement for baseball integration. Branch Rickey's engineering of the Brooklyn Dodgers dominated the 1945 season. His construction of an entire league — the United States League — as well as his team — the Brooklyn Brown Dodgers — aimed to place a black onto his white Dodger team. When Rickey held a try-out for two veterans of the Negro leagues, Terry McDuffie and Dave Thomas, at Bear Mountain, New York, hopes among blacks rose higher. The entire season seemed preparation for the signing in 1946 of Jackie Robinson. Anticipation of that event began to draw attention away from the black version of the sport. Finally, on 30 March 1946, the color line fell as Robinson played for the Dodgers against the Montreal Royals in spring training at Daytona Beach, Florida. The Elites worried about Roy Campanella, their most valuable property. When he signed with Rickey and went to the Dodgers' farm club in New Hampshire, their worries were over (and they got no compensation for him).[20]

Jackie Robinson, playing his first two regular-season games in "organized baseball," drew 16,133 (capacity) at Delorimier Park in Montreal and 30,000 (capacity) at Roosevelt Stadium in Jersey City. With Campy gone, the Baltimore Elite Giants opened the season at Bugle Field against the Homestead Grays, playing before a mere 6,729 fans, including McKeldin. Not that the Elites lost popularity during the 1946 season; rather, they played ball on a scale that became more and more difficult not to compare with the overwhelmingly white majors. The Elite Giants played the Grays at Griffith Stadium before 12,000 fans and the Philly stars at the Polo Grounds before 14,000. The combination draw for the East-West All-Star game between Washington and Chicago was 62,000.[21] Baltimore black baseball continued popular among its fans in the late 1940s if only because no Negroes played on Baltimore's International League Orioles.

By the end of 1947 fan apathy, loss of players to the majors, chaotic league conditions, and lack of owner planning (the Elites' redoubtable Tom Wilson died in May of that year) were beginning to spell the end of Negro baseball. Only cities with strict segregation or good black ballparks or both could survive as hotbeds of African-American baseball. To understand the sport's final chapter in Baltimore one must remember that the city was an anomaly — a Northern/Southern place steeped in segregation and long lacking a major-league club. Fan interest in the Monumental City's local teams was irrepressibly high.

The black press typically disdained black-baseball management. In 1948 Wendell Smith, then sports editor of the Pittsburgh *Courier*, complained of black owners like Mrs. Effa Manley deserting the sport "now that times are bad." At the end of the 1949 season, when Cleveland's black team folded, newspaper columnist Marty Richardson shed a tear, but not for the owners.

> Unlike some of my contemporaries who accepted a load of good, hard cash from Negro league club owners to fight against the entrance of colored players into the majors, I have been very much attached to the Negro leagues as a necessary thing. The colored leagues ... represent an institution which could give colored fans good baseball without subjecting them to the Jim Crow turnstile.... Here is what is killing Negro baseball: lack of support, bad faith with the public by the owners, indifference to the players, over-eagerness to turn a fast buck, mismanagement, generally....

Richardson doubted that the entry of blacks into the majors was killing the black leagues, which, he also believed, had the positive effect of drawing people away from playing the numbers. R. S. Simmons in the Chicago *Defender* called for preserving Negro baseball as "the goose that lays the golden eggs." "If Negro baseball dies," he declared, "there are no other means of preparing Negro players for the majors." In Pittsburgh Jack Saunders argued that it was exactly the high caliber of play in the black leagues which fueled the integration of organized baseball. Still others predicted a revival in black baseball after 1950, when, they predicted, the magic of integration would wear off.[22]

Bill Gibson of the *Baltimore Afro-American* was always critical of Eastern League teams and watched the yearly organizational machinations with great amusement. His colleague Sam Lacy saw the situation from the governing economic perspective. After 1949, Baltimore's biggest problem was the lack of a ballpark, and Lacy realized that the Elites' shaky finances prevented the team in 1950 from renting the new Memorial Stadium.[23]

The 1949 Baltimore Elite Giants championship team (courtesy of Babe Ruth Museum, Baltimore).

Financial structure and the erosion of fan support had become problems common to most black teams. West Coast black baseball, always isolated because of the high cost of travel, had no rivals in major-league franchises in the immediate postwar years, but they nonetheless quit league action when stars like Johnny Ritchey signed to play in the previously all-white Pacific Coast League.[24] Even the Cleveland Buckeyes, a team with its own ballpark (seating thirty thousand), could not compete with integrated teams for fan support. In 1948 the Cleveland Indians won the World Series while drawing 2.5 million customers to giant Municipal Stadium. Many of them were black, for the team's owner, Bill Veeck, rejected Jim Crow. Blacks were welcome at the park; and two of the team's leading members, Larry Doby and Satchel Paige, were African Americans. Badly in debt (served with a summons at home plate during pre-game ceremonies on opening day), the Buckeyes' owner took himself and the team to play in segregated Louisville.[25] By 1950 other teams with proud names such as the Homestead Grays, New York Cubans, Newark Eagles, and Brooklyn Royal Giants were either dead or had moved south to segregation. The only strong clubs to remain after 1951 were the Kansas City Monarchs, Chicago American Giants, Indianapolis Clowns, Philly Stars, Birmingham Black Barons, and Atlanta Black Crackers. These teams played a mostly barnstorming schedule and as late as 1961 attempted to keep alive the East-West game in Chicago. For most northern and border cities, however, black baseball was no longer a regular event after 1950.

With Wilson's death and Vernon Green's move from general manager to owner, running of the Elite Giants fell to the same Dick Powell who in 1938 had helped attract the Nashville team to Baltimore. Powell had an interest in the community and a belief in the fan support in Baltimore. Coming off of the golden years of local black baseball, 1942–47, Baltimore was in a good position to support a black team for several years to come. Besides the quality of the team and the relatively good location of the park, the city had the dubious asset of being still virtually segregated. Possibilities of seeing blacks in big-league uniforms were limited to eleven appearances of the Cleveland Indians in Washington each year, and eleven appearances of the same club in Philadelphia against the all-white Athletics. The Phillies could offer eleven appearances of Jackie Robinson and the integrated Brooklyn club. The International League Orioles remained all white and had Jim Crow ticket policies on a discreet basis at Municipal Stadium. That left Baltimore's black fans with the pleasant prospect of watching future big-league stars such as Jim Gilliam and Joe Black perform in the comfortable surroundings of honey Bugle Field, now nearly twenty years old. There was still plenty of local enthusiasm for the team. Bob Elmer, a former assistant to booking against Eddie Gottlieb, remembered a 1952 promotion between Satchel Paige's All-Stars and the Indianapolis Clowns at Westport Stadium. "We were down at the ticket windows at 4:00 P.M. for a game that was to start four hours later," in Elmer's memory. "all I remember is selling tickets and taking money so fast that the dollar bills were falling out of my pockets. The final gate for the game was over seven thousand."[26]

The *Afro-American* account of the game and the activity of such teams as Yokely's All-Stars, with Laymon Yokely still pitching, demonstrated strong interest in the game. Perhaps the best baseball in town (Dick Powell later so agued) had, in fact, been played by blacks or between the Elites and barnstorming major-league whites.[27] Why, then, in view of this evidence of vitality, did the city lose its regular Negro league representative after the 1951 season? The answer, as usual, lay with finances, lack of community interest on the part of the owners, and the absence of planning and organization.

Blame for the team's end in Baltimore cannot be placed on Powell. Though he never owned the club, he tried after Wilson's death to develop some permanence in the least of Bugle Field. His dealings with Matt Rheinholt, the former Oriole Athletic Club boxing promoter who managed Bugle Field, were strictly year-by-year arrangements. Worried about the possible sale of the land and the threat of ouster (going back to 1944, when the parkless Orioles were looking for a home), he was always assured by Rheinholt that no one would ever want the land and, if the park were on the auction block, that he would be notified in plenty of time to search for a new home. On the other hand, Powell's efforts to convince Green either to buy the property or attempt to acquire land for a permanent park also were futile. "I asked Vernon every year to either buy Bugle Field or buy some land," Powell recalled later. "I even hired an architect to draw up some plans for a combination park and recreation center. He wouldn't go for the idea, though, probably because he was interested in immediate money and he thought the sport was dying."[28]

With Green's death in 1949 Powell received power of attorney from Green's widow and assumed virtual control of the club for the 1950 season.

His long-term dreams for the club did not include occupying Bugle Field. "I wanted to develop a park-rec center," he later said, "and have a semi-pro club that played good enough ball for black fans who were Jim Crowed here and in Virginia and the Carolinas. I wanted to develop players and sell them to the majors. By 1950 though," he continued, "we needed to have a park and some prosperity for a few years for me to carry this off."[29]

The park became the rub for Powell and the Green family. In August 1949, without warning from Rheinhold, the Galloway sisters sold the property to the Lord Baltimore Press. The Elites, with their best team ever (including Black and Gilliam), were winning the 1949 league pennant and were allowed to finish the season in the park. The day after the campaign was over, however, wreckers moved on the old wooden stadium and ended the Elites' residence thee forever.[30] During the winter of 1949–50 bulldozers cleared another Baltimore site, Municipal Stadium, which literally was plowed under to make way for the construction of a conventional all-purpose park — supposedly roofed — for both football and baseball. Sans roof, the new park was ready with nineteen thousand seats in the lower deck by the beginning of the 1950 season.

Called Memorial Stadium and controlled by the Baltimore City Park Board, it was supposedly open for the rental of any organization that needed it. The Elite management, totally parkless by late April, approached the board seeking rental of the new facility for Sunday games when the prime tenant, the International League Orioles, were on the road. Powell recalled the meeting and the subsequent first game in the stadium:

> They [members of the park board] didn't know who we were or acted like they didn't They figured out I wouldn't show and that they could just pass on by our request and deny it without us there. I went in with sheer muscle, though. Dr. Bernard Harris didn't want us to use the stadium. He was afraid there would be trouble and that our (black community's image would be hurt. I had to tell them that we had been in Baltimore for more or less fourteen years and had had a successful operation. We got the stadium and there wasn't any trouble. They had monitors there to make sure we didn't tear up the place. Afterward, they said that we were the best behaved crown they had seen there in a while.[31]

Financial arrangements for the Elites were nonetheless devastating. They were charged a flat rental of $1,000 per date plus 20 percent of the gate receipts. The Orioles paid seven cents per head flat rate. The Elites, playing their first game in the stadium, drew a gate of 10,115. If the Orioles had drawn that crowd, they would have paid little more than $700. The Elites' bill came to more than $3,000. Sam Lacy decried this discrimination, but park board officials were determined to hold to it for the remainder of 1950 and 1951 as well. Faced with a dilemma, Powell turned back to Rheinholt, who knew of some open land (also owned by the Galloway sisters) in Westport on the edge of Cherry Hill. On a hillside next to the then-rural Old Annapolis Road, Rheinholt in mid–April began constructing an earthen and concrete stadium to accommodate five thousand persons. Later known as Westport Stadium, the park would cater specifically to the Elites and barnstorming black teams, much as had the city's old black parks, Bugle and Maryland Park.[32]

Completion of Westport Stadium in time for the May 1950 slate of Elite home games saved the club from either hitting the road or going broke on 33rd Street, but it was no panacea. Westport's location, back near the original pioneering area for Negro baseball parks, posed fans a transportation problem. Unlike the original Westport Park of 1918, which advertised street cars direct to the Bush and Russell Street location, the new park was hard by the side of narrow, unlighted Annapolis Road. It was a dangerous walk from the most southerly Baltimore Transit Company bus stop in Westport. The Baltimore and Annapolis Railway buses charged a full round-trip fare to Annapolis of fifty cents for their runs, which left Baltimore and Charles streets and stopped at the park on their way to Annapolis.[33]

The problems of the club and its changing role as an organization kept Powell hopping throughout the 1950 season. Westport, which Reinholt thought "good enough for Negroes," had no infield grass; a constant wind stirred up the grit. Players, who received a percentage of the gate rather than a regular salary, struck for more, but Powell had no extra cash. Typically for a Negro-leagues owner, he thought of the team as a nursery for players destined for the majors (recall that the team had earned nothing for releasing Campanella in 1946). Alex Pompez, owner of the Cubans in New York, trained players for his Polo Grounds landlords, the New York Giants. Powell's relations with the integration-minded Brooklyn Dodgers improved after the National League club paid him $10,000 each for Joe Black and Jim Gilliam following the 1950 season. He even employed a player whom the Dodgers had released from probation in North Carolina. A stint with the Elites served as his rehabilitation before he was allowed to try out for the Brooklyn club.[34]

In order to pump more money into the organization, Powell promoted his team and special pre-game attractions more than had any Baltimore Negro-team owner since George Rossiter of the ill-fated Black Sox. One such promotion, a resounding success, was the game between Satchell Paige's All-Stars and the Elites. The Elites' young ace pitcher, Tome Coleman, was to oppose Paige himself for at least three innings, saving nothing for later in the game. More than five thousand fans flocked to the dusty South Baltimore bowl, proving that interest in the club was still considerable. In 1950 Sunday baseball at Memorial Stadium had to average attendance of ten thousand to break even, and it did. A year later, with the Elites spending most of the season on the road (like Rossiter's 1931 Black Sox, who also had ballpark problems), Powell staged a pre-game old-timers affair for the benefit of Provident Hospital. With the game scheduled for Memorial Stadium and old Black Sox favorites such as Yokely and Jud "Babe Ruth" Wilson featured in the pre-game exhibition, two thousand fans paid their way in. "They were interested in the Elites and Memphis," Yokely remembered, "but I got the feeling that they were happy to see us. Pitching on that nice field made me feel like I came along too early."[35]

By the end of the 1950 season the Green family back in Nashville was interested in unloading the team while it still had some value. Local Baltimore interest in purchasing the Elites existed only in the person of Eddie Leonard, the white Howard Street restaurateur. When the Green-Leonard deal fell through, William S. Bridgeforth, former owner of the Nashville Stars of the Negro Southern League, purchased the club. Bridgeforth operated the club through Powell, mostly as a road club with occasional appearances in Baltimore, through the 1951 season.[36]

The team left Baltimore for good in 1951, surviving for one year as the Nashville Elite Giants. Powell, his ideas for Baltimore Negro baseball finished, came back to the city and resumed his job with the federal government. Thereafter in Baltimore the sport was confined to a few remaining barn-storming teams that played occasionally at Westport Stadium under Gottlieb's auspices.

Studying black baseball in Baltimore means unmasking "philanthropy," black and white, and noting the hard nature of business dealings in a spectator sport. Before Wilson's purchase of the Elites, white owners of Baltimore black clubs had run them much the way Wilson and Powell did — never owning the parks they played in and worrying only marginally about fan comforts or convenience. Owners of these clubs, black or white, used promotions for institutions such as the Chick Webb Recreation Center or Provident Hospital to expose fans to the club, draw greater crowds, and generate community good will. However laudable, such events were part and parcel of the baseball-business venture. Wilson's refusal to purchase land for a park was in the same class with his Black Sox predecessor's allowing old Maryland Park to deteriorate. It represented common-sense business logic when applied to a questionable asset, the owning of a Negro baseball team.

How wide and deep was enthusiasm for the game? Black-community support for baseball surfaced in the many black-enclave clubs that played on the fringes of the organized game — teams like the Edgewater Giants of Turners Station and the Catonsville Social Giants. Yet long after the Elites folded Powell had complained to sportswriter Sam Lacy that Baltimore African Americans never had truly galvanized around his black franchise.[37] Powell's organization of community leaders to attract a franchise was itself a fleeting phenomenon — brief if effective. The degree to which whites joined blacks in attending games is open to dispute, but whites supported the clubs more noticeably before World War II, in the days of white team ownership. For whites, going to see the Elites was something like seeing the Globetrotters in the mid–1950s, when the National Basketball Association was largely made up of white players. For blacks the Elites (and Black Sox before them) of course offered much more than entertainment, for places like Bugle Park brought pleasant escape from the embarrassments of Jim Crow. Fans could sit where they wanted to, bring food into the park, and be relieved of the name-calling that was a part of a trip to an Oriole game. At bottom Baltimore's black-baseball fans liked good baseball, and the results of black-white exhibition games in the period of segregation (most of them won by blacks) left no doubt of the quality of play in the black leagues.

Perhaps the most important truth to come out of this study is the richness of the black pastime itself. As the professional game, played by both races, tends to become stiffer and more characterless (with the architectural exception of Oriole Park at Camden Yards), one can only harken back to the descriptions of the great days of the black sport. Beer in the ballpark, informal dress, fans greeting regular seat neighbors, and the spectacle of powerful, unorthodox athletes such as Satchel Paige and Josh Gibson (who once hit eighty-nine home runs in a season), remind present-day fans of what a natural, delightful piece of entertainment Negro baseball was.[38] It is ironic that the progressive, integrated world might never again provide a naturally attractive social experience to equal Negro baseball.

Part III

TRANSCENDING RACE

Jackie Roosevelt Robinson put on his Montreal Royal uniform in 1946 at just the right time for baseball and the nation. The national game, and the nation it had long mirrored, could no longer ignore its racial failures in the wake of the overseas war against racial fascism. Born twenty-seven years earlier in a year marked by seventy-six racial lynchings in the South and twenty-seven race riots in the nation, the son of a Georgia sharecropper would soon help to lead his country out of its racial miasma. It took a special kind of man to spearhead this reformation. Athletic, intelligent, proud, and in the words of one sportswriter, "unconquerable," Robinson made baseball the social laboratory for testing American democratic ideals.

Racism, so deeply imbedded in American life, would not dissolve easily. In the case of Baltimore, a thoroughly segregated southern city with a team in the International League where Robinson would play in 1946, the test seemed daunting. Several generations of racially separate worlds were unlikely to quickly merge in a city not known for change in social affairs. Still, Baltimore's vibrant and proud black world was ready to welcome a new day in race relations and there were enough whites, touched by the slow rise of racial reformism in the nation, to blunt the bigoted fans who taunted Robinson. In his essay that blends historical scholarship with personal recollections, "Jackie Robinson in Baltimore: History and Memory," Thomas Cripps describes how this sociological watershed came to be.

A quarter-century later Robinson reflected on his Brooklyn Dodgers experience. Speaking to a group of athletes and sportswriters on the occasion of *Sport Magazine*'s special tribute to him as the most important sports figure of the previous twenty-five years, Jackie's acceptance speech is transcribed for this book. In it he credits the people who made his success possible, most notably Branch Rickey, Robinson's mother, and his wife, Rachel. In a previously unpublished interview conducted that day, Robinson tells Ted Patterson about the Brooklyn Dodger teammates who contributed most to his achievements. Rounding out the segment on Robinson, Patterson shares a later interview he conducted with one of these teammates, Carl Erskine. Erskine's recollections of the Robinson years reveals players as much caught up in winning games as scoring moral victories. Nevertheless, Erskine places Robinson in the forefront as a national leader who changed the lives of white Americans as he did African Americans. No longer a mirror of America, baseball had become a transforming agent in 1947, though not without subsequent foot-dragging that the ever-honest Robinson noted a year before his death in the 1971 interview.

In the midst of the Robinson revolution a much quieter social transformation occurred in baseball. In 1951, an affable Cuban, Orestes "Minnie" Minoso, became a fixture with the Chicago White Sox. Latinos who followed him in the major leagues surely were aware of the social consequences of Minoso's milestone as a Hispanic star. Tim Wendel, who is becoming well-known as a pioneer historian of the Hispanic transformation of baseball, summarizes it in his essay, "Minnie Minoso and His Footsteps." Wendel describes the evolution of the sport in Latin America, its distinctive style of play, and Minoso as a role model for others who followed him north. As Wendel's observations on the process of cultural assimilation reveal, baseball continues to play an important social role in the nation.

10

Jackie Robinson in Baltimore: History and Memory

Thomas Cripps

In Countee Cullen's short poem "Incident" (ca. 1925), a child's hope for a happy day is spoiled by another kid, who "poked out his tongue, and called me, 'Nigger.'" In six months of exploring the city of Baltimore, says the poet, that was all that he remembered."[1] This essay is the story of how another racial incident twenty years later overshadowed and warped the meaning of a single day in a historic moment, the debut of the African American baseball player Jackie Robinson into formerly lilywhite professional baseball. In its way it mimed a common truism — as old ways fade and the new rise, both share a moment, a "watershed," when the traits of both coexist. Often, the actors, like Cullen's small boy, are marked by the last sting of the *old* before the onset of a *New World A-Coming*, as Roi Ottley's 1943 book title put it.

Such a tipping point in 1946 was the debut of Jackie Robinson into the "farm system" of the Brooklyn Dodgers. In that same Baltimore, on his first road trip with his team, Montreal, he and his wife stood up to the *old* even as they ushered in the "new world." Generously, he called his memoir of his heroic act *Baseball Has Done It* (1964), a title that glossed over the laggard racial history of Baseball during World War II, a war whose propaganda catch words included "unity, tolerance, and brotherhood."[2]

Already, in the summer of 1944, as Baseball snubbed such democratic ideals, Robinson, then an officer in the U.S. Army, stood up for these values that were his country's war aims. He refused to sit in the back of a bus, an early skirmish in the nation's internal fight for "integration."[3] At the same time, Baseball perversely stiffened against what had become a core of liberal war aims. It was a "people's war," said the Southern progressive, Will Alexander, a sentiment that FDR caught in his "four freedoms" speech of 1942 as did Norman Rockwell's four *Saturday Evening Post* covers inspired by it. By war's end, membership in the National Association for the Advancement of Colored People had increased tenfold, and the historian, Thomas C. Cochran could write "'Democracy' had become the major slogan of the period."[4] That is, Robinson's offense against Southern custom and his arrest for it, took its place in a *movement*. Even before he was court-martialed for it, the Pentagon had appointed Judge William Hastie, late of Howard University, as civilian counsel to the Army to deal with hundreds of such racial incidents, eventually resigning in protest of the Army's slowness in acting on them. His successor, a black lawyer, Truman Gibson, became Robinson's counsel, and got him off with an honorable discharge.[5]

Even before the war, racial change had been in the air. FDR often sought counsel from a "black cabinet." His wife as often addressed black women's groups. And when the Daughters of the American Revolution denied its concert hall to the black singer, Marian Anderson, Mrs. Roosevelt persuaded the Secretary of Interior to open the Lincoln Memorial on the Mall for her concert that drew 50,000 on Easter Sunday 1939—earning a favorable Gallup Poll rating of 2:1! In 1940, when A. Philip Randolph of the Brotherhood of Sleeping Car Porters called for racial equality in war industries or risk a massive march on Washington, FDR signed executive order 8802 creating a Fair Employment Practices Committee. Already, both college and professional football drifted toward facing these new realities, as movies and theatre soon would do.[6]

Some racial changes were graphically caught in news film. In the summer of 1936 Jessie Owens won four gold medals in the "Nazi Olympics" in Berlin thereby throttling Nazi racial theories and graphically linking black victory with America's. Two years later in Yankee Stadium, Joe Louis reaffirmed the linkage by knocking out the German champion, Max Schmeling in the first round of their bout, thereby avenging an earlier defeat. In black circles at home the annual Penn Relay in Philadelphia, noted for its openness to black athletes, won the tag of the "Negro Olympics."

This sensibility was reflected in the nation's most routinely popular cultural medium, movies. As early as September 1941, three months before Pearl Harbor, Walter Wanger's *Sundown* was released. It was a soldierly yarn, set in a British outpost in East Africa, threatened by the Afrika Korps' drive eastward to the Suez Canal. Previously, Walter White of the NAACP had lunched with Wanger while promoting new black roles in the coming war. What was the war to be about? The answer is clear in one sequence of the film. An Arab trader lands her airplane nearby and is welcomed in the British officers' mess tent, but at a segregated table outside the netting. One officer, clearly the voice of the two Walters, joined her. I "know what this table means," he says, upon which he interjects with a line that might have been written by the NAACP. "The England that's going to win this war is going to do away with a lot of this nonsense."[7] Even *Gone with the Wind* (1939) swung to the beat of the times. As David O. Selznick told his scriptwriter, Maxwell Anderson, "the picture must not emerge as anything offensive to negroes ... in these fascist-ridden times." And a B-movie man, Sol Lesser, hired the black actor Clarence Muse and the poet Langston Hughes to write "the colored man's point of view" into his *Way Down South* (1940).[8] Thus even prewar movies began to see the image of Americans and *African* Americans as one.

Back east, in Manhattan, "it became the thing to do" to join with the singer Billie Holiday in Café Society, a cellar club in the Village, for a few bars of "Strange Fruit," a protest against lynching written by a white Brooklyn school teacher: "Black body swinging in the Southern breeze," it ran, "Strange fruit hanging from the poplar trees."[9] In fact, the war let white fans musically "cross over": They knew Billy Eckstine and made Billy Daniels' "That Old Black Magic" a crossover hit. They saw Lena Horne in *Stormy Weather* and *Cabin in the Sky*. Duke Ellington played Carnegie Hall. Black versions of opera opened—a *Black Mikado* at the New York World's Fair, *Carmen Jones* on Broadway. Paul Robeson played *Othello* beside a white Desdemona. And everywhere he sang "Ballad for Americans" or "Ol' Man River," changing the lyrics of the latter to fit the times: "get a little drunk and you lands in jail" became "show a little grit and you land in jail." The war against overseas racism enhanced the liberal mood and its plea for tolerance in Frank Sinatra's short, featuring the song "House I Live In." In much the same way, Kate Smith sang "God Bless America" on radio while pleading that we should end racism, "not at a conference table in Geneva," she said, "but at our own kitchen tables." The staccato columnist, Walter Winchell, followed up with an *Open Letter on Race Hatred* on his own network radio program. Meanwhile on Harlem's WLIB, Roi Ottley named his talk show after his book, *New World A-Coming*. A *Variety* headline in 1945 aptly caught the moment: "*Gear Show Biz Assault on White Supremacy.*" In tune with the times, three books appeared, each touting the mood of racial liberalism: Ottley's *New World A-Coming* (1943); the historian, Rayford Logan's *What the Negro Wants* (1944); and a scholarly analysis of African American life, Gunnar Myrdal's *An American Dilemma* (1944).[10]

The black press picked it up when William Nunn's *Pittsburgh Courier* ran a weekly page-one feature that called for a "Double V"—a double victory over foreign fascism and domestic racism. Walter White praised Nunn's "fight for liberties here while waging war against dictators abroad." That is, everywhere "it became the thing to do." Except on the baseball diamond where moss backed bosses shielded their eyes from the times and covered their heads with the sand of indifference.

The rest of us too were touched by the coming war. My parents' upbringing in the *Allgemeine Deutsche Waisenhaus*—the German Orphan Asylum in Baltimore made us *German*—sort of. In March 1936, as a child my father took me to Fells Point to see the German battle cruiser Emden on which I had my picture taken with a sailor's cap proudly on my head. Then four years later, we again visited the waterfront, this time to see the *City of Flint*, a small tanker that had been set afire by a German U-boat. Our mood had changed; this time my father bridled at the hurt done to *us* Americans and became an air raid warden. At the same time, a German family, on the run from Nazism, took over our corner store. My father gave them an icebox and I saved their kid from a ragging by warning him off wearing *Lederhosen* to school.

My father had always harbored a strain of empathy for people in need of a break, particularly "colored people," perhaps arising from the orphanage or the hard life that followed it, along with the mood of the coming war. On his half-day Saturdays (many workers did a half-shift on weekends), I sometimes rode for the fun of it and to see "downtown." As we drove through the black ghetto he pointed to white steps "as clean as ours" or to "Kerr's Kill-a-Kough" drugstore where "a colored man invented" cough medicine or, when we began taking the streetcar, he would buy an *Afro-American* from the black newsie who worked the 'cars.

Of all the media, Hollywood movies reached the largest sector of American opinion. An alliance of the Office of War Information in its new office at Hollywood and Vine, studio liberals, and the NAACP sought to make movies to reflect the times. The 1940 Republican candidate, Wendell Willkie, sat on the board of Twentieth Century–Fox and as general counsel for the NAACP. "Let's go out to Hollywood and talk with the more intelligent people," he had told White. The trade paper, *Variety*, caught the mood in a banner headline: "*Better Breaks for Negroes in H'wood.*" It was, said Walter White, "one of the opening guns" in the battle to better "the status of the Negro in the war."[11] This was no easy matter. Moviemakers had inherited a glut of nineteenth century stereotypes from the whole range of popular culture—comic postcards with their grinning pickaninnies, minstrel shows, even the boxes of Uncle Ben's rice and Aunt Jemima's pancake flour. In movies, the fiftieth anniversary of the Civil War from 1910 to 1915 was marked by D.W. Griffith's epic, *The Birth of a Nation* (1915), that defined the movie Negro for decades. Thomas Dixon, its author, meant to teach the North of the South's despair during post–Civil War Reconstruction. Dixon, no mere backwoods preacher, had studied at the Johns Hopkins University where he met Woodrow Wilson in whose White House his movie premiered. The hot books of the day were Charles Carroll's *The Negro a Beast* (1900) and R.W. Shufeldt's *The Negro: A Menace to Civilization* (1907).

The resulting Hollywood system, with its fear of the "southern box office," its self-censorship of material that might "offend" social groups, its romantic view of the South, and its stables of black actors whose careers rested upon their faithful renderings of old types, spent the ensuing years up to World War II "whistlin' Dixie," that is playing to Southern legends.[12] To win a role as a cop, crook, or cowboy, black actors could turn only to low budget "race movies" made for the so-called "chittlin' circuit."

Despite this history, the wartime studios, pressed by the NAACP and by the OWI, anticipated Jackie's goal in baseball "to break the color barrier." They tried scores of scripts, finally settling on a formula that we might call "the Jackie Robinson role," the long, flawless black figure, plunked by chance into a privileged lilywhite circle. Four major war movies featured this "Jackie" role. In MGM's *Bataan*, he was a black demolition man who destroys a key bridge—"One of the outstanding merits of the picture," said the *New York Times*. *Sahara*, Columbia's contribution, included a black African soldier in the Saharan desert war; thence to a submarine in *20th's Crash Dive*; and then in Hitchcock's *Lifeboat*.[13]

We have no sure way of knowing whether Jackie Robinson saw these movies, but almost certainly he saw at least one wartime film — the Pentagon's own documentary, *The Negro Soldier* (1944). During his checkered hitch in the Army he would have been ordered to see it either in his role as morale officer or as required of all recruits after 1944. Written, directed, and acted, in part, by Carlton Moss, a Morgan College alumnus, the film sought to teach both white and black soldiers the history of black America. As in the Hollywood genre, it opens on a lone black figure, this time the real Joe Louis, first seen defeating the German champion, Max Schmeling, in one round, then as "team" leader of US troops in boot camp, he is centered in an epic struggle between "our way and their way — the American way or the Nazi way."[14]

The Negro Soldier was such a smash that the Army, under pressure by the NAACP, ordered that it be seen by every recruit, a version played civilian theatres to raves in *Time* and even in *Vogue's* "People are Talking About" column. Soon, any school board could get free copies for classroom use. In a cameo in Warner Bros.' *This Is the Army* (1943, Sgt. Louis *reasserts* his role on the American team — "I'm just glad to be on God's side," he says. For critics who saw him as too soft on racism, he learned a stock phrase, "there ain't nothing' wrong with Americans that Hitler can fix."[15]

Such ideals in the summer of '44, it must be said, were *fragile*. The Congress soon denied postwar funding to OWI and other "liberal" agencies. Yet in 1946, the "Jackie role," played by Ossie Davis (his first on Broadway) was in *Jeb*, a play about another returning black vet who, like Ossie himself and Jackie, returned, seemingly to face business as usual. But Jeb, wounded and unable to pick tobacco — his old job — turned to white man's work, on an "adding machine," a skill the Army had taught him, so he became the play's Jackie! In a way, Jeb/Jackie reminded me of an old friend, a captain in our "black" army, who returning from the war, still dressed in uniform, went to an old line Baltimore department store, was measured for his first civilian suit, but upon returning for it, was told he must put on his captain's uniform in order to claim the suit — war borne racial change was indeed *fragile*.

Meanwhile, the real Jackie, fought a half dozen scrapes with Army racial custom — classic black crimes — including the case of the seat on the bus, entering the wrong PX door, balking at playing for Jim Crow Army teams when so ordered. Only when he found that Officer Candidate School was "for whites only," did he learn to game the system by means of an insider. Joe Louis sent him to his own "friend at court," Truman Gibson who had replaced Judge Hastie in the "black section" of the Pentagon, and had fought to get *The Negro Soldier* a civilian audience by arguing to a General that "All races play every position on one big team."[16]

After the war, activists on the left struggled to keep the movement alive. The United Auto Workers was the angel for *The Brotherhood of Man* (1946), a widely seen animated cartoon that its makers saw as part of a "permanent front" against racism. The Army joined in by offering its films free to the country's schools. And Hollywood reenlisted in 1946 when Sinatra's *House I Live In*, won an Oscar and a Golden Globe. In Jackie's major league year came *Gentlemen's Agreement* (1947) attacking genteel anti–Semitism, and *The Quiet One* (1947), set in a favorite crusade of Mrs. Roosevelt's, the Wiltwyck School for black youth. Capping the movement in March of 1949, four major movies appeared — Darryl Zanuck's *Pinky*, Stanley Kramer's *Home of the Brave*, Louis DeRochemont's *Lost Boundaries*, and MGM's *Intruder in the Dust*, each pitching for racial change.

In parallel arcs, the careers of Jackie Robinson and Sidney Poitier marked the mood of the times. By 1946 Jackie had won his honorable discharge, signed on with the *all–black* Kansas City Monarchs, met "Mr. Rickey," broken in with Montreal, then finished the 1940s with Brooklyn. Sidney Poitier, in a similar path, moved from acting in an Army training film, *From Whence Cometh My Help* to a "race movie" called *Sophia Cinderella*, then to an all-black road company of *Lysistrata* before breaking into the "big leagues" starring in Joseph Mankiewicz's Twentieth Century–Fox film, *No Way Out* (1950). Indeed, their careers symbolically merged in 1950, when Jackie played himself in *The Jackie Robinson Story* while Poitier played a beleaguered black doctor in *No Way Out*.

Also in Jackie's debut year, President Truman himself, perhaps having seen a widely published photography of "Dingman's Alley," a slum block of wooden shacks foregrounding the majesty of the capitol dome, ordered a study of racial practices in the nation's capital. The result was *To Secure These Rights* (1947), a pamphlet which found its way into the Democratic platform of 1948. Pressed by the NAACP, the pamphlet received wide circulation. How to account for this progressive ferment at war's end? The historians, August Meier and Elliot Rudwick, in their book, *Black History and the Historical Profession*, held that the politics of ordinary folk had "shifted considerably to the left in the social and intellectual context of the New Deal and World War II." Everywhere but in Organized Baseball.[17]

Why, at mid–twentieth century, was the game of baseball so resistant to social change? A partial answer lay in its claim to ancient origins founded in the fable of a Civil War officer in the quaint village of Cooperstown. Wrap it in the flag and we have "the national pastime" with its almost theological claim to have shaped our national character. Over time, then, changelessness became a virtue. Indeed, in the half century after 1903, almost nothing changed — franchises, their cities, even its anthem, "Take Me Out to the Ball Game" (1908). Moreover, after the benchmark *Plessy v. Ferguson* Supreme Court case in 1896 both law and custom cast the races into two rigidly separate spheres. In the 1870s and onward, fifty or so African Americans had played in recorded games in white leagues; indeed, in 1887, "a banner year for colored talent," according to a black observer, the magazine *Sporting Life* once referred to the International League as a "colored league." But in the 1890s, as Steven A. Riess reports, a club owners' emerging "unwritten policy" had became law and Baseball and America were as one in a common racial culture.[18]

By 1901, only five years after Plessy, the subject of racism had become only a training camp joke. John McGraw, the legendary player-manager of the Baltimore Orioles, toyed with the new etiquette of race in spring training in Hot Springs, Arkansas. His second baseman one day was a bellman in a local resort, brown-skinned Charlie Grant, playing under the American Indian *nom de jeu* of Chief Tokahoma. Like a punch line in a gag, one tale has him exposed by Charlie Comiskey of the Chicago White Sox, one of the "gentlemen" whose "agreement" kept baseball lilywhite while in another Grant's black fans exposed him by cheering for "our man."[19] By the 1920s Landis, miffed at barnstorming big leaguers who only broke even against black teams, forbade major league teams from playing black teams, particularly in the Caribbean. Henceforth, only white pickup teams of "all stars" strove to uphold the honor of the race against blacks.

Even under the reformist New Dealers, such racial arrangements persisted as they adroitly walked a line between reform and the need to cultivate Southern support, leading a few blacks to haze the National Recovery Administration (NRA) as "Negroes Ruined Again."[20] Nor in baseball were their vocal African American audiences (most blacks still lived in the South), scouts covering the Negro leagues, owners or players who spoke for the left. Thus "Organized Baseball" came down on the side of stasis. At best, a rare white owner might, like Clark Griffith of the Senators, predict the arrival of African Americans but always, "not far off."[21]

A final turn of the screw of segregation followed the "Black Sox" scandal in the World Series of 1919, a sordid tale of crooked gamblers and fixed games. As a sign of their wish for a cleaner game, the owners appointed a commissioner—a czar, as they liked to say—federal judge Kenesaw Mountain Landis. In the 1920s, miffed at barnstorming major leaguers who barely broke even against black teams, Landis allowed barnstorming games only between black teams and white "all stars" to discourage comparison between actual black and white teams. The point was stressed in reports such as that of Dizzy Dean who once confessed that against the fabled black pitcher, Satchel Paige, "my fast ball looks like a change of pace."[22] Only the influx of new people— less inured to these racial strictures—masses of urban immigrants from Europe, along with black migrants to the North, driven by the residues of slavery, supplied new fans (and eventually) new players of baseball.

In fact, in the 1930s of Joe Louis and Jesse Owens, segregated sports began to seem pointless. The absurdity hit Sam Lacy, then of the Washington *Tribune*, later sports editor of the Baltimore *Afro-American*, when the University of Maryland hastily canceled a football game with Syracuse whose player, Wilmeth Sadat-Singh, despite his Sikh stepfather's name, proved to be an African American. Two old allies of black America began to argue the case: the black press and the Communist Party. Through the depression decade, Lacy and other black writers, such as Wendell Smith of the *Pittsburgh Courier* (whose interviews with managers revealed only two who would balk at black players), pressed the owners for meetings that were either put off or abruptly ended. Yet, voices of all colors and origins—trade unions, baseball writers, the NAACP's organ, *Crisis*—all pleaded for an open door.[23]

For its part the CPUSA, and its *Daily Worker*, joined the chorus of keeping with its historic focus on "the just grievances of the Negro people." Beginning in 1939, the *Worker* interviewed players, circulated a petition that garnered 50,000 signatures, and in the war years pressed for tryouts of black players. As its Lester Rodney wrote, "Can you read, Judge Landis? Why ... your silence ... when we are at war ... to end Hitlerism?" Such barbs led baseball men, even Jackie's champion, Branch Rickey of the Brooklyn Dodgers, to smell "reds" or see "a sickening red tinge," and Larry MacPhail of the Yankees, to cry, "Agitators." "No Good From Raising Race Issue," said the *Sporting News* during the 1942 season. As the tension rose, Joe Bostic's column in Adam Clayton Powell's *People's Voice* (which the FBI thought "red") so enraged the Yankees that in 1943 he lost his press box seat.[24]

During World War II, baseball survived unchanged, partly as a result of FDR's sense that it boosted morale. Yet rumors abounded—the Pittsburgh Crawfords to replace the inept Phillies, or Bill Veeck of the Milwaukee Brewers to buy the team and stock it with black players (a deal Veeck once thought "done"), or to scatter black players on the rosters as replacements for drafted whites. In fact, several players went through the motions of wartime tryouts, including Robinson and Roy Campanella, even as Dodger manager, Leo Durocher, claimed he would sign black players if permitted. Coyly, Judge Landis insisted that "Negroes are not barred from organized baseball ... and never had been."[25] Sam Lacy, in the spring of 1945, just after Landis's death, boldly called for a committee to act and got an audience with the owners. But Rickey himself at times despaired at the owners who "always had some excuse." A slim hope for action was dashed in owners' meetings in Detroit and then in New York when they picked Landis's successor, a malleable former Senator from Kentucky, A.B. "Happy" Chandler.[26]

News of Rickey's quietly forming plans for Jackie Robinson led the owners to assail not only his motives—a mere "publicity dodge"—but the threatened ruination he might bring to the Game. "We question [Rickey as] another Abraham Lincoln," said one man; a "menace" stirred by "the carpetbagger white press," wrote a southerner; W.G. Bramham, a sort of "czar" of minor league baseball, cast Rickey as a man of the "carpetbagger stripe" whose mission on behalf of blacks was driven by "selfish interests."[27] At stake for them was the end of the flag-draped American game itself. In reality, they had lost a wartime moment when baseball might have embraced the war's meanings rather than cling to its old order. Instead, it would be left to Jackie Robinson to link war aims to the later civil rights movement.

But what of Baltimore in this story? As the southernmost city in the league chosen by Rickey to "season" Jackie, *it* would be the field upon which Baseball would be tested, with the city cast as the unwitting "heavy" in a melodrama that might reveal the owners as correct all along in their resistance to change. Unconsciously, they may have needed Baltimore in this role because the northerly teams— Syracuse, Rochester, Newark, Toronto, Jersey City, Buffalo, and Jackie's own Montreal team — might not act out enough racism. Baltimore was perfect —"a Southern city, below the Mason-Dixon line" whose own press feared "a possible riot," according to Arnold Rampersad, Jackie's best biographer.[28]

There was nothing to fear from its black community that would welcome racial change. In 1946, Baltimore was racially segregated, its white neighborhoods cordoned off by a paper wall of covenants, deeds, and "red lines," its African Americans on bottom rung, its schools divided into white "haves" and black "have nots," its halls of power closed to its colored citizens. So in black circles inside *their* Baltimore — led by a layered, richly cultured, self-conscious, black bourgeoisie — there was cynicism mingled with hope. Their forebears had known slavery but of a unique sort. In the 1860 census, of its 27,000 black residents only 2500 were slaves mostly for hire as dockers, barbers, caterers, and teamsters, and lived apart from their often remote owners. As a result, the black city lived with its own heritage. As Frederick Douglass, himself once a rural slave, and later renowned abolitionist, said, "Even the air smelled freer in Baltimore."[29] And the black sage, W.E.B. Du Bois later kept for a time a home in Baltimore.[30] True, many blacks faced low wages, lived in shabby houses, and learned in worn out schools, but a tier of black strivers that began a century ago with teamsters, haulers, coal-and-ice men, and caterers, along with marginal industrial jobs, and eventually a thin elite in the law and medicine, all in a network of churches, lodges, orders, newspapers, schools and colleges, fought in civil rights groups going back to the Sons of Liberty, a forerunner of the NAACP.[31] For them Jackie would become an heroic figure.

These strivers' pressure against formerly lilywhite housing became a theme of the city's history beginning as early as 1910, when a lone black man moved into an all white block. Back then, the *Sun* warned of "encroachment," whites formed "protective" associations, and white kids tarred the offender's white steps.[32] After World War II, as Jackie made his debut, this racial pressure heightened. War workers had come up from the South in numbers enough to render the city 9,000 houses short. In one typical row house, two stories and 14 feet wide, two boarders were taken in and children slept in the coal bin. Old bathhouses and "comfort stations" from the Progressive Era reopened. The word on the street was that the city was "swarming" with "loafers" and "scum."[33]

So Jackie came to a city made tense by new conditions that pressed against the stock of housing. Scarcer housing made for pressure against old racial lines. The *Sun* and the *Afro-American* both ran ads asking "why pay rent." "Wise Home Buying Urged with Outlawing of Restrictive Covenants." Move northwest to "porches, garage space, and ... flower or vegetable gardens." So, the gates were forced by wartime savings, Federal Housing Administration and "GI Bill" funds, an auto-driven white rush to the suburbs, and the "outlawing" of covenants. The mood lent itself to "blockbusters" who scared fleeing whites into selling cheap then "flipping" at dearer prices to blacks. As citizens wrestled with the shock of the new, its reformist mayor, Theodore R. McKeldin, called on them to face the "urgent necessity of breaking the ... deadlock in the matter of Negro housing."[34]

By time of Jackie's arrival, the ghetto had burst its seams. In the classified pages old white blocks had shifted to the "Colored" column—ready for "immediate possession," they said, addressing the pent up black cash the war had provided them to buy the houses that broke the noose of the ghetto that had been defined by "redlining" banks and federal mortgage "guidelines." Whites were moving to suburbs with names like "Forest" and "Glen."[35] For them, the war had been against fascism, anti–Semitism, and racism—their schools and movies said so—but *why* so close to home. But Peace and Jackie Robinson had arrived by spring 1946.[36] It was *this* Baltimore, struggling to live with change that greeted Jackie. "Southern," yes, but neither more nor less racist than New York (there, blacks mainly stayed in the Hotel Theresa in Harlem), and not the bugbear that baseball used to justify its own racial foot-dragging.

Not that it was an easy step for whites. True, things were swinging for "Negroes," but at a price. The old white semi-pro soccer league with its teams—Our Lady of Pompei, Kearny Scots, and Hakoah—waned. Sandlot baseball began to dry up. The guys on the corner drifted off. Benkert's *Biergarten* closed. Heintzman's and Kurtz's beaches (with their "restricted" signs at the gate), were made remote by rationed gas. And my father and I had a spat over his selling the house out from under us; he might have stuck it out, he said, but he was "not a pioneer."

To soothe the *angst* of white people who feared uncommonly rapid change, progressives of all sorts invoked the war as the catalyst of change with Jackie, as Adam Clayton Powell put it, "a definite step toward winning the peace." A "fitting" end to "a great war to preserve liberty, equality, and decency," said the Oakland *Tribune*. A few Southern writers agreed, imagining that if Jackie played well and with dignity, his color would fade, and he would assume the mantle of Joe Louis as "a credit to his race."[37]

Baseball, however, persisted in its denial of change and in its predictions of dire consequences. The *Sporting News*, "the bible of baseball," sampled opinion among writers and concluded that baseball was "far from a satisfactory solution." One Southerner wrote Rickey was a "menace" roiled by "the carpetbagger white press." "We are "happier with segregation in athletics," wrote another.[38] Rickey's own downer came in a "secret" meeting in 1946; after Robinson signed on but "before he had played a game," Rickey's colleagues "condemned" his work as "well intentioned" but unanimously warned that "the use of Negro players would hazard all the physical properties of baseball."³⁹

Surely, baseball needed such forbidding images as evidence of the wisdom of decades of Jim Crow baseball in spite of emerging racial awareness elsewhere in white circles. For example, the *New York Times* and the Baltimore *Sun* both covered the Negro leagues' teams, the Black Yankees and the Elite Giants while New York's white jazz fans frequented clubs in Harlem as surely as Baltimore whites safely went to Gamby's or the Casino on Pennsylvania Avenue in their town. Yet, in the spring of 1946 baseball was alive with rumors of fans chafing to resist the assault upon their old ways, so much so, that General Manager Herb Armstrong of the Orioles called on legislators for extreme measures against the miscreants.⁴⁰

Yet, Jackie Robinson's first game in Baltimore was played casually. Almost nobody showed on a late April Saturday—a boycott, guessed a few baseball cassandras. But the slim house (reportedly 3415) was merely *cold* while other locals either warmed at home or at a movie or in one of hundreds of corner taverns with a cold National Bohemian, the local beer of choice. C.M. Gibbs, the *Sun's* second tier columnist, reviewed it as an ordinary spring game, but with a rookie to whom attention must be paid. As he scanned the lineups, he allotted Robinson only one line of type—"then comes Robinson, the Negro star at second." In the game itself, Jackie played only passably in contrast to his four hits in the league opener. "It was a good humored crowd out to see a ballgame," wrote Gibbs. "Disturbances in the stands were exceptionally scarce," he said as though expecting worse. The *Afro* focused on Jackie's sense that "all of the fellows seem to be pulling for us," an echo of a *Sun* note that "the fellows ... have been swell to me." Of the city itself, he offered only an appropriate wisecrack. "They told me this was the southernmost city in the league, but last night I felt like I was playing in Alaska," he said. "Man, was it cold."⁴¹

Then came a warm Sunday doubleheader that contrasted starkly with the cool opener. The spring day, along with Robinson, drew some 25,000 fans. "Warming up in a pepper drill" before the game, Jackie "appeared completely relaxed and undisturbed by the large turnout of fans," said Jesse Linthicum in his "Sunlight of Sports" column. As for the game and the weekend series, the editor reviewed his play as they might have any new rookie—"not particularly impressive ... only two hits, but has played acceptable ball in the field."⁴² The *Afro* awarded Jackie his place in the black firmament, pushing the Elite Giants off the first sports page, running his box scores each week, counting the "dust off" pitches he took, praising his base running flair that distracted pitchers, and noting his place in the city's black life when he threw out the first ball in Druid Hill Park as Carver High defeated Dunbar.⁴³

Then on May 2, next weekend, the *Afro* ran an unsigned sidebar to the story. "It was tough on Jackie Robinson to have to listen to the slurs which came from white fans," it said. "How human beings could be so prejudiced

... [while] his charming wife was right there to hear it all." Calmly, she had smiled and said, "it was worse here than in Florida." Reported epithets were "midnight express" and "the ink spot." Pointedly, the paper took pride in the cool of black citizens. "Hats off to you colored fans," it cheered. "While the cops took out three white drunks (and were they drunk) and two white youths for rowdyism, the colored fans seemed to have everything under control."[44]

Except for Sam Lacy's angle on good black behavior, the beat writers gave the story a pass until later when the *Afro* lit into the "too ignorant to read" fans who rode Robinson, failing to see his superiority to them not only as athlete but as a UCLA alumnus. As for Sam Lacy, he focused on baseball, writing an "open letter" to Clay Hopper, the Royals' manager, prodding him to treat Robinson as any other player. After a misplay, "if you didn't give him hell, you should have," he wrote. Even reports on "bean balls" were normative; Jackie was hit by a pitch only six times in the season (three by Orioles), hardly a compelling figure in a game in which rookies are usually initiated with such pitches.[45]

Later, the Royals made a second and a third road trip to Baltimore. By then racial barbs seemed to mingle with more conventional razzing; the Montreal third baseman, John Jorgensen, recalled a certain ambivalence — "people no doubt liked to see him play, *but* there was still that tension." Tygiel had a similar sense in describing a rhubarb after a last-out play at home plate: the crowd "erupted" onto the diamond, but merely, he wrote, "in support of the hometown Orioles." True, after the game, with Jackie idled by an injury and already in the clubhouse, a crowd of diehards did form, chanting "Come out here, Robinson, you son of a bitch." But Jorgensen and two other "southern" players waited them out, escorted him to a bus, and took him to his hotel in the black west side. Then in August when Montreal again arrived for a series, Sam Lacy of the *Afro* heard "a number of unreconstructed whites" make Jackie the "target" of "'unfunny humor.'" He "oughta be behind a pair of mules," said one. But Orioles manager, Tommy Thomas, more "persistently" ragged the Royals than Jackie, aiming at their bleak futures when more blacks will "all be coming now" and white players would "all be out of a job."[46]

Over the years, the story varies, enlarging some, and growing lurid, as though with the passing of time writers reckoned Jackie's heroism needed puffing. In *My Own Story*, "as told to" Wendell Smith, (1948) he heard rumors, "but I never encountered trouble there" except "some ugly name-calling." His memoir, *Baseball Has Done It* (1964), Art Rust, Jr.'s brief "*Get That Nigger Off the Field*" (1974), Maury Allen's later *Jackie Robinson: A Life Remembered* (1987), and Rachel Robinson's own *An Intimate Portrait* make no mention of Baltimore. Not until his autobiography (with Charles Duckett), *I Never Had It Made: An Autobiography* (1972), do "two racist types" appear, shouting "nigger son of a bitch," a mood that spread "all over" the park. Then in 1995, the *Afro*'s two hoodlums that the "cops took out," morphed into a mob in David Falkner's *Great Time Coming: The Life of Jackie Robinson* (1995). The old park itself, the Orioles' home after their own burned in 1944 became a villain. Its length obliged all players, with few police in view, to dash to the lockers, ducking young fans seeking autographs or pats on their backs. Only Falkner, perhaps citing later road trips, records a chorus of "threats" by "vigilantes ... lurking" until "early hours," and cries of "We'll getcha, nigger s__ of a b_____!"[47]

The point here is not to minimize a vile racial history, nor to diminish Jackie Robinson's heroic hand in its eventual demise in a defining moment in Baltimore. If, indeed, "mobs" had appeared it would have affirming Baseball's secret meetings to preserve Jim Crow baseball. That is, Baltimore would have served Baseball's worst instincts. Instead, as Jackie told it in *My Own Story* (1948), except for "some ugly name-calling" in the first game there they "treated me well" and later even "gave me a great ovation for stealing home."[48]

Indeed, it was easy to misread Baltimore's racial ethos. "Two years later," Rampersad, Jackie's biographer, wrote, "a group of blacks and whites would be arrested for playing tennis together in the city's Druid Hill Park." True, but their *point* was lost. Two young women, Mary Coffee, a Morgan State College student, and Mitzi Swann a young artist, and their friends, mostly members of local Young Progressives who, in fact, in the spirit of Robinson, had *invited* the cops. They and their allies, as they intended, were busted for disturbing the pace. H.L. Mencken, the barbed essayist of the Baltimore *Sun*, wrote a wry piece about it. "The public parks are supported by the taxpayer," he wrote, "including the colored taxpayer.... It is high time all such relics of Ku Kluxury be wiped out in Maryland." Besides, he said, there was no law, only a "Park Board rule [that] is irrational and nefarious."[49] On its face, this story testified not only to the seeming success of the late war's propaganda of unity, brotherhood, and tolerance, but also to the need for a Jackie Robinson and a Branch Rickey to press on with it.

Oddly, less than a year later, I performed in a tragicomic version of both Mitzi's and Jackie's histories. One Sunday we, my white sandlot team, played a prelim to a game between two *black* teams, the Baltimore Elite Giants and the New York Cubans. Bugle Field, the Elites' home diamond, held a good crowd of men, some in Sunday suits and snappy fedoras, and a few women mostly in dresses, a few with hats like flowery crowns. But, sadly, that season the Elites won their last pennant and then their league folded, the unintended victim of Jackie's *beau geste*.

11

Jackie Robinson Interview

TED PATTERSON

TP: In Jackie Robinson's rookie year with the Brooklyn Dodgers in 1947 a new magazine hit the stands, *Sport Magazine*. Unlike similar publications on sport, this one lasted 25 years. On this special anniversary *Sport Magazine* is honoring Jackie Robinson as the Man of the 25 Years Award. Jack, this must be a great honor for you, considering that magazines and people tend to remember recent things, but you have been out of the game for over ten years.

JR: Well, it is a tremendous honor and I think a great deal of credit must go to *Sport Magazine* and its editors for recognizing an achievement that doesn't relate perhaps to an individual. The award signifies to me that there was an accomplishment that required Mr. Rickey, the baseball fans, and baseball players other than myself. I think it's a wonderful kind of a thing to see Sport recognize this achievement rather than the abilities of all of these other tremendous athletes who are at the luncheon today. Any one of them could have been recognized as the outstanding athlete of the quarter-century, but to recognize an achievement to me is something that I'll always be grateful for.

TP: To see you out there on a baseball diamond, you didn't look the part of someone like Jim Brown as far as physique, but you tried harder and this is probably something that a lot of athletes that don't have the great physical attributes could make it on.

JR: I've always been an athlete who felt that you had to give 100 percent all the time. There were certainly many times that I was out there on sheer courage and guts alone because of incidents that were happening, but we had a great bunch of guys that I worked with. I think when you deal with the kind of guys like we did on the Brooklyn baseball club, they had incentive to achieve whatever you attempted to do. So all this adds to the significance of this award—when you had teammates like I did. Knowing what they did and what they had to go through makes it all the more meaningful.

TP: Your achievement is one that not every Negro athlete could have done. You took an awful lot. Did Mr. Rickey research this before he brought

Ted Patterson interviews Jackie Robinson at Mama Leone's restaurant on the night of Robinson's acceptance of a *Sport Magazine* award, 1971 (courtesy Ted Patterson).

you onto the scene and said you're the one that's going to embark on the trailblazing of the color line in baseball?

JR: According to the reports I had from Mr. Rickey, he had scouted Latin American countries and gone out into different areas where blacks were playing looking for someone who could do the job. The important thing was I found later, he was looking for more than just baseball talent because of the kind of problems that he foresaw. As far as I'm concerned, had it not been for Mr. Branch Rickey it could not have been a success. He continuously called us in to give us the kind of guidance and counseling that was necessary and it enabled me to be prepared for any eventuality. I believe very frankly that with Mr. Rickey and my wife and the kind of encouragement I got from fellas on my own ball club, it made it possible. I just don't believe had it not been for these combinations that the first couple of years could have been what they were. It may have taken another 10 years or so to really break the barrier had it not been for the Rickey's and the Reese's, the Erskine's, the Labine's, and guys like that who really did a good job and had the understanding that was necessary.

TP: 25 years later as you look back, is there still a lot more to be done? Are you satisfied with the growth of baseball or is it lacking in a lot of ways?

JR: Well, it's lacking in a lot of ways. I make my protests by simply saying "no" to going to old-timers games and not participating in athletics any longer. A lot of people say it doesn't accomplish anything, but on a personal basis, I think it does accomplish something. I think basketball has moved along, but baseball, in spite of the fact they were the first, in spite of the contribution that they made, in spite of the contributions that black athletes are making today, they cannot go to the manager's role. They cannot go to the front office. They're just trying to kid people when they talk about the reasons why we don't have any black managers today. In my opinion, it is purely prejudice and bigotry on the part of club owners who are still wallowing around in the nineteenth century unable to see the forest for the trees. For had it not been for black players since Mr. Rickey broke the barrier, I don't know where baseball would have been. Certainly it wouldn't be in competition with the other two sports who use their black athletes and if they have the ability they do get a chance in most instances to go on — especially in basketball.

TP: The Negro leagues went through so many years without being recognized. Satchel Paige is now a full-fledged Hall of Fame member. Is this a step in the right direction?

JR: Yes, and I think the only reason that Satchel Paige is in the Hall of Fame is because Willy Mays spoke out. I remember speaking out saying it wasn't right. Well, I sincerely believe that had Willy Mays and Hank Aaron had not spoken out against it, it would not have happened. Because if I were one of the few again standing out against these kinds of prejudices and bigotries as I saw, the results would have been basically the same. There he goes again yelling and really the only guy or one of the few speaking out. But today its' great to see the Bill Russell's, the Kareem Jabar's standing up for their blackness and proud of their blackness. And, I think this is the thing that Americans have to understand. These guys are saying to the world, we're proud of what we are. You've got to recognize that. If you don't give us the credit, then there is not anything you can do to change the way we feel. I think that if we would only just take a page of our baseball's book in the early days when we as a team worked together — if we did this as a nation, we'd be much further along making this the kind of land we want it to be. But, until we do, we are going to have the frustrations and the problems that we've had for a long, long time. As a matter of fact, it could very well get worse.

TP: Jackie, to sum up have you read or gotten the chance to look at Roger Kahn's book *The Boys of Summer*?

JR: I certainly have and of course being part of it and looking at some of the stories, I'm particularly proud of Carl Erskine. Carl and I have always been pretty good friends. The things that he had to say in that book about the early days and how he felt about not being able to do anything about the conditions under which we had to live in was very impressive to me. Carl had an understanding the likes I'd never seen about what was going on and I just am as proud that our friendship has carried on over the years. He's just a great guy.

Jackie Robinson Speech

Thank you very much ladies and gentlemen. Thank you. Thank you very much Roger [Kahn]. I think Roger and everybody close to Roger knows how much I appreciate his friendship and sincerity over the years. I've known many newspaper men, but few have left the mark as Roger has on me and our relationship has been one of sincerity and respect. I'm more than pleased Roger that you took the time to come here and be with us today. I find it a bit difficult ladies and gentlemen. I have prepared a speech because I wanted to be sure I said the things that I feel very deeply.

But to have Bill Russell stand here before you this afternoon as he has, to have said the things that he did, kind of leaves me pretty much numb because I don't know of a man in athletics that I have admired more than Bill Russell. Not so much because Bill Russell was a great, great basketball player with the kind of leadership abilities that he had, but because Bill Russell is a man. A man proud of his blackness and a man that has been a tremendous leader in terms of letting us know exactly where we're going and how we are going to get there. To have him speak as he did left me certainly with tremendous thrills. I'm sure all of you know how much I appreciate this honor. I humbly accept it because of what it means.

The most significant athlete award is related to a great deal more than my performance on the playing field. It does have much to do with what happened on the playing field, but it also says to me that a man can be rewarded for standing up for his convictions and must have meaning to all those who played a part in making a difficult task much, much easier. There were certainly those who did not want us to succeed, but for every one of them there were hundreds that were rooting for our success. It's good to see so many of

Jackie Robinson at Ebbets Field, shortly before being promoted to the Brooklyn Dodgers in 1947 (National Baseball Hall of Fame Library, Cooperstown, New York).

you out here today, but I can't help but feel saddened that two of the three people who played leading roles in those early days and who gave me the necessary strength to reach the goals we set are not here with us today — my Mother and a truly great, great guy — my friend Mr. Branch Rickey. They've departed, but I know that they not only left a mark on me that will always be an inspiration. I'm sure they left a mark — especially Mr. Rickey — on those of you who care about where we are going in this country of ours. Without them we certainly wouldn't be here today — especially me receiving this honor. The religious strength they provided gave me the courage and determination and there were times when I felt Mr. Rickey was filling the role of a father I never had and some how I felt I was helping to ease the loss of his own son. That was our relationship and I'm certainly proud of it.

My Mother — a tower of strength gave so much of herself that it made me proud to see her proud of our success. But, Rachel is here — a strong a powerful mother and certainly a loving wife. She's been by my side through it all and there must not be any mistake about it. Without her I could not have withstood the agony and the pressure that went with being the focal point in the experiment that was at best questionable in the eyes of many Americans. Rachel has been the inspiration behind everything I've attempted to do. And besides being the strength in our family, she had a true and understanding meaning of what was going on and know how to deal with practically every bad situation and good one that we faced. Rachel's strength was my strength and the warmth of our relationship made the job a great deal easier. She was more than a wife, more than a mother to our children — she was the guiding light behind whatever successes we've had.

Rachel and I lost our eldest son, Jack. Jackie had more guts and courage than I ever had. He fell victim to drug addiction, but he had the guts to fight back. To have the courage to overcome this tragedy required great understanding and love and we loved our son. His courage made us proud and because Daytop Rehabilitation Program and its director, Kenny Williams, who was like a father to Jack — helped him so much. I'm certainly grateful to *Sport Magazine* that it has made a contribution to help them continue its great work. As I said before, drug addiction is a deadly blow to our young people, but I believe it is a great deal more important to help the Kenny Williams' all over this country who are exploring the minds and attitudes of our young and we must take a closer look at our priorities.

I'm quite proud that my daughter is here. She's so much her Mother's child and really my secret love. Sharon knows how much she means to me and I certainly want Sharon to stand and be recognized because she's a great, great girl. *[Applause]* I'm deeply proud of the achievement that she is making as a student at Howard University. While Sharon knew very little of what was going on in my early baseball career, her presence is of great significance.

And then there is my youngest son, David. David had the benefit of being the third child. He grew and took advantage of what we learned from Jackie and Sharon. While David isn't here — he's on his way back from a trip that covered most of Africa — I certainly feel that since he knows about this, that he's quite proud. And I certainly think that young David is going to move along in a great way in a short period of time He's quite a talented young man, even if I am a prejudiced father at this particular point. *[Applause]* And ladies and gentlemen there are so many of my friends here today that meant so very much to me during my baseball career, but more importantly, after my career was over — people who I've leaned on heavily. People like Ambassador Frank Williams who started me off in the civil right struggle. *[Robinson proceeds to identify many other people who helped him]* I can't help but to say how pleased that I am that there are guys here that mean so much to me, guys who I'm sure had to withstand great pressures to make the old Dodgers the team that we were.

I heard many things that happened on the playing field, but the things that I didn't hear about — the pressures from family and friends must have been tremendous on those players who cared. There are many incidents that could prove my point. Some eased away — others caused many problems, but there is one that stands out in my mind — one that was a simple gesture, but with tremendous meaning. Back in 1948 as we took our positions for infield practice, some Boston players thought that Pee Wee Reese, being a Southerner, would react to their taunts about playing along side of me on the Dodgers. There wasn't the viciousness as compared to the taunts of a Ben Chapman and some of the Phillies, but it was strong enough. Well, Reese did react. He left his shortstop position, came over to me at second base and placed his arms on my shoulder and said something. I don't remember the words and I'm sure that Pee Wee doesn't either, but his actions had great meaning. The heckling stopped and the bench cleared in no time. Pee Wee Reese, by his gesture, said simply, yell and scream as much as you like — we're a team — we came to play ball together. Because of attitudes like that, Roger, the Dodgers won six pennants in that 10-year period — not five. *[Applause and laughter]* And while we were only able to conquer the Yankees once in those six tries, I think we made our mark on things and on the game and on the nation. I can't help feeling that if Americans today would take a page out of Pee Wee Reese's book — if we could develop this kind of understanding in today's troubled world, how much further along as a nation we would be. We must — all of us — be willing to extend the same hand as the Dodgers and baseball fans the country over did to me or we will continue to face the bigotry and prejudice of a Forest Hills and the shooting and senseless killings of police in many sections of our country. We succeeded in baseball and I'm sure as we start out on our new venture with Artie Sutton and his associates what we need to do in this country is convince more guys to do more in terms of race relations. Artie Sutton and his associate and I are an integrated construction company and we believe very strongly in working closely together. We'll show them we can succeed in business and in our daily lives. We must succeed in bringing understanding or we shall all fail. The old cliché — a house divided against itself cannot stand — is certainly applicable today. There were some Dodgers who never knew or understood what was truly happening in those early years. However, there were those who knew and there were those who cared such as my good friends Clem Labine and Carl Erskine. Clem and I discussed many times things that caused us both concern and I also have a special feeling and admiration for Carl Erskine. In my opinion, no Dodger — none — understood more about what was happening than Carl did and Carl today doesn't hesitate to express himself publicly and all the Dodgers knew how much I appreciated their role.

But more importantly I know that each of them understood the pride and dignity that was mine — that I won their respect without being subservient. There was one newspaper man here in New York who suggested that if I continued my aggressive stand for civil rights I would lose some awards. Well, I told him that if one had to sacrifice dignity and self-respect for an award, if one must do the things that pleased others in order to be given an award, that award could not be worthwhile. He knew and knows today that as far as I'm concerned his self-bigotry — his hint at loss of awards would not change me or my pride in my blackness. Since that time there have been many snide remarks and columns about my firm belief that a person will have trouble living with others if he cannot live with himself. While I know I've lost some awards because I believe as I do, today's award has even greater significance. Those responsible are very much aware of how I feel. I had the pleasure of knowing Al Silverman for a long, long time and I have known him to be a man of courage and of sterling character. And I believe that *Sport Magazine* believes this very sincerely as its editors selected the Man of the 25 Years. In times where the emphasis was on the big play on the field, the people of *Sport Magazine* had the courage to put the emphasis on the achievement that required the help of great numbers of people. They know this is an award that must be shared by many. It's bestowed upon me only because I played a role that was created by a great American and was helped along by thousands. For all of these reasons, today is a very, very proud day for me and my family, and, I'm honored to share it with so many greats of the athletic world. Anyone of them I'm sure could have been selected for this award without any controversy whatsoever and as I share it with them, I hope they understand why this most significant award has a special meaning to me. Thank you very much.

12

An Interview with Carl Erskine

Ted Patterson

TP I've been looking forward to talking to our guest tonight on the early part of the program on WCBM. He was one of the great right handers in Dodger history in their Brooklyn days. He's one of the "Boys of Summer." He's written a book *Tales from the Dodger Dugout.* He's spun a couple of no hitters in his career, had a tremendous 1953 season in which he won 20 ballgames and lost only six. Altogether he won 122 games. I was talking with Stan Williams the other day, the big former right hand pitcher who is now a scout for the Dodgers. He said that if Carl Erskine had Williams' body, with Carl's heart and his ability, he'd of won 300 ballgames. Let's go to Carl Erskine in Anderson, Indiana right now. Carl, how are you?

CE Great. I liked what I was hearing there. I didn't know you knew my Mother. That's the way she used to talk about me.

TP Well, you're were only 5'10", 165 and yet you had a great fast ball and a probably even better curve ball.

CE I never thought of myself as being small. I'll tell you what happened though. I was wiry. I could pitch on hot days in St. Louis. Newcombe used to wilt a little bit once in a while — big Don was a hard worker, but they'd pitch him the night game on Saturday night and hold me for the afternoon game on Sunday. It would be about 110 and about that much humidity. But that always helped me to be kind of wiry.

TP And an excellent athlete besides. Of course, your team that has been romanticized in the "Boys of Summer" — had pretty much the same lineup, except maybe in left field, I think for about 10 years. Did you ever think then that the team was special–when you were playing on it?

CE No, you know the Jackie Robinson era, of course, is the time that you are talking about — the late 40's, mid 50's. No, I don't think we sensed so much being a piece of history because our attention was pretty much taken on keeping our jobs. The Dodgers had a big farm system — 26 farm teams— lots of great talent. There were about 800 players under contract and you couldn't get on the disabled list. If you were a little bit off for some reason, injured a little bit or whatever, you got sent to the minors and somebody else would come up. So, it was a very competitive time and I don't think we sensed completely the piece of history that was there because day-to-day, hour-by-hour we watched Jackie overcome a lot of obstacles and prove himself. But, it was in the course of trying to win another ballgame and win another pennant and so I don't think we sensed the history there.

TP You were in Fort Worth and then Montreal when Jackie came up in '47 and then you joined the team the next year for a little bit. Had most of the animosity gone by the boards by that time or was it still pretty heavy in some towns?

CE I think you got to sort it out. I think the media and history sometimes takes some liberties or plays up the more sensational side. I think the straight truth was that baseball is a game that is pretty rough — they ride on you pretty hard from the other dugout, especially when you are new in the league. They give you a good test to see if you can take it. And, part of what happened to Jackie was just normal baseball stuff where the opposing team was calling him names and getting on him big time. He's black, he stood out like everything in a white Dodger uniform and man you couldn't miss Jackie. Well, some of that was not racism so much as it was just hard-nosed baseball. I think the media made it out that baseball was very racist. Parts of it were, but there was something else going on, too. St. Louis used to segregate the crowd. The black fans would sit in the pavilion in St. Louis and the white fans in the stands. That, in itself, just brought lots of energy to the game because when Jackie stole a base or got a base hit, the pavilion would just erupt with black fans cheering him. If he struck out or got thrown out on the bases or made an error, the white fans, would erupt. So this was the atmosphere in baseball. The racism didn't come so much on the field as it did that explanation I just gave you about the way the fans were segregated. For a couple of years hotels did not permit Jackie to stay with us. So when he put his civvies on after a ball game where he had thrilled the crowd with his great play, and went out on the street, he was just a black man in America — like all the other black men who were not privileged to go into restaurants or have certain privileges because of their black skin. And so baseball was quick to accept Jackie really, but society was a lot slower.

TP That reminds me of that memorable comment from Branch Rickey saying "Jackie I want you not to have the guts to fight, but the guts not to fight — kind of hold it in and just prove yourself on the field" and he certainly did that.

CE I think if you asked me what stood out the most during the nine seasons I played with Jackie, and we were very close friends besides being teammates, if you asked me what is one quality that stood out — it was his self-control. It's obvious he was a great player-he was a four letter man at UCLA and there was no question about his huge ability. He was a college man, so he was intelligent and he was polished and all those things were characteristics of Jackie. But if you asked me what was his special quality I would say it was his self-control. He was a high spirited guy with a real wholesome militant make up, but he sensed that the price was too great for him to erupt and spoil the "experiment"—as Mr. Rickey—called it, being the first black player in the league or in baseball and so he contained himself under great pressure. I'm not a high volatile personality, but I don't think I could have handled some of the things Jackie took. The abuse from the stands, from the field, restaurants and other things where he was not treated like a major leaguer in any sense, but he contained himself and history will not show any place where Jackie punched a guy, shoved him, spit on him or in any way lost control and that is remarkable.

TP Carl, he thought a lot of you. He thought a lot of Pee Wee too, but now we're talking to Carl Erskine—outstanding right-hander for the Dodgers—primarily the Brooklyn Dodgers who did go to LA in 1958. In 1971, Carl, I had a chance to meet Jackie and I interviewed him and the occasion was he was the *Sport Magazine* "Man of the 25-Years" He gave a speech and this was part of it. "There were some Dodgers who never knew or understood what was truly happening in those early years and there were those who knew and those who cared, such as my good friends Clem Labine and Carl Erskine. Clem and I discussed many times the things that caused us both concern and I also had a special feeling and admiration for Carl Erskine. In my opinion, no Dodger—none understood more what was happening than Carl did and Carl today doesn't hesitate to express himself publicly and all the Dodgers knew how much I appreciated their roles. But more importantly I know that each of them understood the pride and dignity that was mine—that I won their respect without being subservient."

TP That's Jackie giving that speech and he really singled you out Carl, and that has to be nice to hear.

CE I've never heard that before. I only knew from talking to Jackie one time after I had stopped outside the clubhouse and spoken and spent some time with Rachel—his beautiful wife and his little son, Jackie, Jr. I stopped and just said hello to them and spent a few minutes chatting with them. And it was out in the presence of a lot of fans who were out circling around the clubhouse. He came to my locker the next day and thanked me for what I did. I said what was that? He said you stopped out there in front of everybody and you talked with Rachel and little Jackie and spent some time with us. I said hey, come on, you can give me a handshake and a pat on the back for pitching a good ballgame, but what I did was as natural for me to do as taking the next breath. Jackie and Rachel, they were class people. They are really dignified individuals and they earned your respect quickly as soon as you got to know them.

TP Carl, right after that speech I had a chance to sit with Jackie and at that particular time Roger Kahn's book was just coming out and this is my question to him and what he had to say. Jackie, to sum up have you read or gotten a chance to look at Roger Kahn's book *The Boys of Summer?*

JR   I certainly have and of course being part of it and looking at some of the stories, I'm particularly proud of Carl Erskine. Carl and I have always been pretty good friends. The things that he had to say in that book about the early days and how he felt about not being able to do anything about the conditions under which we had to live in was very impressive to me, but it's Carl Erskine. Carl had an understanding the likes I'd never seen about what was going on and I am just as proud that our friendship has carried on over the years. He's just a great guy.

TP   Carl, I don't know about you, but that kind of gives me goosebumps.

CE   I've not heard that and Ted, I would just love to own that piece. I don't brag about any part of the "experiment" as Mr. Rickey said with Jackie, but I'd say looking back over history I'd have to think Jackie had more impact on America and how we looked at ourselves and looked at each other than maybe even Martin Luther King did with his fantastic civil rights and human rights efforts. Jackie lived it out on this beautiful spotlight of major league baseball. A pure — there couldn't have been a purer-stage to do that. It was affirmative action in it's purest form — Jackie fielding a ground ball and throwing it because nobody could help him. He had to be completely on his own and handle it in front of the world, in front of this pure stage of major league baseball. I think that impact on America was deep and I think it made America say, hey, we have been wrong. This is the right way and this man — this black man — has opened our eyes. And so, I really believe that Jackie, through his efforts in baseball, and through Mr. Rickey's wisdom, impacted on America as maybe one of the most significant events of the whole century.

TP   What about some of the other Dodgers, such as Roy Campanella. Wasn't he more easy going?

CE   Campy and Jackie were teammates and there was never any kind of a problem in the clubhouse. There was never any snubbing. There was never any discussion, but they both had a philosophy that was really kind of on the opposite sides. Jackie always said don't think that we've accomplished anything just because I made it. Just because I'm here. Just because I've got the uniform on. I'm in the big leagues—that is not solving the major problem we have in America with civil rights and with racism. Campanella, on the other hand, was a poverty kid out of Philadelphia. He grew up with the poor and poor as dirt and he got into baseball and it gave him a way out. He played winter baseball in the Caribbean and Cuba, and Mexico. He played in the Negro League and then when he got the chance to play in pro baseball and then finally to the big leagues in 1948, Campy came, and he said don't rock the boat — hey we finally got here. Don't mess it up. And he wouldn't let any of the younger players like Gilliam. Joe Black, later Sandy Amoros, and Dan Bankhead in his early years a pitcher, complain about their locker or the size of their uniform. He'd say hey — shut-up — were here and don't mess it up! Well, he was so grateful and I admired both of those positions, but they did not gel to each other because Jackie wanted to rough the waters. He wanted to shake them up because there were inequalities. But Campy said shut-up and don't mess it up, and so that was the two of them. But, to their credit never did it interfere in the team spirit, the effort on the field or in the clubhouse — that was kept well away from anything that had to do with our playing together.

TP And Carl, as we sum up, *Tales from the Dodger Dugout* is a very easy read because you have, you know, chapters that last just one page, but it must have been a lot of fun because it brings back a lot of memories of people like Preacher Roe and some of the high jinx he did with a little bit of saliva on the ball, and Rex Barney who has endeared himself to Baltimore — you know he was around here for a lot of years. Was he one of the hardest throwers you saw?

CE You know I can quote Joe DiMaggio when you ask me that question. In the 1949 World Series, Rex Barney had just had a tremendous second half of the season for the Dodgers in '49. We won the pennant by percentage points and Rex pitched in one World Series game and DiMaggio commented after the game that he was faster than Feller. Well, that was a pretty dramatic statement coming from Joe D himself. I don't know how hard Rex threw because we didn't have the gun in those days. The only thing I can tell you, there was nobody in the league that threw as hard as he did in the '49 season. He had overpowering stuff — he was just unhittable. And then a mysterious thing that happened after that was when he lost control and it was like he'd never known how to pitch. He just never could regain that. But a super guy and I know he had a wonderful career at Baltimore — endeared himself to the fans there as one of the field announcers. Rex was a good friend and I always admired him because when I joined the team in Vero Beach, Florida and I walked in and on the doors down the hallway of the old barracks we stayed in, were the names of Branca, Barney and Banta — 3 top right-handed pitcher the Dodgers had in those days. I felt so privileged to be there. I was feeling so good with just being in uniform with those guys.

TP Well, you were a guy that actually caught attention while pitching in the Navy. A lot of the guys had their careers messed up because of the service, but for you it started it I guess. Gee Carl, we could go on and on here. I just want to thank you for this time you have given us tonight, and I'm going to get that tape with Jackie to you.

CE My family would like to hear that. My sons. I've told them a lot about Jackie but to hear his voice again — you know he spoke clean, clear English. He was a very dignified man. You saw him late. He'd probably lost his eyesight pretty much by the time you saw him. He had sugar diabetes. I think he died in '73 [1972] or so. But Jackie was a human being you know. He wasn't a superman. He bled and he hurt and he cried when he lost his son, Jackie, Jr., in a car accident. It broke Jackie's heart. It just really leveled him. He was a human being but he did do a historic thing. He helped us all. I told him one time — Jackie you helped my race more than you helped your own, and I believe that.

TP Good luck with the book *Tales from the Dodger Dugout*. We've heard a few of them tonight and we'll be in touch.

CE Great. Thanks so much and my best to all the good fans in Baltimore.

TP Thanks very much. That's Carl Erskine. Goodnight Carl. He won over 100 ballgames — 122 ballgames to be exact with the Brooklyn Dodgers and threw two no-hitters. And he came within one walk of a perfect game. He walked the Cubs pitcher, Willard Ramsdell, or else he would have had a perfect game in '52.

13

Minnie Minoso and His Footsteps

TIM WENDEL

In 1993, while watching rough edits from the Public Broadcasting Service television series *Baseball* with its director Ken Burns, we viewed snippets of a game between the old Brooklyn Dodgers and New York Giants. Burns commented that you didn't see that style of play anymore in the big leagues. In the images of grainy black and white, players routinely went from first to third base on any hit to the outfield. Pitchers threw inside and, if knocked down, batters simply dusted themselves off and stepped back in, eager to put the next offering in play. The game was so different in the 1950s than what it became forty years later with many major league managers still emulating Earl Weaver, the legendary manager of the Baltimore Orioles—praying for the three-run home run. I told Burns that the old style of baseball still existed in places like Havana and Santo Domingo, and thanks to Latinos, such a style and passion for the game was rapidly being brought back to our shores. Today, many of the game's best sluggers (Albert Pujols, Alex Rodriguez and Vladimir Guerrero) and pitchers (Johan Santana, Francisco Rodriguez and Mariano Rivera) are of Latino descent. They have become just the newest wave of immigrant players that are rejuvenating the game of baseball. What has been lost in the current attention to Hispanic stars, however, is the history of this phenomenon.

They have been playing baseball in Cuba for almost as long as they have been playing the game in the United States. Nemesio Guillo, a Cuban studying in the United States, brought the first bat and ball home to the island nation in 1864. Almost immediately, the game took root there and subsequently gained such an enthusiastic following throughout the Caribbean region that it would become the national pastime in that part of the Americas, too. A migration to the Promised Land of the major leagues in the North would follow. Cuban hurler Adolfo Luque, the "Pride of Havana," compiled a 194–179 record in the U.S. major leagues from 1914 to 1935. His stint included a 27–8 year with Cincinnati in 1923 and 4⅓ innings of shutout that relief helped the New York Giants capture the 1933 World Series.

Baseball in the Caribbean would also pave the way for the racial mixing of the game in the Major Leagues. Negro League stars such as Josh Gibson, Martin Dihigo and Satchel Paige, while barred from the white majors, played winter ball in Mexico and Cuba where colors became mixed on the playing field before Jackie Robinson officially broke the color barrier in North America in 1947. In the years after Robinson, such black stars as Hank Aaron, Willie Mays, Bob Gibson and Reggie Jackson took center stage. Now, Hispanic stars such as A-Rod, Guerrero and Rivera, are gaining the most attention while some teams embrace the Latino influence. The older division between white and black is giving way to another hue. To crib from commentator and writer Richard Rodriguez, the prominent color for the grand old game has become brown.

This new colorization of baseball had its pioneers the same way the earlier integrationist process had its courageous forerunners. In saluting Robinson's achievement, it's often too easy to forget about those who soon followed in his footsteps and not all were African-Americans. At the head of the line of pioneers stands Orestes "Minnie" Minoso — the Latino Jackie Robinson. The legendary Roberto Clemente once tried to explain the unique position of the Latino ballplayer in the years after Robinson. Clemente said it was like being "a double minority," singled out for being dark skinned and unable to speak the language. "Before Minnie came on the scene in the late forties, there had been around fifty Latin players who had played the game, all of them light-skinned because of racial policies," wrote Marcos Breton, a sportswriter with the *Sacramento Bee* and the co-author of *Away Games: The Life and Times of a Latin Ballplayer.* "None of them had ever made a real big impact on the game until Minnie. He really put Latin players on the map in Major League Baseball."

Minoso came to the Chicago White Sox in 1951, the first black player to don a White sox uniform, and he became Hispanic America's first superstar. He homered against the New York Yankees in his Chicago debut and joined with Nellie Fox and Chico Carrasquel to lead the new darlings of the baseball world, the "Go Go" White Sox. Although Minoso would play for three other teams during his seventeen-year major-league career, he would remain so popular in Chicago that he still serves as the team's goodwill ambassador. Decades after his final at-bat, he's mentioned in the same breath with his air ness, Michael Jordan.

"Believe me when I say that Minnie Minoso is to Latin ballplayers what Jackie Robinson is to black ballplayers," Orlando Cepeda wrote in his autobiography *Baby Bull.* "As much as I loved Roberto Clemente and cherish his memory, Minnie is the one who made it possible for all of us Latins. Before Roberto Clemente, before Vic Power, before Orlando Cepeda, there was Minnie Minoso. Younger players should know this and offer their thanks. He was the first Latin player to become a superstar. Luis Tiant once told me that Minoso was his idol because "he was the first one to stand up for black

Cubans—guys like myself. You see somebody like that make it and you have some hope. You start to believe that maybe one day you can reach the big leagues, too."

Minoso withstood his share of abuse to prepare the way for others to follow their dream. Before the Havana-born outfielder came to the U.S. to play ball, the early Latino scout, Jose Pasquel, warned the young Cuban star about setting his sights on the majors. He told Minoso that in North America the young ballplayer would be "treated like a dog," simply because he was black. To his credit, Minoso came north anyway and began his new career with the New York Cubans in the Negro League in 1945. He soon realized that Pasquel was right: Segregation was rampant in New Orleans, where the team had its spring training home. The young Cuban became a quick student of accommodation to racial prejudice there and in the majors when he broke in with the Cleveland Indians in 1949 before being traded to the White Sox in 1951.

Minnie Minoso, the Latino pioneer with the Chicago White Sox in the early 1950s (courtesy Tim Wendel).

Decades later Minoso described for this author what he experienced as an Hispanic racial pioneer in the 1950s. "First you had Jackie Robinson. Then Larry Doby and then you had me," he explained. "I was the first black-skinned ballplayer to play in the city of Chicago. I tried to take everything as it comes. I never let the world hurt me. The world didn't break me. They used to call me terrible things, but I let it go one ear and out the other. None of it stayed with me. I never wanted them to know my feelings on the inside. On the outside I just gave them my smile. Smile all the time."[1]

When asked if that was difficult, he answered, "Sure it was. But what can you do?" Beginning with the Chicago press' insistence on dropping his proud Cuban name Orestes in place of "Minnie," Minoso swallowed his pride and ultimately changed it to his legal name. Then he compared the insults and threats to experiencing a prolonged batting slump. "With both, you have to be strong in the mind. Not let it hurt you. Sooner or later you're going to have a slump and that's when you need to be strong. Ted Williams told me that.

He also told me I could hit and I cannot tell you how good that made me feel. How I remembered that when I was going through difficult times, on or off the field."

"This is what the world is like, my friend. You cannot let anyone run your life because they call you names or tell you that you can't play. When I played I sometimes had to play the clown. I had to listen and laugh, even if I was crying inside. But never did I let them see that it bothered me. I tried to answer with my bat. Always my bat. It's like if you're a singer. If you hear noises out there, people may not like how you're singing, are you going to stop and tell them to be quiet? Of course not. You're going to keep singing." Minoso's persistence paid off and he lead the league in hits in 1960 and between 1951 and 1961 he scored more than 100 runs four times and more than ninety runs nine times.

The runs he scored underlined the distinctive style of play that Minoso brought with him from Cuba. He ran the bases like Jackie Robinson. In his first three years he led the league in stolen bases, in triples the next year, and doubles three years later. Moreover, he would do whatever was necessary to get on base, including getting in the way of fastballs. In sixteen seasons, he set the American League record by being hit by a pitch 189 times. Over seventeen years he averaged .298 at the plate overall while his defensive skills averaged out to .974. Minoso provided the first glimpse into the kind of game common to Latin America where runners relish taking the extra base at every opportunity and pitchers aren't reluctant to challenge hitters. This quicker, passionate, even more confrontational style of play would enliven the game that was losing its panache and some of its pride in performance. "Of all the sports, we Latins believe that baseball requires the greatest amount of skill," Cepeda once told me. "That's why we take such pride in playing it well."

How well Latinos perform in their newly adopted country requires more than acquired athletic skills. It also takes managerial leadership and major league teams are now doing much more to acculturate young Hispanics to the new world than they did in the days of Minoso. The assimilation came slowly at first. In the early 1960s, San Francisco Giants manager Alvin Dark declared that only English would be spoken in the clubhouse and dugout . His edict might very well have kept a team filled with Latino stars, Cepeda, Juan Marichal, and the Alou brothers, from ever winning a World Series. In the hypercompetitive world of professional sports, such division in a locker room is poison for team chemistry. Now many major league teams, and some at the minor leagues, have bilingual coaches, trainers, and Hispanic front office personnel. Moreover, the Cleveland Indians and the New York Mets teach their top Hispanic prospects English and send them to schools in the Dominican Republic to help them get a high school education while they're playing for the organization.

Major League baseball has increasingly prepared their prospects for their lives to the North. Junior Noboa, the former second baseman for the Montreal Expos, operates one of the 30 or so baseball academies now in the Dominican Republic. Establishments such as Noboa's are modeled, in large part, after Days Inns or Holiday Inn Selects. The effect can be jarring to a visitor to the island. Dirt roads in the jungle dead-end at vast complexes with emerald-green fields and residence hotels that would be at home off any U.S. interstate. "We try to make it as close as we can to what they'd find in America," Noboa told me. "If we don't, the odds of them making it aren't too high." Major League Baseball (MLB) has its own type of a guest-worker program. Ahead of the rest of the country it has learned the importance of preparing immigrant labor from Central America for legitimate citizenship in the U.S. This approach has allowed the sport to foster young stars and a new fan base on both sides of the border.

Orlando Cepeda, a Puerto Rican star who started with the San Francisco Giants in 1958 (courtesy of Tim Wendel).

In becoming what has become the largest minority in the U.S., Latinos have mirrored what's going on in the major leagues. While native-born American youth are often placing their athletic dreams in other sports or activities, more than one quarter of the players on U.S. major-league teams were foreign-born by the 2007 season. Most of them were Latino or of Latino descent. At the minor-league level, overseas players make up 45 percent of the roster openings, with the majority coming from the Dominican Republic, which is the top exporter of baseball talent. Fans who might object to Hispanic day laborers competing with them for jobs or not speaking English have little problem cheering on immigrant stars. MLB's attendance, despite the steroid scandals, has reached all-time levels in recent seasons because of them. "Without the influx of Latin players, we certainly wouldn't have 30 major-league teams," Chicago White Sox executive Roland Hemond told *The Kansas City Star*. "So they've been a great boon for our game, its growth in franchises as well as in quality of play."

Every day during the season, when teams take the field, baseball's own model of assimilation provides lessons for the nation undergoing a debate over the fate of other Hispanics in the country. At the major league level, David "Big Papi" Ortiz and Manny Ramirez not only led the Boston Red Sox to another championship in 2007; they were accepted by their teammates as well. "Manny being Manny" became a rallying cry not only for a ballclub, but for a community as well. "Even if they fail as ballplayers, they are given tools that enable them to go on with life," said Alan Klein, author of *Growing the Game: The Globalization of Major League Baseball*. "This isn't the case in other (U.S.) industries making use of temporary workers."

Unlike the early days of Minoso, today's Hispanic players can fold more fully into U.S. society — whether they become U.S. citizens or not. The days are gone when Latino ballplayers are simply treated like better paid migrant workers. Ortiz from the Dominican Republic, for example, has become a folk hero in Boston. Another Dominican star, Vlad Guerrero, is a crowd favorite in Southern California. In New York, Omar Minaya, the first Latino general manager at the major-league level, created "Los Mets," with Pedro Martinez, Carlos Beltran, Carlos Delgado and, more recently, Johan Santana. MLB might be providing the country a lesson in cultural assimilation. If other industries dependent on immigrant labor — in the agriculture and construction trades, for instance — would make comparable efforts as MLB to help their workers assimilate, the benefits would flow through U.S. society. It might also lead to a civilized national debate about immigration reform.

The growing presence of Hispanics in MLB has already provided the basis for meaningful bi-racial acculturation in the game. "Many Anglo players who never learned Spanish in school now know some of the language, and they've learned something about Latin American geography and customs," George Gmelch wrote in *Baseball without Borders*. "International players, whether from Latin America or Asia, inevitably also introduce American baseball fans to their countries and culture, whether it is the customs mentioned by TV color commentators or cultural geography introduced through ESPN specials like those that followed Sammy Sosa or Pedro Martinez around their hometowns in the Dominican Republic."

Off the field, Latinos are making inroads into baseball management, too. Arturo Moreno, a Phoenix businessman, stepped up to buy the Los Angeles Angels from Disney a few years ago. Minaya, who was born in the Dominican Republic and made history when he was named the first Latino general manager in the major leagues, kept his Montreal Expos competitive even though the ball club has one of the lowest team payrolls in the game. Not bad for a guy who was passed over by other ball clubs because he didn't have enough "organizational experience." After turning heads in that job, the Mets brought him back to New York and told him to fix their listing franchise.

By 2050, only half of the population in the U.S. is expected to be non–Hispanic white, according to U.S. Census projections; the other half will be people of color, with Latinos representing the largest group. "I was born a minority," wrote author Paul Cuadros, "but I will not die a minority. America is in the midst of fundamental population changes that will forever alter its national character. In the next fifty years, there will be more people that will look like me, and the country's identity will be transformed."

The racial dynamics of the game has surely changed since the early days of Jackie Robinson and Minnie Minoso. The baseball lives of New York Yankee closer Mariano Rivera and his catcher Jorge Posada provide a window into the progressive evolution of the browning of baseball. After first meeting 14 years ago in instructional league, they came up through the Yankees' minor-league system, with Rivera reaching the parent club as a starting pitcher in 1995 and Posada arriving two years later. High-pressure baseball, closing out the big games successfully, has brought them together despite their dissimilar paths to major leagues. Rivera grew up in Panama and was a budding soccer star. But at the age of 15, he was sidelined by an injury. Baseball was the only ticket out of Panama and to a better life. In comparison, Posada was the son of a big-league scout who often quizzed him about the game's fundamentals when they watched the Atlanta Braves on television in their native Puerto Rico.

"If you can talk when things are going bad," Posada said, "you set things up for them to go right." Rivera, who holds the New York Yankees record for saves, once told me that the right words, no matter how brutally honest, can set anything straight. "It's like a marriage," he said. "That's how I'd put the relationship between the pitcher and catcher. That's why you always try to be on the same page."

What many U.S. sports fans are just beginning to realize is that our national pastime also belongs to the rest of the world. Dreams about baseball extend beyond borders, even past the barriers of language. That can truly be a wonder in a world that's seemingly eager to break along class and racial lines at every turn. Many times in the past, baseball has offered us the comfort of continuity, a link from one generation to another. What we're only beginning to realize is that the game also can connect Americans to worlds with which we thought we had little in common. Say hello to the new age of baseball.

Part IV

THOSE DAMN YANKEES AND THE REBELLIOUS CURT FLOOD

The popular Broadway musical of the 1950s that features a player from the luckless Washington Senators who bargains his soul to defeat the hated Yankees provided a lasting motif for baseball fans who endured a long humiliation of their favorite team by the Bronx Bombers in New York. No other team won so many championships for so long, as Henry D. Fetter's evaluation, "The New York Yankees, 1949–1964: The Price of Dynasty," demonstrates. While many contemporary observers failed to gauge the full extent of Yankee power as it emerged, two of its metropolitan rivals, the Brooklyn Dodgers and the New York Giants, did. Reflecting national demographic trends, they moved to the West Coast in 1958 to escape the dominating Yankee presence.

The Yankees' late and begrudging racial integration ultimately hurt the team, and the American League as well. Fetter's careful research into major league data, revealed in charts for this essay, shows how the racial composition of teams affected their standings during this era. The Yankees won the battle for baseball supremacy in New York for sixteen seasons, but its years of dominance cost the American League its earlier domination in attendance figures. The greater black presence in the National League also won the senior circuit more All-Star games and ultimately more World Series championships. Their teams demonstrated that if the game were to remain preeminent in modern America it needed to mirror, rather than resist, the civil rights course of the Dodgers and the nation.

Baseball's reformist course after World War II was revived in another fashion two decades later. In the late 60s, Curt Flood, a great admirer of the Rev. Martin Luther King, Jr., struck his own blow for freedom with his legal challenge to the century-long reserve clause in major league baseball that bound players to one team for life. Flood's assault on baseball's exemption from anti-trust action, a daunting challenge ruled on by the Supreme Court of the United States, failed. But it set in motion skillful maneuvering by the Marvin Miller and the Players Association, that, combined with bold player initiatives, would soon democratize the economic imbalance between owners and players.

The resulting free agency system accomplished Flood's revolutionary goals, if not his own personal gratification. In the process of liberating others, personal demons conquered him and led to his death within a decade of his often lonely battle for economic justice in the national game. Sadly, unlike one of his heroes, Jackie Robinson, who testified in Flood's support at the Supreme Court, Flood never received the honor he deserves for his battle for democracy. Jules Tygiel partially compensates for this neglect in his detailed essay "Revisiting Curt Flood." One of the premier historians of the game, unequalled in the study of the racial factor in the game, Tygiel focuses on legal issues as well as union-management conflicts. His assessment of Flood is true to his reputation for clear-headed honesty. Tygiel's death in 2008 has left a large void in the world of baseball historians.

14

The New York Yankees, 1949–1964: The Price of Dynasty

HENRY D. FETTER

From 1949 through 1964, the New York Yankees achieved a level of success that has not been matched, or indeed approached, before or since, not even by the Yankees themselves. At the same time, major league baseball was beset by novel challenges that the sport struggled to meet. While the Yankees were winning on the field, headlines in the media were reading "Can Baseball Survive?," "Does Baseball Pay?" and "Why Is Baseball in Trouble."[1] The connections between the sport's difficulties and the Yankee's unprecedented success have, however, been left largely unexplored by sport historians. To Yankee players and fans, winning championship banners year after year may have been all that mattered at the time. With the benefit of hindsight, we can also see that by stubbornly resisting the racial integration of its roster, and by exercising a lordly dominion over the New York City baseball that overshadowed the National League's Brooklyn and New York franchises, the Yankees played a decisive role in shaping the contours of recent baseball history.

When post-war America's novel geographies of race and place converged in the middle of the 1960's to topple, at least for a time, the Yankees from their throne, the team had long since established itself as major league baseball's dominant franchise. That status has, if anything, been solidified in succeeding decades. It is a claim that can become tiresome, if not downright offensive to many, if repeated too often by or too loudly by imperious Yankee fans, but it is a simple statement of fact. Since their emergence from the sport's lower depths after World War I, the Yankees have captured 39 American League titles and 26 World Series championships. They have won pennants in every decade since they captured their first in 1921, and World Series in every decade but one (the 1980's). Over that span of 80 plus years, the Bronx Bombers have compiled a record of long-term success that is unmatched, not only in baseball, but in all of professional sports.

If any one era provided the capstone on the Yankee's arch of triumph, it would be the years 1949–1964. Even by Yankee standards, the team's record during those years was nothing short of astonishing, exceeding anything else in the storied annals of baseball's preeminent franchise. In the course of those sixteen seasons, the Yankees won 14 pennants and 9 World Series titles, including five Series in a row from 1949 through 1953. Averaging more than 97 wins a season, the Yankees won 95 or more games fourteen times between 1949 and 1964; all of the other teams in the American League combined managed to achieve that just half as often (Detroit and the Orioles twice each, Boston, Chicago and Cleveland once apiece). Cumulative standings for the clubs of the American League for those years place the Yankees 172 games ahead of the team with the second best overall record, the Cleveland Indians.

The extent of that dominance, in a league that was bereft of competitive balance, is underscored by comparing it with similar cumulative standings for the National League for that same period. In the senior circuit, the Dodgers led the way, averaging 91.4 wins per season, and leading the runner up Braves (of Boston and Milwaukee) by 104 games. The Dodger lead over the three strongest National League contenders (the Giants and the Cardinals, along with the Braves) was less than that held by the Yankees over the Indians, its closest rival. Only the Indians and White Sox were able to crack the Yankee grip on the AL pennant during those 16 seasons; in the National league, by contrast, every team, except for the Cubs and the two expansion franchises added in 1962, won a pennant between 1949 and 1964. This disparity in competitive balance was reflected at the bottom of each league's standings as well as at the top. The worst team in the American League, the Philadelphia–Kansas City Athletics won 531 fewer games than the Yankees; their counterpart in the National League, the Cubs, won just 388 games fewer than the National League leading Dodgers.

Perhaps Yankee power reached its peak on Sunday August 3, 1958. The standings of the clubs that morning reported that the Yankees were in first place by 17 games, with a record of 67–34 for a winning percentage of .663. *Every other team in the American League was below .500.* That month, *Sports Illustrated* saluted the 1958 team as "the greatest Yankee team ever" (with no question mark attached),[2] but prematurely as it turned out. The Yankees lost more games than they won for the rest of the season and then collapsed to a third place finish the next year. Although they rebounded to win five straight pennants from 1960–1964, the Yankee aura was no longer what it had once been as they lost three of those five World Series. But if their once decisive margin of superiority over the National League — the only NL team to beat them in the World Series between 1923 and 1955 had been the Cardinals — no longer obtained, the fact remained that the American League had ceased to exist as a competitive enterprise in the face of the Yankee onslaught.

It was in the years between 1949 and 1964 that the Yankees broke out of the pack of baseball's great franchises to carve out an unapproachable place in the baseball hierarchy. When the 1949 season started, the Yankees had won eleven World Championships, to the next best Cardinals' six. Five other teams had won three or more World Series, the Red Sox (5), the Athletics (5), the

14—The New York Yankees, 1949–1964

From left, Mickey Mantle, Yogi Berra, Whitey Ford, Joe DiMaggio, and Casey Stengel at an old-timers game at Shea Stadium in 1974 (courtesy Hearst News American Photographic Collection in the University of Maryland Special Collections Library, College Park.

Giants (4) and the Cubs (3). Over the next sixteen years, the Yankees won an additional nine titles; the Cards and Giants added one apiece to their previous haul, the Red Sox, Cubs and A's were blanked. As of 1964, the Yankees could claim a total of 20 titles, the Cards 7, the Giants, Red Sox and A's 5 each, the Cubs 3 (joined now by the Dodgers at that mark). At the beginning of the 1949–1964 era, the World Championships collectively won by the Cardinals and either the Red Sox or A's equaled the Yankees' then eleven World Championships; at its close, the Yankee victory total exceeded that of the three next best clubs combined. No longer first among equals, the Yankees were so far out in front that, to borrow the celebrated, if apocryphal, response to Queen Victoria's question at the inaugural America's Cup Race in 1851, there was no second.[3] And so they have remained to this day.

Even on those rare occasions when the Yankees were defeated, it almost always was by a hair. When they finished second to the Cleveland Indians in 1954, the Yankees won 103 games (their second best mark to that date); four of the five World Series they lost were decided in the seventh game. Only the Yankees' mediocre third place finish (just two games over .500) in the American League pennant race in 1959 and the four game sweep administered by the recently transplanted Los Angeles Dodgers in the 1963 World Series clouded their aura of supremacy.

The Yankees' relentless domination of the game on the field was reflected on the sport's business side. The Yanks led the AL in home attendance every season from 1949 and 1964, with the exceptions of 1960 and 1963, when they were second to the White Sox and Twins respectively. They led the League in road attendance every year in that span. One quarter, sometimes even more, of the fans drawn to their rivals' ball parks came out to see the Yankees. Throughout that era, 40 percent of total American League attendance was accounted for by fans buying tickets to Yankee games. The unmatched drawing power of the Yankees lingered even after the dynasty itself crashed in 1965. The suddenly-humbled team continued to lead the AL in road attendance every year thereafter until the pennant-winning Orioles finally broke the spell in 1969.

Given the magnitude of Yankee success during those years, it comes as something of a surprise to learn that contemporary observers were slow to comprehend the full extent of Yankee power. In the spring of 1947, no less an authority than sportswriter Red Smith had concluded that it was "out of the question" that the Yankees, hobbled by "aging and rusting personnel, slackening of managerial command," could reclaim their former status as "the undisputed rulers of baseball."[4] When Casey Stengel was hired to manage the team in the fall of October 1948, Arthur Daley of the *New York Times* described the team, then coming off a third place finish, as a "ball club whose slip is showing" and as "an overage group" whose "once endless replacement system has run dry." Stengel, Daley added, "is confronted by the biggest rebuilding problem since Miller Huggins brought up Tony Lazzeri and Mark Koenig in 1926. And he has no Lazzeri in sight."[5] The Yankees, according to Daley, were a "worn out ball club" and Stengel had "inherited a club which was as badly disorganized as any team could be."[6]

An even harsher prognostication of the Yankees' prospects was offered by Dave Egan, the *Boston Record* sports writer who had been a particular nemesis of Stengel when Casey had managed the Braves. "Well, sirs and ladies, the Yankees have now been mathematically eliminated from the 1949 pennant race. They eliminated themselves when they engaged Professor Casey Stengel to mismanage them for the next two years and you may be sure that the perfesser will oblige to the best of his unique ability."[7] Tom Meany, among the team's most stalwart press box rooter from the days of Babe Ruth onwards, gazed into his crystal ball as the 1949 season got underway and foretold mediocrity in the offing: "The Yankees can finish anywhere from third to fifth depending on how much service Joe DiMaggio can render."[8] Meany spoke for the consensus of experts. In that year's pre-season Baseball Writers of America poll, the Yanks were picked to finish third, garnering only 6 votes for first place as against 116 for Boston and 79 for Cleveland.[9] Nor did victory in that year's World Series change press box perceptions of the Yankees' prospects. They trailed the Red Sox in the BBWA pre-season poll in both 1950 and 1951 by decisive margins (116–38 and 149–32, respectively) and Cleveland (by 114–91) in the 1952 survey. Not until the spring of 1953, after the Yankees had won four World Championships in a row, did the press box experts tab the Yankees as the favorites to win that season's pennant chase, finally getting it right.[10]

Popular opinion likely outstripped the experts in recognizing the sheer dynastic power of the Yankees in those years. Douglas Wallop's novel *The Year the Yankees Lost the Pennant*, as well as its Broadway musical version, *Damn Yankees*, struck a chord with a baseball public more than ready to believe that only supernatural intervention could stop the Yankee juggernaut — although as fate would have it, the book appeared in July 1954 just as Cleveland's quite mortal Indians (as the New York Giants would prove in that year's World Series) were in the process of doing, at least that one year. By then, the once skeptical sportswriters had become true believers in the Yankee's supremacy, having picked them to win the pennant that season, as they were to do in 1959, the next time their pennant hopes fell short.[11]

The surprisingly grudging recognition of Yankee dominance at the time is also found in a rearview literary mirror of history. As early as 1962, A.J. Liebling wrote that "the Yankees are the least popular of all ball clubs because they win, which leaves nothing to 'if' about,"[12] and the retrospective popularity of the team has not measurably increased. In the decade after 1964, the Yankees found themselves all but shut out of an innovative type of baseball writing which was just beginning to appear. Perhaps because they were reacting against what was often derided as the "what Mickey Mantle ate for breakfast" mode of baseball writing, the pioneers of this emerging style often gave the Yankees short shrift, their darlings being the Red Sox, the Dodgers, even the ineptly "Amazin'" Mets— the ultimate un–Yankees.

A harbinger was John Updike's *New Yorker* article in 1960, "Hub Fans Bid Kid Adieu," recounting Ted Williams' last game at Fenway Park, a landmark effort to write about the sport for the general adult reading public. Thanks to Roger Kahn, Brooklyn's *Boys of Summer*[13] preempted all other claimants to the market for 1950s baseball nostalgia, displacing that era's Yankees to such an extent that a recent ESPN countdown of the top teams in baseball history ranked the Dodgers ahead of the team that had, after all, beaten them in four of their five clashes between 1949 and 1956. Neither Roger Maris's 61st home run nor Don Larsen's 1956 World Series perfect game managed to crack the list of top ten baseball memorable moments as chosen by a vote of fans in 2002 (but if it was any consolation for that era's Yankee fans, neither did Willie Mays's catch in 1954, Bill Mazeroski's Series winning home run for the Pirates in 1960 nor even Bobby Thomson's 1951 "shot heard round the world" as the entire 1949–1964 era seems to have vanished from the consciousness of the contemporary fan). Former Indian and White Sox owner Bill Veeck placed his not unbiased, though entertaining, thumb on the scale of baseball history with a lacerating — and enduring — depiction of the Yankees' cold blooded business practices.[14] The *New Yorker's* Roger Angell bade "Farewell My Giants"[15] and embraced the Mets (with a special dollop of affection for the Red Sox).[16]

If anything, pinstriped tradition came off as more of a liability than an asset in a time of social change. The Yanks matched up against the Mets, Jimmy Cannon wrote in 1964, as Rudy Vallee did to the Beatles.[17]

Judging by the attention they did receive, Yankee sensibilities might have been better served by neglect. The book about the Yankees that did find a place in the sports writing pantheon turned out to be former pitcher Jim Bouton's locker room and bar-stool tales about his hard drinking, sex-obsessed Yankee teammates. *Ball Four*'s tales out of school duly outraged the baseball establishment. But it proved just a warm up for the ultimate demolition job on the Yankee Myth: Richard Ben Cramer's 400 page plus (and companion public television documentary) assault on the Yankee Clipper himself, a portrayal of Joe DiMaggio as a miserly, mobbed up, misanthropic, thoroughly miserable sort of human being. Meanwhile, DiMaggio's great rival Ted Williams basked in a halo of unbridled admiration and affection that only intensified with his passing. It was a long way from the time when Hemingway's "old man" had counseled "have faith in the Yankees, my son," and dreamed of going fishing with "the great DiMaggio."

That the Yankee Dynasty took a surprisingly long time to impress those who witnessed it at high tide proved a forerunner of the "slings and arrows" of retrospective disparagement. Both responses diverted attention from important issues that transcended the Yankees' success on the playing field itself. The legacy of the Bronx Bombers entails more than the numerous pennants raised over Yankee Stadium on so many Opening Days. It also reflects the changing dynamics of a sport and a nation in an era of profound social change for both.

In the years following World War II, baseball confronted two demographic challenges. The first was internal—that of breaking down the color line and integrating a lily-white sport whose claim to be the "national pastime" was never more incongruous, if not indeed offensive, in the aftermath of victory in a war against Nazi racism. The second was external—that of aligning baseball's increasingly obsolete half century old map with the shifting population in a suburban and Sun Belt tipping nation.

In 1947, Jackie Robinson broke the color line in the National League as did Larry Doby in the American. Beginning in 1953, long established franchises moved to Milwaukee, Baltimore, Kansas City and most dramatically to Los Angeles and San Francisco. Amidst these fundamental changes, the Yankee Dynasty rolled on, doing business pretty much as usual, notably so when it came to resisting racial integration. Unparalleled, indeed largely uncontested, success enabled the Yankees to place themselves above change. By so doing— or often not doing—the Yankees passed along the costs of resisting change to major league baseball as a whole. The Yankees could evade the changing circumstances that were testing the "national pastime's" claims to supremacy, but the sport itself could not.

As the Yankee dynasty gathered momentum at mid-century, major league baseball stood atop the hierarchy of the sports' world as America's unchallenged "national pastime." Enthusiastic fans kept the turnstiles spinning. In 1949, 20,215,365 fans attended major league games, just short of the record total of the previous year. That season, the Yankees drew more than two million fans to the Bronx for the fourth time in a row, while the Indians topped that once unattainable attendance mark for the second straight year. The explosive expansion of televisions in the nation's households was also turning on a new revenue stream for the sport, especially in New York where television penetration was ahead of the curve. Major League Baseball local broadcast (television and radio) rights were sold for $3.35 million in 1950 compared to $835,000 four years before. Thirty percent of that revenue went to the three New York City teams.[18]

It was not only that baseball was harvesting an unprecedented bounty of income that was all the sweeter having followed fifteen years of Depression and World War. The sport could also celebrate its unchallenged preeminence in the nation's sporting universe. At mid-century, other professional sport had yet to threaten baseball's supremacy. The verdict of the fan was clear. Major league baseball attendance exceeded that for pro football, basketball and hockey combined. Baseball was the choice of 39 percent of the nation's sports fans as their favorite sport, well ahead of football (17 percent) and basketball (10 percent).[19] In 1951, the World Series was broadcast on coast-to-coast national television for the first time — and baseball collected a rights fee of over one million dollars, more than ten times that paid to televise the National Football League's championship game.[20] The World Almanac that year devoted sixteen full pages to Major League Baseball, less than one half of one page to pro football.

The fledgling National Basketball Association was just emerging from internecine conflict between the National Basketball League and the Basketball Association of America, and was struggling to establish a separate identity in a sport that was still largely associated with grungy college gymnasiums. Pro basketball was an obscure, mostly "second tier" city affair, with franchises in such truly "mini-markets" as Syracuse, Rochester, Indianapolis and Fort Wayne. The National Hockey League remained the closely held, cold weather, secret of but six cities, two of them in Canada and all located within 300 miles of the Canadian border. Even boxing, for so long baseball's only significant competitor for the attention of the fan of professional sports, was losing ground, as the "sweet science's" roots in neighborhood fight clubs began to wither under the onslaught of "free" boxing on television and a rising tide of postwar prosperity and increased employment opportunities for the waves of impoverished, minority and immigrant youths who had once hoped that they could climb the ladder of success with clenched fists.

Fifteen years of unparalleled Yankee dominance later, the news from the baseball business was not so good. The sport remained stuck in the long trough that had engulfed it just as the Yankee Dynasty gained traction in the early 1950s. Free television, increasingly run-down and inconvenient inner city ball parks, territorial expansion driven by desperation rather than by strategic vision, and changing leisure patterns had brought the postwar boom years to a halt. Contributing to the sport's woes in the early 1950s was a sharp drop in the numbers of new potential fans, as the "baby bust" of the Depression years depleted the ranks of adolescents and young men in their teens and early twenties. In 1950, there were only 16,500,000 men and boys between the ages of 10 and 24 compared to 18,000,000 in 1940, the first decline ever recorded in the size of that population group.[21] Within a few years, the baby boom would more than refill the pool of youthful potential fans, but in the short term, baseball was pitching its product to a smaller audience.

In the Yankee Dynasty's final season, major league attendance in 1964 was 21,280,341, about one million more than in 1949. Such a slight increase produced no joy in Mudville. In 1964, there were 20 big league teams rather than 16 and each was playing 162 games, not 154. Average per game attendance had dropped from about 16,000 to 13,000. Even more troubling was the state of the sport in its traditional bastions, the cities that had fielded teams throughout the sport's organized existence and that had remained fixed points on the baseball circuit in the era of franchise shifts and expansion. Attendance in these cities—New York, Boston, Chicago, Cleveland, Detroit and Washington in the American League and Chicago, Cincinnati, Philadelphia, Pittsburgh, St. Louis and New York in the National—had actually declined between 1949 and 1964. Two moments highlight the dwindling hold of baseball on the sporting imagination in those years: Ted Williams's last game at Fenway Park in 1960 was attended by only 13,000 fans and Roger Maris hit his 61st home run the next year in a Yankee Stadium that was two thirds empty.

This downturn in the baseball business and turnabout in America's sporting enthusiasms was occurring even as Major League Baseball was trying to make itself more and more accessible to the sporting public. Until just a few years earlier, after all, most of the country had been physically shut off from the sport by the geographies of time and space, which had confined it to daylight hours and the northeast quarter of the nation. Traditional big league baseball had hardly been a spectator sport at all—for most of its fans, most of the time, it was vicariously experienced through newspaper stories and box scores, radio broadcasts, and World Series newsreels, not direct contact. Now, just as major league baseball was becoming more readily accessible—with night games, expansion to the West Coast, and national television—its once unchallenged hold on the popular imagination was slipping away.

On the accelerating treadmill of public taste in mid-twentieth century America, baseball was running faster—and farther, but by the 1960s, the self-styled national pastime was losing ground. True, some putative claimants to its crown were either fading themselves or only prospective. Boxing's heavyweight title won by Cassius Clay, soon to be Muhammad Ali, in 1964, provided the sport with a compelling personality who claimed the attention of a public otherwise less interested in a sport that continued its trajectory away from the center of sporting life. Ice hockey remained locked within its six frozen cities circuit. The National Basketball Association, however, was positioning itself for a future challenge to baseball's position in the sports hierarchy. The NBA expanded to the West Coast, transferred franchises out of the provincial byways that had once been so prevalent (Syracuse was the last to go, the Nationals moving to Philadelphia and renamed the 76ers in 1963), and more intensively recruited black playing talent. But one contender was already poised to deliver baseball a damaging body blow—professional football.

As baseball stagnated, football surged. By 1960 it had cut baseball's lead in polling for the nation's favorite sport from 22 points to 13. One decade later, it had grabbed a decisive lead as 36 percent of those polled picked football as their favorite sport compared to 21 percent for baseball.[22] Pooling television revenues and rigidly enforcing a home game black out policy that even extended to the championship game itself, the National Football League was so successful that it even spawned a rival, the American Football League in 1960. Television loved football and football fans loved watching the game on television, even to the point of driving to motels out of black-out range to catch the action on TV. With a solid base of season ticket holders, and long waiting lists to fill the rare openings, NFL teams attracted crowds that far outnumbered those turning out for baseball at the venues they shared with big league ball clubs. In seven fall games at Yankee Stadium, New York's football Giants drew about one-third as many fans to the Yankee Stadium they shared as did the Yankees who played ten times as many games there. Two weeks before Roger Maris brought his season long quest to break Babe Ruth's home run record to a successful conclusion before fewer than 24,000 Yankee Stadium fans on September 30, 1961, the Giants had opened their home football season in the House that Ruth Built with 58,000 spectators cheering them on. Baseball's presumptive status as the "national pastime" was under unprecedented attack.

It would be unreasonable to think that the Yankees—or any other team for that matter—could have single-handedly reversed these trends. But a "before and after" snapshot of major league baseball in 1964 as compared to 1949 suggests that the largely uncontested reign of the Yankee Dynasty during those years imposed costs, whether directly or indirectly, wittingly or unwittingly, on major league baseball as it struggled to hold its own in a time of an unprecedented change.

The Yankee's recalcitrant response to baseball's internal demographic challenge — the racial integration of its playing personnel — strikingly illuminates the Dynasty's ability to steer a course that may have served its own immediate interests, but was not in the "best interests of baseball." It would, if anything, be an understatement to say that it was a challenge that the Yankees did not rise to meet. By moving slowly to integrate their roster, the Yankees set a laggardly pace for its American League competitors. This was the opposite of the effect that the Brooklyn Dodgers had on the National League.

In the aftermath of the breaking of the color line by Jackie Robinson and the Brooklyn Dodgers in 1947, the Yankees proved notably, indeed notoriously, slow to integrate. Explanations for their failure to do so can be overly complicated, especially when they resort to the sociological, along the lines of the comment attributed to a Yankee executive that "we don't want that sort of crowd.... It would offend box holders from Westchester to have to sit with niggers."[23] Too sharp a contrast is often drawn between the Yankees, as the team of New York's lily-white well-heeled suburban and corporate elite, and the Dodgers, as the favorites of socially-conscious proletarians. The Rosenbergs may have cheered on the Dodgers even from their death house cells, but Communist Party leaders Earl Browder and William Z. Foster were Yankee fans who enjoyed spending occasional afternoons at the Stadium. It was the fannies of New York's working classes that occupied Yankee Stadium's 30,000 general admission and bleacher seats and it was not the city's carriage trade that quaffed longtime broadcast sponsor Ballantine's decidedly non-premium brew.[24]

Management personalities certainly played a role in shaping the Yankees' unenthusiastic response to the assault on the sport's color line. The team's front office hardly shared Branch Rickey's or Cleveland's Bill Veeck's integrationist impulse. In particular, postwar Yankee president Larry MacPhail's persistent efforts to block baseball integration, within the ruling councils of both New York city and baseball government, have been exposed by Rickey aide Arthur Mann in his semi-official *Jackie Robinson Story*, and Jules Tygiel in his classic study of *Baseball's Great Experiment*.[25] But the best explanation for Yankee foot dragging is the simplest — they had no competitive reason to do so. They were on top — why take any risk, however slight it might prove to be, with the chemistry of a winning team? The teams that integrated were less engaged in the pursuit of social uplift than in the business of winning ball games on the field. Unlike the color line–breaking 1947 Dodgers (who had ended the 1946 regular season in a tie for first place before losing a pennant playoff to the Cardinals), the teams that fielded black ball players almost invariably did so in the aftermath of weak performances the year before, as the following table illustrates:[26]

Team	Year Integrated	Prior Year Standing
Brooklyn (NL)	1947 (April 15)	2 (lost playoff)
Cleveland (AL)	1947 (July 5)	6
St. Louis (AL)[27]	1947 (July 17)	7
New York (NL)	1949	5
Boston (NL)	1950	4
Chicago (AL)	1951	6
Philadelphia (AL)	1953	4
Chicago (NL)	1953	5
Pittsburgh (NL)	1954	8
Cincinnati (NL)	1954	6
Washington (AL)	1954	5
St. Louis (NL)	1954	3

Team	Year Integrated	Prior Year Standing
New York (AL)	1955	2
Philadelphia (NL)	1957	5
Detroit (AL)	1958	4
Boston (AL)	1959	3

Even the Yankees, it might be noted, integrated only after finishing behind the Indians in 1954—the equivalent of a second division finish for them.

In the National League, integration upset the traditional hierarchy of power. The Dodgers leveraged their readiness to sign up black ballplayers into a decade of unprecedented success. Together with the Giants, who were similarly in the forefront of baseball integration, this advantageous tolerance secured National League pennants for New York City in eight of the ten years after 1947. The Braves, who were close behind in seeking out black talent, succeeded them as the leading power in the National League by the latter half of the 1950s. Meanwhile, the border state–based St. Louis Cardinals—the dominant team in the National League from the mid–1920s to the mid–1940s— were slow to sign black players and dropped from contention after the 1949 season. The once mighty Cardinals did not again make a serious run for the pennant until 1963. Although falling short of the National League title that year, in 1964 the Cardinals, now rich in black playing talent, would defeat the Yankees in a classic World Series.

The American League as a whole paid the price for its gradualist approach to racial integration. Year after year, American League teams fielded no more than one half as many black ball players in their starting lineups as their National League counterparts through the middle of the 1960's. The difference was qualitative as well as quantitative. Between 1949 and 1964, eleven NL MVP Awards were won by black ballplayers; in the American League just one (by the Yankees' Elston Howard in 1963). Nine blacks were National League rookies of the year during those years; none took that honor in the American League.

That the Yankees were able to buck the tide that had doomed the similarly slow-to-integrate Cardinals in the National League was largely due to the fact that the teams best positioned to contest their dominance proved even more reluctant to integrate. The Tigers and the Red Sox, the Yankees' only well funded rivals in a league that was otherwise comprised of financially strapped franchises, refused to integrate for over a decade after Jackie Robinson's debut, and were the final two teams to do so. Spurning the opportunity to outmaneuver the Yankees on this promising new front in the quest for baseball talent, the Tigers and Red Sox sank into the second division as the 1950s unfolded. Even when the Yankee dynasty crumbled at last, they would not be the first claimants to the suddenly vacant throne. It would be the Minnesota Twins, led by Cuban born outfielder Tony Oliva and African American pitcher Jim "Mudcat" Grant would bring the curtain down on the Dynasty in 1965.

The Yankees after winning their fifth straight American League title in 1953, before proceeding to win a fifth straight World Series (courtesy Hearst News American Photographic Collection in the University of Maryland Special Collections Library, College Park).

The Yankees were also bystanders with respect to the unfolding of baseball's second great postwar demographic challenge — the need to align its half century old map with the changing distribution of population in a Sunbelt-tilting nation — that reached its climax with the move of the Brooklyn Dodgers and New York Giants to California after the 1957 season. From time to time, the Giants expressed interest in securing a future in New York by moving from the Polo Grounds to Yankee Stadium, but the desultory discussions that ensued went nowhere. There was no reason for the Yankees to go out of their way to try to accommodate the Giants and they certainly did not.[28] Nor did city officials push for such a solution. In retrospect, detaching the Giants from the Dodgers' West Coast planning may been the best chance of discouraging a move by the Dodgers themselves, whose pitch for support from National League team owners worried about increased travel expenses was premised on the economy of scale of a two team move. In all likelihood, nothing could have been done to prevent the Giants from saddling up for Walter O'Malley's West Coast wagon train. The Yankees did not play an active role as these fateful events unfolded. However, the Yankees, and particularly their monumental Stadium, may well have set that still resonating drama in motion. As a result, major league baseball — in New York City at least — paid yet another price for the Yankee Dynasty.

Despite all that has been written on the subject, Walter O'Malley's motivations for the move remain something of a mystery.[29] He had a good thing going for him in Brooklyn and no guarantees about what would await him in Los Angeles. But it surely gnawed at him that the Dodgers played in the shadow of the Yankees, both on the field and at the box office. O'Malley's team lost four out of five World Series to the Yankees between 1949 and 1956. Its ball park seated half as many fans. Its season home attendance was half a million or more lower than that of its Bronx rivals. However beloved they may have been by its ardent fans, the Dodgers simply did not compete on even terms with the Yankees. "Yankee Stadium was a place," broadcaster Lindsay Nelson remembered, "where you took your guests, your clients, your out of town visitors ... you went in the same spirit that you went to the UN or the Statue of Liberty. You were going to see something, not to take part in it."[30]

It was just as surely the case that Brooklyn itself was losing traction within the changing distribution of power, wealth and prestige of the City of Greater New York to which it had been amalgamated in 1898, let alone the rapidly growing suburbs beyond the expanded city's limits. By the early 1950s Dodger owner Walter O'Malley himself had moved out of Brooklyn to suburban Long Island. Long-time Dodger announcer Red Barber had made his own home in Manhattan, commuted to Ebbets Field, and had little apparent interest in the life of the borough beyond what he observed from the radio booth. Indeed, Barber himself defected to the Yankees' broadcast booth after the 1953 season. Nothing did more to demonstrate the Dodgers'—and Brooklyn's—relative impotence in the corridors of metropolitan politics than the resounding failure of Walter O'Malley's efforts to enlist governmental assistance for his plans to build a new ball park for the Dodgers in Brooklyn.

Nor, truth be told, did Brooklyn's fans do their part in the Dodgers' final Ebbets Field seasons to encourage O'Malley to reject the siren song of Los Angeles and commit to a local future for the team.[31] In years past, the borough that had once been the fourth largest city in the nation could proudly claim a full complement of homegrown cultural institutions, businesses, newspapers—everything, as the old saying went, except a railroad station. After two decades and more of stagnation and even decline, it seemed, as one fan plaintively wrote to New York's Mayor in the 1950s, that "the only good thing we have in Brooklyn is the Dodgers."[32] By then that "only good thing" was in trouble too.

Brooklyn fans had simply stopped anteing up at the turnstiles and the usual alibis—old ballpark, inconvenient location, lack of parking, deteriorating surroundings—don't hold. The Dodgers were winning the pennant, or contending for it, every year, with a team of talented ballplayers who were also compelling personalities, but attendance was stuck at a bit more than one million year after year, about 40 percent lower than the postwar peak just a few years earlier. True, attendance was falling everywhere, but "everywhere" was not offering the same product that the Dodgers were, yet attendance was often comparable. Perhaps the most dispiriting moment for anyone hoping for a Dodger future in Brooklyn came in the last days of the 1956 season. As the Dodgers battled down to the wire in a "death struggle with the Milwaukee Braves for the pennant," the generally half full Ebbets Field grandstand was compared to a "deserted village" and Sal Maglie's crucial no-hitter against the Phillies on the night of September 25 was cheered by only 15,200 fans. "Is that civic pride?" a sportswriter asked.[33]

In 1955, the World Champion Dodgers shared one "distinction" with the last place (by 38 games) Pittsburgh Pirates—they were the only teams in the National League drawing fewer fans than in the last pre-war season of 1941. When he made his memorable appearance at Ebbets Field during the 1944 presidential campaign, FDR proclaimed that he had rooted for the Dodgers but had never been to a game at Ebbets Field.[34] By the middle of the 1950s, this was a sentiment that was common among the team's increasingly television room bound fans.

"Don't think that [construction of a new ball park] will solve the problem," *New York Times* columnist Arthur Daley warned. "The new 'home' ... will provide more seats to stay away from."[35] In the course of his very public jousting with the Dodger owner over plans for a new Dodger ballpark, New York City parks and planning commissioner Robert Moses questioned the commitment of Brooklyn's fans to their team, wondering "what proportion of the 3 million and more residents of Brooklyn really care a great deal in view of the slim attendance at Ebbets Field."[36] As was often the case, Moses was being aggressively tactless, but as was even more often the case, Moses had a point.

It was not simply in the somewhat speculative psychological and geopolitical realms that the Dodgers were being overshadowed by the Yankees as the changing contours of postwar New York emerged. In the most hard-headed practical terms as well, that is to say in dollars and cents, the looming presence of Yankee Stadium bred dissatisfaction with the Dodgers' Ebbets Field home. Whatever the drop in regular season attendance, come the fall and Ebbets Field was simply too small to maximize the profit potential of the World Series. In September 1941, the overwhelming demand for tickets to the first Series in Flatbush in a generation precipitated talk about playing Brooklyn's home games in Yankee Stadium, which could accommodate crowds of 70,000, twice the capacity of the Brooklyn ball park, a possibility that would surface again as the Dodgers clinched the 1947 pennant.[37] Into the next decade, Ebbets Field's cramped seating capacity became an accelerating source of frustration. Playing World Series games in Ebbets Field was costing the Dodgers (and with their inevitable opponents, the Yankees) a substantial amount of money.

The 1955 World Series highlighted the costs of doing business in an Ebbets Field that capped attendance far below its potential in the Fall Classic. That year the Dodgers and the Yankees each earned $330,000 from the live gate. Had the seating capacity of Ebbets Field been equal to that of the 65,000 seat Stadium, earnings for each team would have increased by $75,000.[38] Multiplied by the six World Series that the Dodgers co-hosted in Brooklyn between 1947 and 1956, the total "opportunity cost" exacted by Ebbets Field to the Dodgers exceeded half a million dollars. It was a number that spurred Walter

O'Malley's insistence that Ebbets Field had outlived its usefulness and weighed heavily on the scales that would tip decisively against a Dodger future in Brooklyn. With O'Malley's efforts to build a new ballpark in Brooklyn stymied, the 1958 season would open with the Dodgers in Los Angeles and the Giants in San Francisco. The half century old battle for baseball supremacy in New York City had ended in a decisive win for the Yankees.

If that counted as a victory for the Yankees over its home town National League rivals, it failed to herald a triumph for the American League as an entity. The years of Yankee dominance between 1949 and 1964 witnessed a revolution in the overall balance of baseball power to the detriment of the American League. In 1949, the American League had led the National attendance by 10,730,647 to 9,484,718. In 1964, the tables had turned with the National League out drawing the American 12,045,190 to 9,235,151 and four NL teams attracting more fans than the Yankees, the AL's top gate attraction. In particular, it was the old guard American League cities that bore the brunt of the decline mentioned above in attendance in those traditional baseball centers, where there was a slight drop in the National League cities but a drop of over 40 percent in those of the American:

American League	1949 (thousands)	1964 (thousands)
Chicago	937	1,250
Cleveland	2,233	653
Detroit	1,821	816
Boston	1,596	883
New York	2,283	1,305
Washington	770	600
League Totals	9,640	5,507
New York	1,218	1,732
Chicago	1,143	751
Cincinnati	707	862
Philadelphia	819	1,425
Pittsburgh	1,449	759
St. Louis	1,430	1,143
League Totals	6,766	6,672
Both Leagues Combined	16,405	12,179

Baseball had managed to lose much of its core audience, at least as paying customers, in the course of that decade and a half of Yankee supremacy. As the above table illustrates, it was the Yankees' own American League that bore the brunt of that loss. Meanwhile, the same gap between the leagues, and again to the detriment of the American League, manifested itself in the territories into which the sport had expanded. This alone had stemmed what would otherwise have been an even greater collapse in baseball's drawing power. In 1964, these new major league baseball cities (Minnesota, Los Angeles, Kansas City and Baltimore in the American League and Los Angeles, San Francisco, Houston and, Milwaukee in the National) had contributed 3,725,000 of the

AL's total attendance of 9,232,000 but no less than 5,367,000 of the 12,039,000 total in the NL.

While the Yankees reigned supreme, above the fray and securely ensconced in their still grand Bronx home, the National League had decisively outmaneuvered its rival circuit in the expansion wars. The senior circuit shifted three pennant contending teams to richly receptive markets, while the American League dumped two of its worst teams on cities that had already been rejected by major league baseball when it had consolidated operations at the turn of the century. The Braves moved to Milwaukee, the Dodgers to Los Angeles and the Giants to San Francisco. The American League planted a threadbare flag in the less promising precincts of Baltimore, and Kansas City. The National League thereby gained a preemptive foothold on the West Coast that it has never relinquished. Fifty years earlier, the upstart American League had outflanked a National League that stretched west along the Ohio River axis of an older America via Pittsburgh and Cincinnati, by establishing franchises in Cleveland and Detroit along the more dynamic Great Lakes perimeter of the rapidly industrializing nation of the new century. Now, the National League had turned the tables on its younger rival. Whether in the sport's established venues or on its new frontiers, the National League had gained the upper hand.

The shift in relative stature was just as pronounced on the field. In the 15 All-Star games prior to 1949, the American League had triumphed 11 times; in the 20 contests played from 1949 to 1964 (from 1959 to 1962 two games were played each year) the National League won 13 and lost 6 (the second game in 1961 ended in a tie); in the 15 games played from 1965 through 1979, the National League won 14. The two times that the American League sent out a team other than the Yankees to contest the World Series, the outcomes were anything but satisfying for junior circuit pride. The 1954 Cleveland Indians, after winning more games than any AL team in history, were blanked by the underdog Giants in a four game sweep. The "Go Go" White Sox in 1959 were decisively beaten by a Los Angeles Dodger team that had won only 86 games during the regular season, and reached the World Series only after defeating the Braves in a two game playoff.

To the extent this shift reflected, as it surely did, the failure of the American League to match the pace of racial integration in the National League, there was indeed a competitive price to be paid for that failure. The Yankees managed to succeed despite their foot-dragging over race, but the American League as a whole did not. The sport's self proclaimed status as the national pastime also suffered at a time when the cause of civil rights was moving from the periphery to the center of the nation's political and social life. The era of maximum Yankee power was not a good one for the American League as a whole.

If the American League lost ground during the era of the Yankee Dynasty, so too did major league baseball in general. It did not take long for baseball to pay a price for the departure of the Dodgers and Giants in the nation's sporting imagination. Ushers, peanut hawkers and beer vendors at Ebbets

Field and the Polo Grounds were not the only collateral damage from their employers' move west. New York's sports writers had lost two of their prime "beats." Writers who had been covering major league baseball now found themselves at college track meets, horse shows, and harness races when the spring of 1958 rolled around.[39] Suddenly displaced from long established and highly enjoyable routines, reporters and columnists viewed baseball with a newfound cynicism. Tommy Holmes, who had covered the Dodgers since 1924 (first for the *Brooklyn Eagle* and then for the *Herald Tribune*), labeled baseball a "sick sport here [in New York]" and wrote that there "shouldn't be any great surprise that fans aren't packing the big Bronx stadium."[40] Bereft of the Dodgers and Giants, a suddenly baseball starved — and resentful — New York media, with an already well developed ability to set a national agenda for sports enthusiasms that had been enhanced by the rise of New York-based network television immediately discovered a new passion — pro football.

It certainly helped refocus the press box perspective that New York's football Giants happened to be fielding a particularly stirring team and that a little more than a year after the departure of the Dodgers and baseball Giants, squared off against Baltimore's Colts in what was quickly dubbed "the greatest football game ever played."[41] The NFL Giants and pro football, in general, filled the void that had so suddenly opened up in the city's sporting affections. The New York press and sports-minded public needed a new object for their affections and they had found it.

In November 1959, Giant linebacker Sam Huff appeared on the cover of *Time*, which saluted pro football as "A Man's Game." One year later Huff starred in a CBS television documentary chronicling "The Violent World of Sam Huff." As the 1960 baseball season approached, even Roger Kahn — who would single-handedly invent the adult baseball book a decade later with *The Boys of Summer*— was writing that "football's taking over" and asking "can anyone argue well that the sport still retains its old grip on the imagination of America? There is unquestionable a stillness at second base. The noise is coming from the football fields. It may be the sports sound of the future."[42] The Yankees may have still been winning on the field, and they had secured a monopoly — at least until the birth of the Mets in 1962 — on major league baseball in the nation's largest city, but the sport they continued to dominate was no longer as central to the sports life of the American people as it had been just a few years earlier.

By the time that the Yankee Dynasty had run its course with the end of the 1964 season, the American League had lost ground to its rival National League circuit and baseball itself was losing traction as the nation's pastime. That is not the complete balance sheet on the legacy of a team that enjoyed greater success than any other team in the world of professional sports. But it is one that deserves to be included — or rebutted — in any final reckoning of the post–World War II Yankee Dynasty and its place in the history of baseball.

15

Revisiting Curt Flood[1]

JULES TYGIEL

On June 2, 1970, Joe Garagiola testified in the New York courtroom of Judge Irving Ben Cooper in the trial of *Curt Flood v. Bowie Kuhn et al.* The former journeyman catcher had spent nine undistinguished seasons primarily warming the bench for four major league teams. He might have appeared as a witness on behalf of Flood's assault on the reserve clause — the arcane artifact of nineteenth century baseball that owners inserted into all player contracts to control athletes throughout their careers and drive down their salaries. Instead, the always dapper Garagiola, now a successful sportscaster and *Today Show* regular, exchanged pleasantries with Judge Cooper and then launched into a defense of baseball's status quo. "When people ask me and use the words I have been hearing about modifications and we should have some changes and we should do this, to me this is the best system so far. Nobody's come up with anything better," argued Garagiola.[2]

Over the next several decades, Garagiola did his best to make amends for his misguided testimony. He apologized to Marvin Miller, the director of the Players Association that had underwritten Flood's suit. In the late 1980s he recommended Flood for the presidency of the Senior Professional Baseball League. When Flood was dying of cancer, Garagiola's Baseball Assistance Team helped to defray the costs. Upon Flood's death in 1997, Garagiola explained, "I thought if the reserve clause went baseball was going.... I was so wrong, I can't begin to tell you."[3]

Garagiola's turnaround exemplifies the totality of Curt Flood's ultimate triumph. Finding defenders of the reserve clause today is a difficult proposition. But when Flood filed his suit in January 1970 questioning the legality of baseball's longstanding exemption from federal and state antitrust laws the majority of sportswriters, owners, former players, and even many of his major league contemporaries excoriated Flood for his audacity. At the trial, owners and their representatives predicted the total ruination of the national pastime if the reserve clause fell: the most profitable teams would garner all of the best players, eliminating competition, and driving weaker clubs out of business; if a player could change teams from one season to the next, a key error committed against his future employer might raise suspicions of collusion, destroying the integrity of the game; without the reserve clause investors would shy away from the game, driving down the value of existing franchises. "Baseball as we know it," testified Commissioner Bowie Kuhn, "simply could not survive."[4]

When the reserve clause was finally eliminated in 1975, none of these prophecies came to pass. Instead, baseball flourished: competition increased, the integrity of the game remained unsullied; attendance soared; businessmen vied to enter the ownership ranks; and sale's prices of teams continually escalated. So thoroughly was the reserve clause eradicated, that several generations of baseball fans have no memory of it or an era in which most players earned salaries in the thousands or low tens of thousands of dollars, rather than the millions and tens of millions.

Flood, himself, has become a legendary figure — the man who courageously challenged the establishment, sacrificing everything he had, receiving nothing in return — in a struggle to right an ancient wrong and achieve human dignity. At his funeral, the mourners, who included many of the greatest baseball stars of the 1970s and 1980s, now far wealthier than they ever dreamed they would be, heard a tribute written by President Bill Clinton and read by a U.S. Congressman, and eulogies from conservative columnist George Will and liberal gadfly Jesse Jackson. In 1999 *Time* magazine included Flood among its "ten most influential athletes of the century."[5] Indeed, given his current status, one can easily forget that Flood actually lost his case and that the victory over the reserve clause came not due to the overthrow of baseball's antitrust exemption, the key element of his suit, but rather through arbitration gained via collective bargaining, the resolution advocated, however insincerely, by the owners in their defense.

The popular image of the Flood case stands firmly fixed in the public mind. But over the past two decades a body of memoirs, academic and journalistic studies, revelations about the Supreme Court, and most notably three books published in 2006 — *Baseball's Reserve System: The Case and Trial of Curt Flood v. Major League Baseball* by Neil F. Flynn; *Stepping Up: The Story of Curt Flood and His Fight for Baseball Players Rights* by Alex Belth[6]; and *A Well-Paid Slave: Curt Flood's Fight for Free Agency in Professional Sports* by Brad Snyder — offer many fresh insights into Flood and his crusade.

In this essay, I will focus on three aspects of the case: Why Flood sued baseball? Could Flood have won? And what is the enduring significance of Curt Flood's challenge to the reserve clause?

Why Did Curt Flood Sue?

Flood always presented his motivations for challenging the reserve clause in the most idealistic of terms. He considered baseball's labor constraints little more than a modern form of slavery and the core issue one of human dignity. "What I really want out of this thing is to give every ballplayer the chance to be a human being," he told a reporter in 1970.[7]

The reserve clause derived from section 10(a) of the Uniform Player Contract that every major and minor league player had to sign to be allowed to pursue a career in baseball. Section 10(a) stated that if a player and an owner could not reach agreement on a new contract by March 15, the owner could unilaterally renew the pact for another year. If the player refused to sign, he would not be allowed to play. Once he did sign, argued the owners, he had obligated himself to the reserve system for yet another year. Thus, when a player agreed to his first contract, the rights to his services belonged to the club into perpetuity, unless the team reassigned those rights elsewhere. The player had no say in where he would play from year to year. Flood had initially signed with the Cincinnati Reds in 1956 when he was 18. After two seasons the Reds traded him to the Cardinals. In 1969 the Cardinals wanted to trade him to the Phillies. Although now a veteran of 12 full major league seasons, Floods' only conventional options were to report to the Phillies or retire.

A pensive Curt Flood wears a World Series ring at a Supreme Court hearing, 1970 (courtesy Hearst News American Photographic Collection in the University of Maryland Special Collections Library, College Park).

Flood, however, choose a third course, contesting the legality of the reserve clause. In all other American industries the type of employer collusion necessary to enforce the reserve system would have constituted an illegal conspiracy in restraint of trade, a per se violation of federal antitrust laws. But in 1922 the United States Supreme Court in the case of *Federal Baseball Club of Baltimore, Inc. v. National League of Professional Baseball Clubs*, with the legendary Justice Oliver Wendell Holmes, Jr., writing the majority decision, had ruled that organized baseball was not engaged in interstate commerce and was thereby exempt from the Sherman and Clayton antitrust acts. In the 1953 *Toolson* case, the Court acknowledged that the baseball industry was indeed a form of interstate commerce. But the decision deemed it the responsibility of Congress, which had created the exemption, to remedy the matter.[8]

Thus to invalidate the reserve clause, Flood had to convince the Supreme Court to overturn its two earlier decisions, neither of which represented the epitome of legal reasoning.

Flood's lawsuit occurred against the backdrop of a series of player-owner confrontations in the late 1960s. Other athletes had begun to bridle under the restrictions of the reserve clause. In 1966 Los Angeles Dodger pitchers Sandy Koufax and Don Drysdale had engaged in a celebrated holdout.[9] The two stars not only demanded higher salaries, they injected several new elements into contracts talks. Koufax and Drysdale attempted to bargain jointly rather than individually. They requested equal pay, demanded multiyear rather than one-year contracts, and engaged a lawyer to negotiate for them, rather than place themselves at the mercy of the team and its attorneys. Rumors circulated that they might contest the reserve clause in the courts. Koufax and Drysdale agreed to sign when the Dodgers made major salary compromises. But the team pointedly balked at joint negotiations, equal salaries, and multiyear contracts, and refused to acknowledge working with the pitchers' representative.

As the Koufax-Drysdale drama played itself out, a far more significant, yet less noted development had occurred. In March 1966, the Major League Baseball Players Association selected Marvin Miller as its new director. The former Steelworkers' Union official would revolutionize labor relations in baseball, but in these early years he had relatively modest aims. He needed to secure an independent funding stream to gain the Players Association independence from the owners; negotiate a formal Collective Bargaining Agreement (CBA); and win concessions on salaries, the pension, and working conditions to gain the confidence of a largely unenlightened union membership. By the end of the 1968 season, he had largely attained these goals. When in the off-season the owners attempted to cut back on their contributions to the pension plan, Miller convinced union members to refuse to sign their contracts until an agreement could be reached. Confronted with this unprecedented action which threatened to delay the opening of spring training, the owners not only withdrew their proposed cuts, they made considerable concessions that greatly improved the plan.[10]

Amidst this emerging environment, in 1969 several players expressed their discontent with the reigning regime and produced indications that athletes possessed greater leverage than previously thought. Montreal Expos outfielder Donn Clendenon announced he would retire rather than accept a trade to the Houston Astros. After Commissioner Bowie Kuhn stepped in to mediate, Clendenon won a substantial raise and a rare two-year contract.[11] New York Yankee pitcher Al Downing objected to a pay cut in the team's proffered 1969 contract. He considered honoring the reserve clause and playing out that season, but refused to sign a new contract. The Yankees told him that if he did not sign the contract, he could not play. Downing approached Players Association director Marvin Miller to discuss his options, but ultimately signed after Miller gave a dire prognosis for successfully challenging the reserve clause and the Yankees increased their offer.[12] In April Ken "Hawk" Harrelson rejected a trade from the Boston Red Sox to the Cleveland Indians. Kuhn again intervened and convinced the Indians to offer a higher salary to lure Harrelson out of "retirement." In June, Expos shortstop Maury Wills threatened to retire unless Montreal traded him to the Dodgers, whom he wished to play for. The Expos met his request.[13]

Flood's actions after the 1969 season marked both a continuum and a break from these trends. In none of the above cases, save that of Downing, did the players approach the union for assistance. Once he had decided to sue, however, Flood immediately consulted Miller. Most people suspected that Flood, like Koufax, Drysdale, Clendenon and Harrelson, simply sought a better bargaining chip for a higher salary. If offered the proper amount of money, he would report to Philadelphia. But Flood cared more about obtaining a modicum of influence over where he played than the monetary rewards he might accrue. He expressed no hesitation when Miller warmed him that even if he won he would probably receive no damages in the judgment. He assured the Executive Board of the Players Association that this was not a bargaining tactic. When pitcher Jim Bunning asked him if he would forsake his determination to the reserve clause if offered a million dollars as a settlement, Flood promised, "If the Players Association commits to help me in this lawsuit, I will make the commitment that I will not withdraw the suit."[14] Flood took his stand on principle not in pursuit of monetary gain or personal enhancement. As Red Smith observed in 1971, "If he wins his suit, everybody else will benefit. The fetters will be eased for all other players present and future.... The only one who has nothing to gain is Curtis Charles Flood."[15]

Most commentators agree, however, that Flood's actions cannot be viewed in a social vacuum. Flood was an African-American man, during a time of great racial upheaval, a self-confessed "child of the sixties." When questioned by the Players Association Executive Board as to whether racial motivations underlay his decision to sue, Flood replied, "I'd be lying if I told you that as a black man in baseball I hadn't gone through worse times than my white teammates.... I think the change in black consciousness in recent years has made me more sensitive to injustice in every area of my life. But I want you to know that what I'm doing here I'm doing as a ballplayer, a major league ballplayer."[16] Nonetheless recent writers have rejected Flood's more moderate tone and interpreted the race issue as more central to Flood's protest. Michael Lomax, for example, views Flood as emblematic of "the disillusionment with white society which set the tone for the Civil rights movement as it entered the Black Power phase."[17]

Flood, himself, emphasized his experiences as a black man in America most explicitly in his angry autobiography, *The Way It Is*, written during the course of his initial trial and in between bouts of heavy drinking.[18] He revealed his shock, after a relatively idyllic racial upbringing in Oakland, at the segregated conditions at spring training in Florida, the brutal racism that he faced during two minor league seasons in the Carolina and South Atlantic Leagues, his suspicions that his first team, the Cincinnati Reds had traded him to avoid playing an all-African American outfield, and his treatment at the hands of Cardinal Manager Solly Hemus, whose prejudices obstructed the emergence of Flood and pitcher Bob Gibson.

There can be little doubt that these realities shaped Flood's perspective and influenced his personality. It is probably also not coincidental that of the five players who bucked the baseball establishment in 1969, four were African American and the fifth, Ken Harrelson, sported long hair and mod, sixties type attire. Yet, there is little in Flood's narrative or his later comments, to support the image of Flood as a late 1960s black militant. Flood bears no noticeable hostility to whites as a group. Throughout his life he expressed gratitude to white patrons who eased his path — legendary Oakland baseball coach George Powles; businessman Sam Bercovich; friends John and Marian Jorgensen; and manager Johnny Keane. His social and political gestures all speak to a vision of the traditional civil rights movement. He protested segregation in spring training, appeared with Jackie Robinson at a rally in Mississippi in 1962, and made headlines when a white homeowner attempted to block him from renting a home in an all-white neighborhood in 1964.[19] Flood took great pride in his efforts on the Cardinals to "deliberately kick over traditional barriers to establish communications" with white players and the creation of a team "as close to being free of the racist poison as a diverse group of twentieth century Americans could possibly be."[20] The portrait of Martin Luther King, Jr., released bearing Flood's signature in the aftermath of King's assassination, testified to his sympathies.

What Flood does not convey is any sense of the rising tide of Black Nationalism and Black Power. In the early 1960s when invited by Muhammad Ali (then Cassius Clay) to a Nation of Islam meeting, Flood disapproved when the speaker decried white devils.[21] In *The Way It Is*, published in 1970 at the peak of the Black Power movement, Flood does not invoke its doctrines as inspiration. As late as 1994 when Flood explained his actions on the Ken Burns Baseball documentary, he cited civil rights marches, race riots, the Kennedy and King assassinations, and the War in Vietnam as formative influences. He does not mention the Black Panthers, the protests at the 1968 Olympic Games, or any other signposts of the era's black militancy.[22] Race plays a key role in Flood's actions, but he remains more a child of the fifties and early sixties, imbued with dreams of integration and civil rights than the separatist demands of the late sixties and early seventies.

Another element, however, is often overlooked in understanding Flood's motivation: Flood's increasingly deteriorating personal situation and mental state. Most accounts generally describe Flood's stability and character at the time he brought his suit. "At least in Curt Flood, we had the right man and the right situation with which to mount the challenge," explained Miller years later. "It was absolutely essential that the man at the center of it could be someone with great personal integrity. As to Flood's personal qualities there could be no doubt."[23] Flood was the co-captain of the St. Louis Cardinals, a team that had won three pennants in five years. He had earned acclaim outside of baseball for his talents as a portrait artist. Other players hired him to paint pictures of themselves and their families, and playfully dubbed him "Rembrandt."[24] In the aftermath of Martin Luther King's assassination in 1968, a St. Louis calendar company asked him to prepare a portrait of the civil rights icon. The painting took on a life of its own. Flood appeared on the *Today Show* to discuss it. The calendar company distributed over a million copies. Flood donated the portrait to King's widow Coretta, who hung it overlooking her desk.[25] Flood also had opened two photography and portrait shops in St. Louis, enhancing, writes Michael Lomax, "his reputation as a businessman."[26]

Unfortunately, as Brad Snyder demonstrates, this image rested on a foundation of quicksand. Camouflaged by Flood's soft-spoken manner and outward confidence, Flood's personal, business, artistic, and even his baseball life was rapidly unraveling. Flood's reputation as an artist was a total fraud. He had some talent, but Flood had contracted with a Burbank, California portrait specialist to paint the pictures and affixed his own name to the finished canvases.[27] His businesses, for which he had minimal patience, were drifting into debt and bankruptcy. Personal tragedy also haunted Flood. His close friend John Jorgensen had been murdered in 1966 in the Oakland engraving shop they co-owned. In March 1969 St. Louis police had arrested Flood's brother Carl, who had a long history of crime and drug problems, for the holdup of a downtown jewelry store. Flood's marriage had collapsed several years earlier. He had little to do with his ex-wife and their five children who lived in California and had fallen behind on his alimony and child support payments. His lifestyle had descended into what he himself would describe as "bedding and boozing." Flood entertained a myriad of women companions and had begun his descent into alcoholism, a problem that ran through the Flood family. This addiction would plague him for the rest of his life. Jorgensen's widow, Marian, had moved to St. Louis in an unsuccessful attempt to help Flood gain control of his business and personal affairs.[28]

Baseball, itself, no longer offered a refuge. From 1964 to 1968 Flood had reigned as co-captain and one of the top stars on the best team in baseball. A *Sports Illustrated* cover story called him the best centerfielder in the game. He was a personal favorite of Cardinals' owner August Busch and took particular pride in the Cardinals close-knit camaraderie and racial harmony.[29] In 1968 the Cardinals won their third pennant in five years. But after taking a 3–1 lead in the World Series against the Tigers, the Cardinals lost the last three games. The key moment occurred with two outs in the seventh inning of the seventh and deciding contest. With the game still scoreless and two runners on, Flood misplayed Jim Northrup's line drive into a triple. Two runs scored, as did Northrup on the next play, and the Cardinals lost 4–1.

The Cardinals' narrow loss occasioned great lamenting. A *Sports Illus-*

trated article published before the Series had already described the Cards as "the world's most expensive team," and wondered if by paying its players "so well the Cardinals are undermining the very structure of baseball." An article in the *St. Louis Dispatch* blamed the Players cupidity for the loss.[30] Cardinal management began to pare high-priced players, most notably team leader Orlando Cepeda, from the roster. Busch, shaken by the loss and even more by the emerging power of the Players Association, condescendingly lectured the team at spring training, attacking what he saw as growing player selfishness.[31] Cardinals entered the 1969 season in a "morose and touchy" mood, according to Flood, and dropped to a fourth-place finish.[32]

Flood's 1969 contract negotiations reveal his growing disillusionment. At Flood's trial Cardinal general manager Bing Devine testified that Flood told him that "baseball had become physically a problem to him, and he was tired mentally and physically, and as he often had thought ... there was something better in this world than playing centerfield."[33] This might be dismissed as a typical bargaining ploy, threatening retirement to force a salary increase. But Flood reiterated the same message to a reporter in March 1969 after he had signed his contract. "I want to get as far away from baseball as I can," he said. "I am just tired of the struggle, the pressures ... the fears, the insecurities."[34] After Flood filed his suit, he confessed to Devine, "that he wished I had shot him down the previous spring ... and I wanted more money than you were prepared to give me.... I wish then you hadn't reached a figure that I could agree with and probably we would never have reached this point and I would have quit a year ago."[35]

Thus, the Flood who took on the baseball establishment in 1970 was a far more complex figure than most people appreciate. He was indeed a "child of the sixties," but one whose values were shaped by the integrationist dream of the early decade. His challenge went beyond what other players of the era had dared, but it followed the smaller, less audacious steps of others. He was driven not only by his considerable strength of character, but also his personal vulnerability.

To be a "child of the sixties," possesses a meaning often overlooked. Confronted by exposes of injustice at home and abroad, many Americans felt compelled to take a stand, to step outside of themselves and make a difference. Flood, argues Snyder, idolized Jackie Robinson, the epitome of personal courage and sacrifice. Like many African-Americans who came of age in the 1940s and 1950s, Flood considered Robinson his role model. As he endured racism in the southern minor Leagues, Flood wore Robinson's number, 42, on his back. In 1962, at a time when many black athletes steered clear of civil rights activities, Flood joined Robinson, at his hero's request, at the NAACP Southeast Regional conference in Jackson, Mississippi.[36] Wracked by personal demons, obsessed by a need to emulate Robinson and make a mark beyond baseball to strike a blow for human dignity, Flood was determined to liberate himself and his fellow baseball players. Robinson himself recognized this.

Testifying at Flood's trial in 1970, Robinson avowed, "It takes a tremendous amount of courage for any individual — and that's why I admire Mr. Flood so much for what he is doing — to stand up for something that is appalling to him, and I think that they ought to give a player the chance to be a man in situations like this."[37]

Had Flood accepted the trade to Philadelphia, or simply retired after the 1969 season, who other than the most avid baseball fans would remember Curt Flood today? Flood gambled on immortality. He lost his case and paid a high price, but won redemption on a far grander scale.

Could Curt Flood Have Won His Case?

Assessing Flood's case as it unfolded in the courts poses yet another level of difficulty. It was a foregone conclusion that the lower courts would rule against Flood. No judge or appeals court would take it upon itself to overrule the clear, if conflicting, precedents established by the Supreme Court in *Federal Baseball* and *Toolson*. Marvin Miller would later question his decision to employ Arthur Goldberg, who in affect abandoned the case to run for Governor of New York, and his failure to encourage other players to appear at the trial to support Flood.[38] But neither of these factors affected the Supreme Court's decision, which relied more on an issue of law rather than the actual trial record. Yet, as Neil Flynn demonstrates in *Baseball's Reserve Clause*, the trial transcripts reveal a great deal about how the Players Association and major league owners approached the Flood suit and how each used it to advance their own, and not necessarily Flood's, interests.

Commissioner Kuhn and his owners always maintained that Marvin Miller had instigated Flood's challenge to the reserve clause. The evidence is firm, however, that Flood, in conjunction with his personal attorney Allan Zerman and chose friend Marion Jorgensen, developed the idea for the suit. When Flood first spoke to Miller in November 1969 he had already decided to pursue this course.[39] Enlisting the Players Association to support him offered Flood many advantages. The union, not Flood, would bear the financial costs of what promised to be a prolonged legal battle. Miller also had greater access to top flight legal talent. Indeed, recruiting former U.S. Secretary of Labor and Supreme Court Justice Arthur Goldberg to represent Flood gave the case greater visibility and legitimacy, and improved its probability of reaching the high court.

In his autobiography, Miller describes taking great pains to explain to Flood how unlikely he was to prevail in his suit. Under the legal doctrine of *stare decisis*, the Court rarely overturned long standing precedents such as those established by *Federal Baseball* and *Toolson*. Nonetheless, noted Miller, several more recent decisions offered some basis for optimism. In the 1957 case of *Radovich v. the National Football League*, the Court had ruled that professional football was not exempt from the antitrust laws and indicated that *Federal Baseball* was "of dubious legality." Since that time professional boxing and the theater arts industry had failed to establish legal rights to an exemption. In a recent case, the Court had rejected the validity of a reserve clause in professional basketball virtually indistinguishable from that used in baseball. Thus, organized baseball's antitrust exemption was now more clearly anomalous from the legal status of other sports and entertainment industries.[40]

Nonetheless, Flood's case also posed a conflict for Miller and the Players Association. Miller had always understood that the reserve clause posed the crucial obstacle to players receiving their full economic value, but he never favored its complete elimination. As a veteran union leader, naturally inclined to making gains through the bargaining process, he viewed the reserve clause as a negotiable issue. The Players Association would force concessions that would weaken the stranglehold that the owners now had, giving the players additional, but not total freedom. Miller believed that a system that controlled the flow of free agents, allowing a limited number of players to openly sell their services each year, would lead to greater bidding wars that would drive salaries higher than one which freed everyone at once. Thus players would be better off with some basic constraints on their movement.[41]

Marvin Miller, head of the Players Association, talks to reporters after players went out on strike in 1981 (courtesy Hearst News American Photographic Collection in the University of Maryland Special Collections Library, College Park).

Furthermore, the Players Association had implicitly accepted the legitimacy of the reserve system, if not the specific details, by including the Uniform Players Contract, complete with Section 10(a) in the first Collective Bargaining Agreement (CBA) in 1968. Miller had had little choice in the matter. To secure the legitimacy of the union, Miller had to reach a settlement with the owners. Management made major concessions on pensions, minimum salaries, and a grievance procedure, but would not accept a pact that did not acknowledge the traditional contract. The fledgling union lacked the solidarity to strike over the issue. Miller informed the owners that the union did not accept the legality of the reserve clause and convinced them to participate in a joint-study committee to consider "possible changes to the reserve clause as now constituted."[42] Yet incorporating the reserve clause into the CBA made it a subject of collective bargaining and possibly limited the ability of a union member to challenge it in the courts. This reality became more critical now that the National Labor Relations Board (NLRB) had recognized the Players Association as the bargaining unit for baseball and assumed responsibility to regulate negotiations.

Flood's request for assistance from Players Association at its Executive Board meetings in San Juan, Puerto Rico in December 1969 came at a propitious moment. The gathering itself marked a declaration of independence for the organization. For the first time the Players Association, which before Miller's arrival had effectively been a company union, would be convening independently of major league baseball's traditional winter meetings. The board, which consisted of a representative from each team, had received a report detailing how the owners' had jettisoned the joint-study committee by rejecting all player proposals while introducing none of their own. When Commissioner Kuhn, who viewed himself as impartial representative of all of baseball, addressed the group, the players adopted a hostile tone, making it clear that they considered him a management mouthpiece. In this environment the Executive Board voted 25–0 to back Flood.[43]

Flood agreed not only to allow the union to select his attorneys and determine his legal strategy, but to drop the suit if it could negotiate acceptable modifications at the bargaining table.[44] Miller always saw the suit as an additional bargaining chip to force the owners to negotiate on the reserve clause rather than a weapon to destroy it. When Flood filed his complaint in January, 1970, Miller informed National League counsel Lou Carroll that the suit would be withdrawn if the owners would liberalize the reserve clause. Goldberg, ostensibly employed to represent Flood, told Bowie Kuhn, "It is my understanding that if appropriate modifications can be made through negotiation, this would satisfy Curt Flood. Therefore, if you want to carry out your legal right to negotiate, please do so."[45]

Flood had readily accepted these conditions and was perfectly willing to sacrifice his own interests to those of his fellow athletes. But as Flynn points out, this emphasis greatly compromised his position in the courts. Flood's complaint specifically called for the elimination of the reserve clause, arguing that it violated numerous state and federal laws.[46] To win, Flood's attorneys had to convince the court to overrule *Federal Baseball* and *Toolson*, which allowed baseball to ignore these statutes. Establishing the illegitimacy of the reserve clause and the damages that Flood and other players had suffered from it would further this end. Instead, the union's lawyers focused minimally on Flood himself, and more on the failure of the owners to bargain in good faith on this issue. It is telling that Flood appeared on the stand only once at the start of the trial, while Miller testified three times. Flood, in his complaint and on the stand, supported the proposition that "the whole reserve system should be scrapped." Miller and all of the other witnesses enlisted to support Flood, including former players Jackie Robinson and Hank Greenberg and maverick owner Bill Veeck, called for a resolution that entailed modifications to the reserve system, not its elimination.[47] This essentially conceded the right of the owners to limit player movement, if done within the context of collective bargaining.

The owners effectively seized upon this distinction in their legal defense. Major League Baseball remained confident that the courts would validate its antitrust exemption and render Flood's challenge to the reserve clause moot. But what if the Supreme Court overruled its earlier decisions? To address this contingency the owners developed a secondary strategy to save the reserve clause. Although they had done everything in their powers to undermine the Players Association — releasing and trading player representatives, undermining the joint-study committee, and using sympathetic sportswriters to demonize the union in the press — the owners now agued that the bargaining table was the appropriate arena to resolve this dispute. Baseball's lead negotiator John Gaherin testified, "We certainly have all of the ability in the two sides to sit down and in the free arena of collective bargaining resolve a matter of this nature.... We are quite willing to do so."[48] In the event that the union felt that the owners were not engaged in legitimate negotiations, it should take the matter before the NLRB as an unfair labor practice, not to the courts.

In the post-trial brief, the owners pointedly asked, "Who is the real plaintiff in this action?" The union, they argued, not Flood had instigated the suit. Snyder charges that this presentation "sought to make Flood and his personal sacrifices irrelevant, to remove the human face from the lawsuit."[49] Flynn maintains that the ill-conceived strategies of Flood's own lawyers had already made this a reality.[50] Judge Cooper, who had shown great disdain of Flood and his lawsuit from the beginning of the trial, also accepted Flood's marginalization. In his closing remarks he commended both sets of lawyers and glorified the game of baseball. He did not mention Flood.[51] The core of Cooper's subsequent decision rested on his inability to overrule the earlier Supreme Court precedents. But, he cavalierly dismissed Flood's plight by advising him that he retained "the right to retire and embark on a different enterprise outside of baseball." Since both management and labor agreed that the reserve system was a mandatory subject of collective bargaining, Cooper was "convinced that the reserve clause can be fashioned so as to find acceptance by player and club."[52]

As everyone had always known, however, the events in Judge Cooper's courtroom would not determine the outcome of the Flood case. Nor would anything be decided at the appeals level. There Judge Sterry R. Waterman opined that *Federal Baseball* "was not one of Mr. Justice Holmes' happiest days," and that the rationale behind *Toolson* was "dubious," but nonetheless joined the majority to affirm Cooper's ruling.[53] Flood's only hope for victory rested in a hearing before the U.S. Supreme Court.

The workings of the Supreme Court are often shrouded in mystery. However, thanks to several books — most notably Bob Woodward and Scott Armstrong's *The Brethren*; Linda Greenhouse's *Becoming Justice Blackmun*[54]; and now Snyder's *A Well-Paid Slave*—we know a great deal about the Court's maneuverings of the Flood case and how close Flood came, first to being shut out from a hearing, and later to actually prevailing in his suit.

The Flood case arrived at a moment of great transition for the Supreme Court. Justices Hugo Black and John Harlan, two mainstays of the liberal Warren Court, had recently retired. Richard Nixon had appointed Lewis Powell and William Rehnquist to replace them. Indeed, when the Court first considered whether or not to review the judgment against Flood, only seven Justices were seated. Their initial reaction seemed ominous. The Justices voted 4–3 to deny Flood a full hearing before the Court. The narrow margin allowed for a reconsideration two weeks later. At this time Justice Bryon "Whizzer" White, himself a former professional athlete, switched his vote allowing the case to go forward.[55]

Commentators on the Flood case have often remarked on two issues that may have tilted the decision against him — the dismal performance of Flood's attorney Arthur Goldberg before the Court and the influence of the conservative Nixon appointees in the decision.[56] But neither matter proved critical to the final outcome. Goldberg's appearance had elicited much expectation, a rare appearance by a former Justice arguing before the Court. But Goldberg offered a rambling, meandering discourse that failed to advance Flood's arguments and appeared to irritate his former colleagues. Greatly humiliated, he would never argue before the Supreme Court again. In the final 5–3 vote favoring the owners, none of the four Nixon appointees had voted in Flood's favor, leading to speculation that the more liberal court of preceding years might have ruled differently.

The actual debates of the Court expose a more complex reality. Goldberg's embarrassing display did little to advance Flood's cause, but it probably did not doom it either. More significantly the ebb and flow of support for Flood on the Court reveals a less partisan divide. In the vote on whether to hear the case, liberal Justice Thurgood Marshall, the only African American on the bench, opposed Flood. The Court's initial polling of opinions favored Major League Baseball by a 5–4 margin, with Marshall still against Flood, and Nixon appointees Warren Burger and Powell supporting him. Even William Rehnquist, who voted to continue the federal anti-trust exemption, expressed doubts as to whether this protected baseball from state anti-trust claims.[57] Harry Blackmun received the assignment to express the will of the Court. He responded with a long paean to baseball as the national pastime and a shorter, unconvincing defense of the need to retain the game's antitrust exemption. With the exemption intact, Blackmun did not address whether or not Flood's complaint was a labor relations issue, one of the main points of contention at the original trial.

By this time, alliances on the court had shifted. Rehnquist, White, and Potter Stewart reluctantly indicated support for Blackmun's draft. But Marshall shifted sides. He prepared a dissent rejecting baseball's anti-trust exemption and remanding the case back to the lower courts to determine if this was indeed, as the owners had argued, a collective bargaining issue.[58] Marshall's switch would have given Flood a qualified 5–4 victory. Flood would have knocked down the antitrust exemption, but the issue of his free agency would have to await the outcome of yet another trial. But Lewis Powell, one of Flood's supporters, had not withdrawn. Powell held stock in Anheuser-Busch, which owned the Cardinals. At his nomination hearing he had come under heavy questioning about his stock holdings and how they might affect his decisions. Even though he favored a verdict that would have gone against the interests of Anheuser-Busch, Powell disqualified himself from the case.[59]

Marshall's change of heart and Powell's withdrawal left the Court deadlocked at 4–4. If Flood's supporters could convince one more Justice to defect to his side, he would win. If the tie persisted, baseball's antitrust exemption would stand, but upon even shakier legs than in the past, giving Flood at least a moral victory.[60] Instead Justice Burger blinked. Burger, Blackmun's best friend since childhood, announced that while he did not agree with Blackmun's underlying logic in sustaining the earlier court decisions, he had become a "reluctant affirm." "The least undesirable course," he wrote, "is to let the matter rest with Congress." Burger never explained his rationale for abandoning the position he had held since the earliest stages of the debate.[61] Thus, in effect, in the bottom of the ninth inning, Flood had lost by a 5–3 score.

The Significance of the Curt Flood Case

Flood's defeat before the Supreme Court in 1972 points to one of the ultimate ironies of his case. Flood had neither terminated baseball's antitrust exemption, nor won free agency for himself. On the surface, his defeat seemed total. From a legal standpoint the doctrines laid out in *Federal Baseball* and *Toolson* stood. Baseball's attorney Paul Porter called it "a clear cut victory for baseball." Yet *Flood vs. Kuhn* had already changed the landscape of labor relations in baseball and moved the issue of the reserve clause into the forefront of both player and public consciousness. As John Gaherin, who represented the owners in collective bargaining negotiations with the Players Association, told his employers, "After the Flood case, it wasn't a question if the reserve structure would be restructured or annihilated, but when."[62]

Once again, as the *Federal Baseball* and *Toolson* cases, the consideration of baseball had inspired the Supreme Court to the height of irrationality. Blackmun in his decision acknowledged Appeals Court Judge Sterryman's view that baseball's antitrust exemption was "unrealistic, inconsistent, and illogical," but defended this as an "established ... aberration," an "inconsistency and illogic of longstanding" resting on "a recognition and an acceptance of baseball's unique characteristic and needs." Blackmun invoked a peculiar doctrine, that of "positive inaction" by Congress to bolster his argument. By failing to act to negate the Supreme Court's decision, Congress had given its tacit endorsement to the antitrust exemption. The remedy, therefore, lay in the legislative, not the judicial branch.[63]

Blackmun's opinion opened the Court to widespread criticism and ridicule and weakened public support for the reserve clause. In his dissent, Justice William Douglas attacked Organized Baseball for its "predatory practices," and made it clear that any contract "which forbids anyone to practice his calling is commonly called an unreasonable restraint of trade."[64] Marshall, the great advocate of civil rights, wrote, "The importance of the antitrust laws to every citizen must not be minimized," argued Marshall. "They are as important to baseball players as they are to football players, lawyers, doctors, or members of any other class of workers." These rights could not be trumped by the perceived economic interests of the owners.[65]

The combination of the soppiness of Blackmun's paean to the national pastime (which Justice White explicitly refused to endorse) and the weakness of his legal arguments shifted the tide of public opinion with regard to the reserve clause. In a footnote, Marshall implied that this was a decision "contrary to the public sense of justice."[66] Most of the subsequent commentary shared this perspective. Not only sportswriters, but the editorial pages of many major newspapers assailed the Court's verdict and mocked Blackmun's opinion.[67]

Throughout the trial and various appeals, the baseball industry had relied heavily on its fallback position, that even if the game had lost its antitrust exemption, the reserve clause was a matter for collective bargaining. Commissioner Kuhn reiterated this stance in the aftermath of the decision, which he proclaimed opened "the way for renewed collective bargaining on the reserve system after the 1972 season." ("Renewed?" responded a sarcastic Miller. "It has never begun.")[68] Labor negotiator Gaherin recognized the narrowness of baseball's legal victory. The Court had essentially said that if it was starting from scratch, it would never grant the exemption. Without the exemption the reserve clause could never stand. It wanted Congress to take action to remedy this state of affairs. Gaherin advised to owners to make minor compromises with the players to preserve the essence of the reserve clause.[69] Kuhn and the owners instead insisted on collective bargaining "as we know it": stonewalling the issue and making no concessions at all on the reserve clause.

But the Flood case had already given the Players Association added leverage and produced one critical victory at the bargaining table. The 1967–68 Basic Agreement had introduced a grievance procedure whereby the players might take contract disputes before an arbitration panel. The board consisted of a representative of the owners, a second from the union, and, adhering to the fiction of baseball commissioner as a neutral party, the commissioner himself. This constituted less than the impartial arbitration normally included in labor-management pacts. In December, 1969, before Flood filed his suit, the owners had rejected the Players demand for an impartial arbitrator. But the hypocrisy of this stance posed potential problems at the impending trial. As John Helyar writes, "How could baseball argue that Curt Flood was wrong and the industry was eminently fair to players if their only appeal on grievances was to the commissioner?" In May, 1970, just before the start of the trial, the owners conceded the point. An independent arbitrator would replace the commissioner as the third panel member under the new 1970 Basic Agreement.[70]

Had this system been in place one year early, Flood might not have had to sue baseball. He could have taken his protest before the arbitration panel. Thanks in no small part to his efforts this right had now been won, though Flood could not benefit from it.[71] Independent arbitration, however, did offer an alternative path to challenge the reserve clause. Marvin Miller always felt that the owners' traditional implementation misconstrued the reserve clause. Section 10(a) allowed an owner to unilaterally renew a contract for one year. Organized baseball maintained that this right carried over into each subsequent contract into perpetuity. Miller believed that if an athlete played the second year without signing a new contract he had fulfilled his obligation to the team and now became a free agent.[72] Privately, some baseball advisors agreed. Both National League Counsel Lou Carroll and labor negotiator John Gaherin feared the worst. "Don't ever let them try that renewal clause," warned Carroll.[73]

With impartial arbitration in place, a player might now test these rival interpretations. The key was finding a player willing to take this step. The 1972 season almost provided a defining case. Cardinal catcher Ted Simmons, a former teammate of Flood's, declined the team's salary offer. Rather than start the season without their talented young catcher and fearing the power of the union, the Cardinals set a precedent by allowing him to play without a contract. Gaherin immediately recognized the threat posed by the situation. "Get a hold of this, we don't' want to test it. Sign him. Don't let him go through a year without a contract," Gaherin told Bing Devine. When Simmons made the All-Star team, the Cardinals caved in. Devine offered him a two-year contract totaling $75,000.[74] Other players took note.

Determining how much the Flood case actually influenced the course of labor-management relations in these years remains difficult. A combination of Flood's example, increased player militancy, and skilled union leadership produced a series of successes. The 1970 Basic Agreement allowed agents to represent players in contract negotiations. In 1972 disputes over the pension plan triggered the first player strike, with the owners ultimately granting the union demands. This set the stage for negotiations for a third Basic Agreement in 1973, the first to be implemented sine the Supreme Court decision. Players won the right to salary arbitration. More significantly, for the first time, the owners accepted modifications to the reserve clause. Players with five or more years of major league service won the right to reject assignments to the minors; ten-year veterans with five years of service to the same team could no longer be traded without their permission.[75] Thus, the right of a senior ballplayer to exercise an element of control over his future, perhaps the key element of Flood's protest had been won.

In 1973 five players followed Simmon's lead and began the season without contracts. Four ultimately signed, while the fifth was released. In 1974 seven more players took this route. Most reached terms relatively quickly. But New York Yankee relief pitcher Sparky Lyle held out until September before winning a two-year pact that would pay him $180,000. San Diego outfielder Bobby Tolan, another of Flood's former teammates, played the entire season without signing. Gaherin and National League President Chub Feeney pressured San Diego to reach an agreement with Tolan "for the good of the industry." Miller and the Players Association filed a grievance on Tolan's behalf, seeking to test the validity of Section 10(a). In December Tolan signed a two-year, nearly $200,000 contract.[76]

The Simmons, Lyle, and Tolan situations demonstrated the growing bargaining power of the players and the effectiveness of using the ambiguous meaning of Section 10(a) as a tool. The matter of Oakland pitching ace Jim "Catfish" Hunter revealed the potential value of free agency. In early 1975, after Oakland owner Charlie Finley reneged on payments promised in their contract, the independent arbitrator invalidated the pact and declared Hunter free to sell his services to any team. The New York Yankees won the bidding with a five-year $3.75 million offer, terms far in excess of what players had received under the constraints of the reserve clause.

Hunter's success emboldened Andy Messersmith of the Los Angeles Dodgers to make the definitive challenge. Messersmith, a 20-game winner in 1974, opted not to sign a contract for the 1975 season and played out his option. He refused to entertain salary offers from the Dodgers. The case which now also included pitcher Dave McNally, went to arbitration. In December, 1975, the independent panel member Peter Seitz ruled in favor of Messersmith and McNally. Once an athlete had played out his option year, his obligations to the team had ended. The two pitchers, and by extension anyone else who took this course, could become free agents.

In his opinion, Seitz specifically stated that his judgment bore no relation to the Flood case. "It deserves emphasis," wrote Seitz, "that this decision strikes no blow emancipating players from claimed serfdom or involuntary servitude as alleged in the Flood case. It does not condemn the Reserve System presently in force on constitutional or moral grounds.... It does no more than seek to interpret and apply provisions that are in the agreements of the parties."[77]

Baseball's anti-trust exemption remained intact and the legality of the reserve clause itself still stood. Eliminating the possibility of perpetual renewal, however, rendered it ineffective. Nor is it entirely clear that this result would not have been achieved without Flood's efforts. Players had already grown restive and the union had already begun its inexorable march to a more equitable position in labor relations. Yet the Flood case, at the very least, accelerated the process. The path from Flood to Messersmith-McNally seems clear. The Players Association won impartial arbitration earlier than they would have without the threat of the looming trial. It gained additional concessions in the 1973 CBA that compromised the sanctity of the reserve clause. The Supreme Court's strained rationalization exposed the ultimate untenability of the existing system for all to see. Flood's example encouraged other players to envision alternatives to a really defined solely by the owners. Andy Messersmith might have tested the waters in 1975 without Flood, but in all probability the ultimate challenge would have come several years later and been launched in an atmosphere less attuned to the issue.

The demise of the reserve system transformed baseball economics. The Players Association, as Marvin Miller had always promised, negotiated a new system that recognized many restraints on player movement, but allowed athletes to achieve free agency after an initial period of service. Open competition for their services sent salaries soaring. Generations of baseball players earned riches beyond Flood's wildest dreams.

Flood, himself, according to the prevalent narrative, received nothing in return. A brief comeback attempt with the Washington Senators failed. No team would offer a job as a coach or scout to the man who had dragged baseball before the Supreme Court. Even the Players Association never deigned to offer Flood a job. Flood spent much of the rest of his life desperate and destitute, embittered and forgotten. As Flynn writes, "His stance cost him the remainder of this professional baseball career; he was financially ruined; his personal life was in a shambles; and he was banished from baseball ... an ingrate and a traitor."[78]

This interpretation, however, absolves Flood of all responsibility for his plight. Flood's suffering derived not so much from his failed lawsuit or subsequent ostracism, but from his drinking problem. In 1970 Washington Senators owner Robert Short offered Flood a contract to play in the nation's capitol. Attorneys representing both sides in the case agreed that Flood's reappearance would not invalidate his complaint. Flood, no more enthused about playing baseball than he had been in 1969 but desperately in need of money, signed. His return proved short-lived. After thirteen games and 40 plate appearances in which he was able to eke out only seven singles, Flood withdrew. Most people cited Flood's the effects of a year's hiatus in eroding Flood's baseball skills. Others blamed Senators' manager Ted Williams for not giving Flood a "fair shake." But other players had returned from prolonged layoffs and Williams' reservations about Flood had a sound basis. Flood failed because he had become a pronounced alcoholic. During spring training, writes Snyder, "Flood holed himself up ... at the Surf Rider Motel and drank vodka all night until he passed out. He refused to leave the room for breakfast or din-

Curt Flood at the Rustic, a bar he opened on the island of Majorca off the coast of Spain in 1973 (courtesy Hearst News American Photographic Collection in the University of Maryland Special Collections Library, College Park).

ner.... If there was no food, Flood simply drank." Nothing changed when the season started.[79] Flood, in effect, drank himself back out of the game.

Flood drifted through Europe for several years unable to escape his addiction. He suffered a broken arm in a fall, was arrested in Andorra for burglary, and was placed in a psychiatric hospital in Barcelona. He returned to the United States in 1976 and fell and fractured his skull.[80] Flood blamed his inability to find work in baseball on a blacklisting resulting from his suit. "I think people in baseball are holding a grudge. It's a very sad and disappointing part of my life."[81] There may be truth to this. But Flood also was rarely in any condition to hold down a job. His childhood patron Sam Bercovich bought the broadcasting rights for Oakland A's baseball games and insisted on hiring Flood as a color commentator. The role should have suited the well-spoken Flood, but he frequently appeared at games drunk. Even driving to the ballpark proved a challenge for the inebriated Flood.[82] During the early 1980s he temporarily won his battle with the bottle and found work with the Oakland A's Speakers' Bureau. After two years, however, he began drinking again.[83] Under these circumstances, not even the Players Association felt comfortable offering Flood a position.

Flood stopped drinking in 1986. Between his major league pension and money earned signing autographs at card shows and other events, he could now support himself. He married actress Judy Pace, a longtime friend, and moved to Los Angeles where he lived comfortably.[84] In the last decade of his life, until he was struck down by lung cancer, he earned a measure of solace, recognition and self-acceptance. He did not share in the financial bounty that his efforts had helped create for baseball players and other athletes, but he had elevated his life and legacy above that of his fellows who could boast more substantial playing achievements.

On the day after Flood's death in 1997, Representative John Conyers introduced legislation in Congress removing baseball's anti-trust exemption in matters of labor relations. Congress passed the measure as the Curt Flood Act, generally considered a final tribute to his courage and sacrifice. Yet Organized Baseball had exacted the last laugh. The bill removed the anti-trust exemption relating to areas that collective bargaining had already rendered moot. But since the Flood decision, several court rulings had questioned the validity of baseball's antitrust exemption in matters relating to relocation of franchises and umpires. In the Curt Flood Act, Congress explicitly recognized baseball's anomalous exemption in these and other matters, including broadcasting rights, marketing, licensing, the minor leagues, the amateur draft, expansion, ownership issues, and control over minor league players.[85] Under the auspices of the Curt Flood Act, baseball had finally won what it had long sought—clear, unambiguous legal sanction for the anti-trust exemption created on a day that was not among Mr. Justice Holmes' happiest.

Part V

THE GLORY YEARS IN BALTIMORE AND THE GAME'S DECLINE

A half-century after losing its major league franchise, the Baltimore Orioles regained it in 1954. In the following decade they began a run for their own dynasty, though it never matched the Yankees in World Series championships. Beginning with their stunning sweep of the Los Angeles Dodgers in the 1966 World Series and ending with a less decisive victory over the Philadelphia Phillies in the 1983 series, the Orioles were the most dominant team in the American League. Confirming the baseball adage that games are won with starting pitchers, the Orioles often had three stellar ones, and one year they had four twenty-game winners. In 1970 they rolled over the Cincinnati Reds in the World Series. Their defense was equally strong, featuring the human vacuum at third base, Brooks Robinson. The other Robinson, Frank, provided the fire power at the plate and in the clubhouse.

In his essay "The Baltimore Orioles: How They Built a Winner (and Tore It Down)," John Eisenberg relates how their decade-and-a-half success also rested on superior management, beginning with the owners who turned over the team to skilled baseball professionals. The team's winning formula, based on preparedness in the farm system, skillful trades, and inspired field managing by Earl Weaver, became known as the "Oriole Way." When new owners departed from the script in the hope of producing instant championships, a decade of losing seasons followed. Now rebuilding in the team's ebb tide, Oriole fans' hopes rest on the teams restoration of winning the old-fashioned way — the way it was done first in the 1890s and then for an even longer period beginning in the 1960s.

Summertime was synonymous with baseball for most American boys and many girls throughout much of the twentieth century. While hopes of reaching the majors were limited unfairly to boys, no ballpark turned away their sisters as fans. Their love affair with baseball was often a family affair, as the concluding essay, John B. Wiseman's "Fall from the Pedestal," describes. The calamitous players' strike in the summer of 1994 abruptly ended the romance for one member of the editor's family, as it would for a sizeable portion of the larger nation of baseball aficionados. While the decline of the national game had begun decades earlier as a result of a compelling marriage between television and professional football, the unforeseen consequences of the free agency system also took its toll. The players' search for the biggest bidder for their services undermined an important ingredient that had been a mainstay of fan devotion — player identification with one team. The price that players paid for their large, sometimes astronomical, salaries was the severance of a large portion of the faithful nation of baseball devotees.

Those who have remained in the fold have witnessed the metamorphosis of a game quite different from what it was at the turn of the twentieth century. Moreover, players' use of strength enhancement drugs have recently tarnished the major leagues. Still, attendance at many aesthetically attractive stadiums remains high. The major leagues have weathered cheating scandals, labor-management conflict, and fan disenchantment before. What they haven't faced is the competition from so many other organized sports. Baseball is no longer the national pastime, but it surely remains an important part of American life.

16

The Baltimore Orioles: How They Built a Winner (and Tore It Down)

JOHN EISENBERG

When the New York Yankees finally fell into a decline in the mid–1960s after dominating the American League since before the Great Depression, the Baltimore Orioles were unlikely successors to the throne. In more than 60 years as the St. Louis Browns (from 1902–1953) and the Orioles (from 1954–1965), the franchise had won just one American League pennant and never captured a World Series. The Chicago White Sox, Detroit Tigers, and Cleveland Indians had better traditions, and the Minnesota Twins, new kids on the block, jumped ahead of them all to win the 1965 pennant.

But it was the Orioles who took control when the Yankees became just another team. Beginning in 1966, Baltimore went on a 17-year run that included eight postseason appearances, six AL pennants, and three World Series titles. Other teams' fortunes rose and fell during those years (the Yankees rebounded to win back-to-back Series title in 1976 and 1977) but no team in either league won more games overall than the Orioles. They had just one losing season in 17 years (in 1967) and became known as baseball's savviest franchise.

They won their first pennant in 1966 and went on to shock the heavily favored Los Angeles Dodgers in the World Series, sweeping four games. Then, from 1969 through 1971, they won three straight pennants while averaging 106 regular season wins, and added a second Series title by defeating the Cincinnati Reds in five games in 1970. Perennial playoff contenders through the 1970s and early '80s, they won pennants in 1979 and 1983, and captured the franchise's third World Series title in 1983, defeating the Philadelphia Phillies in five games.

Their teams featured some of the best players in baseball history: Brooks Robinson, a third baseman who won 16 Gold Glove awards; Jim Palmer, an elegant right-handed pitcher who won 268 games; Frank Robinson, a fierce outfielder who put the team over the top in 1966 with his leadership; Boog

Powell, a burly first baseman who slugged 339 career home runs; Dave McNally, a left-hander who pitched his best when the stakes were high; Eddie Murray, a switch-hitting slugger who became the first major league player to make $1 million a year; and Cal Ripken, Jr., a homegrown shortstop from Aberdeen, Maryland, who would eventually play in 2,632 straight games, setting a major league record that likely will never be broken. All but Powell and McNally made it to baseball's Hall of Fame in Cooperstown, New York.

But while those well-known figures (and many more) were essential to the Orioles' success, a series of mostly obscure figures who toiled in the organization's front office were just as important. They included Harry Dalton, a former sportswriter who became the team's farm director and general manager; Jim McLaughlin, a scouting pioneer who came with the team from St. Louis; Jim Russo, a superb talent scout; and Cal Ripken, Sr., an undersized catching prospect who joined the front office and worked as an instructor, scout, coach, and manager for years.

As much as the Orioles were known for sound pitching, steady defense, and timely hitting during their glory years, they also were known for shrewd scouting, tireless player development, and peerless overall management. Their success was a testament to what can happen when you hire committed professionals and let them do their jobs.

It all started, ironically, with a series of bad scouting judgments made by one of the Orioles' shrewdest executives: Paul Richards, the team's manager from 1955–61 and general manager from 1955–58. A tall, lean, introspective Texan who owned a pecan farm just south of Dallas, in Waxahachie, Richards was an original baseball thinker — as a minor league manager he once stopped an opponent's fleet base stealer by walking the batter in front of him every time — and was briefly in charge of every aspect of the Orioles organization, including scouting. But he preferred the advice of his cronies to that of McLaughlin's scouts, and was himself not a canny judge of talent. Under Richards, the Orioles wasted scads of money on prospects such as Bruce Swango, a fireballer who couldn't pitch in front of crowds; Bob Nelson, the "Babe Ruth of Texas," who never hit a home run in the major leagues; and Jim Pyburn, a two-sport star at Auburn University who hit .190 for the Orioles and became a football coach.

Richards, the "Wizard of Waxahachie," did score one direct hit that hugely benefited the Orioles. A former minor league player under Richards in the 1930s spotted a sure-handed high schooler playing ball in Little Rock, Ark, and suggested Richards come and take a look. Richards and several others did just that, came away impressed, and the Orioles beat out several clubs to sign the player — an infielder named Brooks Robinson.

But Richards had many more misses than hits, and by 1958, the Orioles' owners had tired of his costly miscues. They relieved him of his scouting duties and brought in a traditional general manager, Lee MacPhail, to run the front office. MacPhail instituted a normal chain of command, and the team began to rely on McLaughlin's scouting network, which he had brought with him from St. Louis and tweaked while Richards was in charge. Humorless and difficult, McLaughlin didn't know talent any better than Richards, but he knew smart scouts and employed many. He was loyal to the notion of fielding a team of homegrown stars, and years ahead of his time with his focus on prospects' mental tools (determination, attitude, etc.) as well as their physical skills.

Every team had a national network of scouts in the years before baseball instituted an amateur draft in 1965, but the Orioles' network outperformed them all. The team signed numerous future stars simply by outworking and outmaneuvering the opposition.

In 1959 Powell was a renowned slugger from Key West, Fla., but his stock dropped precipitously when he bombed at the state high school tournament. A handful of $100,000 offers came off the table, leaving just the Orioles and Cardinals in the running. Both bids were lower than Powell wanted, but Fred "Bootnose" Hoffman, a charismatic Orioles scout who had once roomed with Babe Ruth, talked Powell into signing. Hoffman was undeterred by the tournament flop and convinced Powell had the right stuff.

In 1960 McNally was an American Legion star in Billings, Montana. Both the Orioles and Dodgers wanted him. The Orioles' scout was a former major league pitcher named Jim Wilson. When McNally asked if the Orioles had any good young pitchers, no doubt wondering how quickly he might rise through the ranks, Wilson fibbed and said the Orioles needed help. In fact, they had an array of young pitchers such as Milt Pappas, Jerry Walker, and Steve Barber already starring in the majors. But this was before detailed information on teams was widely known, and Wilson gambled that McNally would believe him. He was right.

In 1962 Palmer was a lanky natural athlete from Scottsdale, Arizona. He had led the state in receiving as a football star, and was so gifted in basketball than powerhouse UCLA offered him a full scholarship. But his best sport was baseball. He could rear back and throw 97 mph fastballs, and every major league team wanted him. The Orioles had a pair of scouts, Wilson and Russo, on the case, simultaneously working his parents and following Palmer's progress in a Montana summer league.

Paul Richards, who by then had left the Orioles to run a National League expansion franchise in Houston, got in the door first. As Palmer later recalled, Richards ate peanuts, practiced his golf putting on the living room carpet and left two contracts, telling Palmer just to sign the one with the terms he liked best and mail it back. Palmers' parents were turned off. When Russo and Wilson came in and made a friendlier pitch, Palmer's mother remarked that they seemed nicer. Palmer signed with Baltimore.

From 1960 to 1963 the Orioles also signed future major leaguers such as infielders Davey Johnson and Mark Belanger; pitchers Tom Phoebus, Darrold Knowles, Eddie Watt, and Wally Bunker; and catchers Andy Etchebarren and

Larry Haney. They signed fleet outfielder Paul Blair off the roster of a low-level team in the New York Mets' system. Their eye was dead-on.

Once they had the players under contract, they put them in the hands of highly knowledgeable instructors and coaches. At one time in the early 1960s, six future major league managers (Earl Weaver, Jim Frey, George Bamberger, Clyde King, Joe Altobelli and Ripken Sr.) were on the Orioles' developmental staff. McLaughlin had hired them all, although, ironically, he was gone, having lost a power struggle with Richards before the Texan left for Houston in 1961. (Dalton, when put in charge later, eventually brought McLaughlin back.)

To round out their teams, the Orioles blended homegrown talent with key players acquired in trades, such as relief pitcher Dick Hall, outfielder Curt Blefary, and infielder Luis Aparicio, a future Hall of Famer. By the early 1960s the Orioles had more talent in uniform than the franchise had ever had in a half century in St. Louis. They were in first place with 22 games to go in 1960, and finished second after succumbing in a showdown with the Yankees. In 1964 they won 97 games, again challenging the Yankees until late in the season. In 1965 they won 94 games and finished third.

Brooks Robinson had emerged as a superstar and fan favorite, earning the AL's Most Valuable Player award in 1964. His fielding was pure poetry. Even though he didn't have natural speed or the strongest arm, his hands were unerring, his first steps were quick, and his throws were always timely and accurate, beating runners by a half-step. Off the field, with his Southern drawl and easygoing manner, he was always available to sign autographs and speak to kids' groups.

With Robinson at one corner of the infield and blossoming Boog Powell at the other, the Orioles had the right cornerstones for a pennant winner. But something was missing; the team always came up short. That lead MacPhail, in his last act as GM (before handing the team over to Dalton), to make the most important deal in franchise history, trading for Frank Robinson in December 1965. The Orioles sent pitcher Pappas to Cincinnati in exchange for the outfielder, who was furious after having been labeled "an old 30" by the Reds' general manager. Intensely competitive to begin with, and now motivated after the perceived slight, Robinson provided the final piece of the Orioles' winning puzzle—fire in the belly.

He lashed a double in his first spring training at-bat in 1966, told his genial teammates not to talk to opponents before a game, and led the Orioles to a blazing 12–1 start once the season began. On an April Sunday afternoon at Memorial Stadium, he hit a home run ball so far off Cleveland pitcher Luis Tiant that it flew all the way out of the stadium and into the parking lot. No batter had ever hit a ball out of that park, and, it turned out, no batter ever did again. After that bomb, the Orioles knew they were on their way to something special. With Robinson capturing a Triple Crown by leading the American League in home runs, RBI and batting average, the Orioles sat atop the standings all season and won their first pennant going away, with 97 wins.

Facing the Dodgers in the Series, the Orioles put on a pitching show that served as a testament to their organizational strength. After winning Game 1 on a superb relief performance by veteran Moe Drabowsky, they won the next three games on shutouts by pitchers they had signed and developed. Palmer, as a 20-year-old rookie, out-pitched the legendary Sandy Koufax in Game 2. Wally Bunker, a 19-game winner at age 19 two years earlier, overcame a sore arm to win Game 3. Then McNally, who had pitched poorly in the opener, came back to win Game 4. Three homegrown complete-game shutouts put the Orioles on top of the baseball world.

After hiccups in 1967 (when Frank Robinson was injured) and 1968, they embarked on their greatest run, winning 109 games in 1969, 108 in 1970, and 101 in 1971. They also swept the new best-of-five AL Championship Series three straight times without losing a game. They were an awesome team. The Robinsons and Powell formed the meat of the batting order, and the top pitchers were Palmer, McNally and left-hander Mike Cuellar, acquired in a 1968 trade. Those three pitchers and No. 4 starter Pat Dobson all won 20 games in 1971, an amazing feat.

But the Orioles only won one World Series in their three-year span of dominance, dropping a stunner to the New York Mets in 1969 before beating the Reds in 1970 and then losing to the Pittsburgh Pirates in 1971. Their lack of Series titles probably kept them from being regarded as one of the greatest major league teams ever. Still, no one doubted that they represented baseball's savviest organization.

Weaver was their manager through these years, having gained the job in 1968 after paying his dues for more than decade in the minor leagues. An irascible, brilliant strategist known best for his bug-eyed tirades against umpires, Weaver defined the winning Orioles as much as their developmental system. He valued pitching, defense, and three-run homers, eschewed bunts, and gave all 25 players on the roster a role. His players alternately loved and hated him, but he cared about winning, not about being popular, and he coaxed the best out of them. Like many of his best players, he ended up in the Hall of Fame.

McNally and Cuellar were slowing by the early 1970s, but the younger Palmer was approaching his peak after having overcome arm trouble in the late 1960s. With his signature high leg kick, blazing fastball and pinpoint control, he won 20 games every year from 1970 to 1973, and in many ways was a fitting symbol for the Orioles: smart, consistent, seldom beating himself. Handsome and glib, he often complained about ailments, driving Weaver nuts, but he usually pitched through the pain to victory. And for all his talk about injuries, he ended up having a long career that ran into the 1980s and featured eight 20-win seasons, 53 shutouts and 211 complete games—all franchise records likely never to fall.

By the 1970s the Orioles needed a new generation of talent, and they were ready, thanks to their strong organization. The draft, inaugurated in 1965, had altered the nature of player acquisition, and the Orioles adjusted well. They

Exuberant Brooks Robinson, Davey Johnson, left, and Mike Cuellar celebrate the moment of World Series victory over the Reds in 1970 at Memorial Stadium (courtesy Hearst News American Photographic Collection in the University of Maryland Special Collections Library, College Park).

swung and missed on a few early picks such as first-rounders Scott McDonald and Ted Parks, but for the most part, Dalton's scouts continued to crank out the hits. In 1967, the Orioles drafted future stars Don Baylor and Bob Grich. The 1968 litter included Al Bumbry, a future AL Rookie of the Year, and five others who would make the majors. In 1969, they selected Wayne Garland, a future 20-game winner. In 1970 they took Doug DeCinces. In 1973 they selected Murray and Mike Flanagan, a future Cy Young Award winner, and also signed a skinny Nicaraguan prospect named Dennis Martinez, who would become one of the greatest Latin American pitchers in major league history. Future Oriole draft classes included infielder Rich Dauer in 1974, and infielder Ripken, Jr., and pitcher Mike Boddicker in 1978.

This sustained success enabled the Orioles to continue winning when their first generation of championship talent grew old. Murray replaced Powell at first base. Grich and Dauer replaced Davey Johnson at second. DeCinces replaced Brooks Robinson at third. Flanagan replaced McNally. Baylor replaced Frank Robinson. Palmer stayed on and on, bridging the generations with his masterful pitching.

There was similar turnover in the front office. When Dalton and McLaughlin moved on, top executives such as Frank Cashen, Walter Shannon, and Dave Ritterpusch stepped in. They tutored young executives such as John Schuerholz and Lou Gorman, who would become general managers elsewhere. When the old scouts retired, new scouts such as Ray Poitevint, Al Kubski, and Don Pries stepped in. (Pries would later head the major league scouting service.) In on-field matters, there was a succession of top pitching coaches (George Bamberger to Ray Miller) and a steady stream of committed coaches and instructors such as Ripken Sr.

For almost two decades the Orioles stood for a way of playing baseball — pitching well, hitting with power and relying on intelligence and fundamentals. It was all written in a pamphlet, titled "How to Play Baseball the Oriole Way," which Dalton had ordered in the early 1960s as scouting director. Various coaches and instructors wrote chapters on how to pitch, hit, and play various positions, and all Oriole teams, from the lowest minors to the majors, followed the instructions. The Orioles continued to play winning baseball as if it were their birthright, racking up division titles in 1973, 1974, 1979, and 1983.

The Orioles of this era didn't have as many All-Stars or future Hall of Famers as their predecessors, but they were resourceful (reliever Tippy Martinez picked off three players in one inning of a key win) and Weaver brilliantly manipulated his talent. John Lowenstein and Gary Roenicke weren't highly productive players by themselves, but as part of a left-field platoon with teammates Pat Kelly and Benny Ayala, they produced winning totals. Rick Dempsey, a strong defensive catcher who struggled at the plate, shared a platoon with no-name Dan Graham in 1980, and the pair totaled 24 homers and 94 runs batted in. Dempsey, who rose to the occasion in the 1983 World Series and was named series MVP, became one of the most popular Orioles ever, entertaining crowds with pantomime acts during rain delays and always playing hard.

The Orioles of this era did have Murray, a perennial All-Star, batting cleanup, and a cadre of brilliant pitchers such as Flanagan, Dennis and Tippy Martinez, and soft-tossing Scott McGregor. But inevitably, just as the Yankees faded in the 1960s, the Orioles also ran out of steam. The departure of so many talented scouts and executives had left a hole, and although general manager Hank Peters, who held the job from 1976–87, was solid, the system stopped producing useful players. When the team's second generation of winning players got old, this time there weren't suitable replacements. After winning 98 regular season games and a World Series title in 1983, they finished out of the running and barely over .500 the next two years, and then fell into a sharp decline. In 1987, they lost 95 games and finished 31 games out of first, and then topped that the next season by losing their first 21 games, a record-setting collapse that made them a laughingstock. Abruptly, their glory years had given way to despair.

Part V: The Glory Years in Baltimore and the Game's Decline

Ken Singleton, Rick Dempsey and Doug DeCinces greet Eddie Murphy after his grand slam at Memorial Stadium in 1981 (courtesy Hearst News American Photographic Collection in the University of Maryland Special Collections Library, College Park).

Instead of symbolizing the game at its best on and off the field, the Orioles suddenly were just another team trying to buy their way to the postseason via free agency. They had a brief period of renewed success after they moved into a glistening new downtown ballpark, Oriole Park at Camden Yards, in 1992. Baltimore attorney Peter G. Angelos purchased the team a year later and spent heavily for a few years, resulting in sellout crowds and back-to-back playoff appearances in 1996 and 1997. But in the end, Angelos' method of operation failed and the Orioles entered the worst period in their history. From 2001 through 2007 they averaged more than 90 losses per season and never contended for a playoff berth. Only the presence of the woeful Tampa Bay Devil Rays in the AL East kept them from finishing last every year.

Their one saving grace (aside from their beautiful park) through these increasingly desperate times was the presence of Ripken Jr. at shortstop. The quintessential local boy-made-good, he gave the fans a reason to cheer, win or lose. Ironically, he became a starter just in time to experience the World Series victory in 1983, catching the last out himself on a soft line drive to shortstop. The team then proceeded to fall apart around him, but Ripken remained a bedrock of consistency, hitting for power and average while anchoring the infield—and carrying himself with a low-key humility that seemed a throwback to an earlier era.

He didn't set out to play in every game of every season, but it became a habit under managers Weaver and Joe Altobelli early in his career, and fortunately, he was big and strong and avoided injury. In the beginning, he played in every inning of every game for more than five years, totaling an astounding 8,243 consecutive innings until his father, now the Orioles manager, ended it in July 1987, believing the streak was burdensome. Ripken continued to play in every game, though, and his streak gained more and more attention as he began to bear down on Yankee legend Lou Gehrig's acclaimed record of 2,130 straight games. And Ripken didn't just play in the games, of course. He was a perennial All-Star, a superb shortstop, and earned his second AL MVP award in 1991, his first having come in 1983.

His career reached an apex when he broke Gehrig's record amid great fanfare at Camden Yards on September 6, 1995. A labor stoppage had forced the cancellation of the World Series a year earlier, and with still-disgruntled fans unsure whether to come back to the game, Ripken showed them what was so great about it. The sports world stopped to watch and cheer his record. He celebrated by hitting a home run and then taking an impromptu victory jog around the field, smiling and slapping hands with the fans in the front row. It was a great night for the Orioles, a return to their halcyon era. But dark days soon ensued.

The collapse of a franchise that had been baseball's best underscored the importance of what made the Orioles so successful for so long. For years, they were just smarter and more stable than everyone else. It was when that foundation wobbled—when they changed how they operated—that their dynasty became imperiled.

The start of the collapse is traceable to owner Jerry Hofferger's decision to sell the team in 1979 to Edward Bennett Williams, a high-powered Washington D.C. attorney. Hoffberger, president of a Baltimore brewery and the team's principal owner since 1965, was a low-key, hands-off owner who sat in the stands alongside fans and let his baseball executives do their jobs. Williams, who bought the team for $12 million, didn't immerse himself in the team's day-to-day operations, but he had his opinions and voiced them. Like many strong-willed modern-era owners, he was less interested in the minor league system than in the major league product, and the Orioles' system suffered because of his inattention. Scouting directors and minor league executives came and went along with scouts, coaches, and instructors. What had once been the best system in baseball was reduced to a mélangle of different attitudes and beliefs. Predictably, fewer players were produced.

In Williams' defense, he had no choice but to invest in free agents when the system failed to produce enough winning players in the wake of the 1983 World Series triumph. But after the 1984 season Williams took matters into his own hands and selected the players to target while Peters, the general manager, was out of the country. The Orioles brought in a handful of established veterans to try to win immediately. Suddenly, instead of having a clubhouse full of players who had grown up together, the Orioles were just like everyone else, an assemblage of high-priced talent. The magic was gone.

After Williams died in 1988, his estate sold the franchise to Eli Jacobs, a New York financier who soon had money problems. The dependence on free agency — and lack of focus on the minor league system — continued under Jacobs. When Jacobs was forced to sell the team in bankruptcy court, Angelos won the bidding to emerge as the team's first local owner since Hoffberger. The fans briefly cheered the return of the team to local hands, especially when Angelos' spending led to playoff appearances, but it soon became clear Angelos was the most hands-on owner in team, history, to the detriment of the on-field product.

In his first year of ownership, he made lineup suggestions to manager Johnny Oates (he wanted a third baseman named Leo Gomez to play) and included his sons in some personnel decisions, shocking Baltimore fans accustomed to a team with a proper chain of command. And unlike the stability that marked the team in the glory years, the Angelos-era Orioles changed managers and general managers constantly, reflecting their owner's chronic impatience. Chaos ensued. In the first seven years of Angelos' ownership, the Orioles employed five managers and four general managers, They briefly had two of the best in the business under contract at the same time, but manager Davey Johnson couldn't get along with Angelos and walked away after being named AL Manager of the Year in 1997, and general manager Pat Gillick departed a year later. A brilliant team builder who had put together a World Series winner in Toronto (and would later build playoff teams in Seattle and Philadelphia), Gillick had become disillusioned when Angelos vetoed a trade that Gillick believed would have stocked the team with young talent. Gillick's replacement, Frank Wren, lasted less than a year.

These repeated changes had a chilling effect on the team's performance, which Angelos ill-advisedly tried to reverse with one bold stroke, the 1999 signing of surly free agent slugger Albert Belle, whose tenure was cut short by a career-ending hip injury. By then Angelos had become a controversial figure in his hometown, facing heavy criticism for his habit of interfering with the team's decision-making. The criticism was warranted, but Angelos wasn't solely responsible for the mounting losses. He had inherited the dysfunctional minor league system, which continued to perform poorly on his watch. In 1999 the team had seven first-round picks in the draft, and only one, second baseman Brian Roberts, developed into a useful player in Baltimore. Roberts was the first everyday player the system had produced since Ripken Jr., who was drafted in 1978, two decades earlier.

Like Williams before him, Angelos lacked the patience to invest heavily in the minor league system and then sit back and wait for the winner to develop. He preferred to spend millions on players such as Belle who were already past their playing peaks, hoping for a more immediate miracle. He even wanted the draft to produce more immediate results. In 2004 he overruled the scouting department on draft day and ordered the team to select a college pitcher rather than a high school shortstop, thinking the college player would be ready sooner. But the team then failed to sign the college pitcher.

Solidifying the minor league system was the key to pulling the Orioles out of their slump, just as it had been the key during the glory years. But the Orioles gave themselves a slim chance of succeeding. Times had changed and an organization needed to have tentacles that reached worldwide, to baseball hotbeds such as the Dominican Republic, Venezuela, Puerto Rico, and even Japan, where major league teams had begun buying up top talent. But as other teams focused more and more on international scouting by shelling out bonuses for top prospects and building campuses to develop them, the Orioles were cutting corners and getting second-rate talent in return. Of the more than 160 major league players who were born outside the United States and eventually played in the All-Star Game, only two (pitchers Dennis Martinez and Armando Benitez) were originally signed by the Orioles.

Management dysfunction became the norm in the first years of the new baseball century. The Orioles employed four managers between 2003 and 2007, ran through a series of scouting directors, and established a succession of curious arrangements at the top of their baseball operations department. At one point, Mike Flanagan and Jim Beattie were co-general managers. Then Beattie was replaced by Jim Duquette. Finally, Andy MacPhail was brought in over the GMs in 2007, leading to Duquette's departure.

The team had led the major leagues in attendance throughout the early- and mid-90s after moving from old Memorial Stadium into Oriole Park at Camden Yards in 1992, but the years of failure and dysfunction discouraged many fans. From a high per-game average of 46,951 in 1994, the average attendance steadily slipped to a low of 26,582 in 2006. The park would be full only when the Yankees and Boston Red Sox visited, and many of the fans who bought tickets were cheering for the opposition. A cadre of true Oriole fans became disgusted, and in September 2006 a local radio station organized a protest. More than a thousand fans paraded through the ballpark during a late-afternoon game, chanting their disapproval.

The 2007 season, which ended with the Orioles below .500 for the 10th straight year, was typical of the Orioles' losing era. Manager Sam Perlozzo preached optimism in spring training, but the team performed so poorly for him that he was fired in June. His replacement, former bullpen coach Dave Trembley — the eighth manager to work for Angelos — took over on an interim basis, instilled discipline, and had the team playing its best ball in several years: in his first 54 games the Orioles had a winning record of 29–25. But on August 22, 2007, the day Trembley was promoted from interim to fulltime manager, the Orioles lost a game to the Texas Rangers by the score of 30–3.

No team had scored that many runs in a major league game in the modern era. A decade of losing baseball was summed up in nine innings.

The epic loss sent the Orioles into a tailspin that lasted for the rest of the season. They won just 11 of their last 40 games to finish again with 90-plus losses, just ahead of the Devil Rays. It had been almost a quarter-century since their glory years ended. That period has become a misty legend, unfathomable to later generations of fans weaned on losing teams. But there was, in fact, a time when the Orioles had routinely defeated the Yankees, Red Sox, and the rest of the American League, and it is informative to look back and see how they built a winner — not by going out and haphazardly buying the best players, but by patiently developing talent in a system populated for years by sharp baseball men who were left alone to do their jobs.

17

Fall from the Pedestal

JOHN B. WISEMAN

In the spring of 1994 my two grown daughters, Caroline and Elizabeth, planned a joint vacation to Chicago when both the Cubs and the White Sox were to be in town. As long-standing Baltimore Oriole fans who had spent many glorious nights in Memorial Stadium, they also loved the game itself enough to want to see teams play in other parks. They booked an air flight, a hotel, and bought tickets for games at Comiskey Park and Wrigley Field. When rumors of a players' strike threatened their much anticipated adventure, they went into a state of denial. It was unimaginable that players could be that unhappy about their outsized salaries, their plush work environment, and their bosses. "Join the real world," the oldest sister, Caroline, thought. "How could you not be happy? You're playing baseball, for God's sake."[1]

When the strike actually happened, Elizabeth was "ANGRY" at the players and the owners ("at baseball at large"), an anger that only subsided with the arrival of three sons. "How could they let this happen?! How could they not care about the fans the same way that we cared about them." Her love affair with baseball ended abruptly, hurt by the game's "one way street where fans paid the emotional price." Caroline's romance with baseball remained intact. She was more forgiving, like the betrayed Joseph in the Chicago production of "Joseph and the Amazing Technicolor Dreamcoat" that she and her sister saw in place of a game that watershed summer for major league baseball in 1994.

This family divide was representative of the emotional division in the nation of baseball believers that the two-month strike left in its wake. For many, including my youngest daughter, Elizabeth, the game fell from its vaunted pedestal. Baseball for her is now only a small part of the larger world of sports. An Oriole event related to her golden era with the team brought her to Camden Yards to see Eddie Murray hit his 500th home run, and she and her husband have on other occasions come back to Baltimore, mainly as social outings, with friends while she occasionally takes her sons to the new park in Washington, D.C. Her young sons play in a t-ball league and the oldest one keeps her posted on major league scores that he gleans from newspapers. But football is the favorite sport in the family and their favorite team is

John B. Wiseman in his back yard with grandsons Henry at the plate, Sam as catcher and David looking on (courtesy of Mark Alves).

the Pittsburgh Steelers, a football team she rooted for as a girl in Western Maryland. Professional football has never betrayed her.

Her older sister, like the half or so of the "baseball nation" that survived, simply refuses to relinquish her love of the game and the Orioles. She still hates the Pirates for their come-from-behind victory over the Orioles in the 1979 World Series, and their theme song that rubbed it in, "We Are Family." The Orioles have become her new family's team, including a young daughter. They all regularly attend games at Camden Yards and their home contains Oriole memorabilia from the past. Her loyalty to baseball is deeply rooted in her personal history with one team. Leaving home for college in Baltimore, she found "the most perfect job in the world" at Memorial Stadium. Even during the Orioles dreadful 1988 season that began with 21 consecutive losses, she could leave the ticket office where she worked in the fifth inning to take a free seat behind home plate. And after ten straight Oriole losing seasons she begins each new year believing a good one for her team lies ahead.

In the mid-to-late 1960s, when my two daughters were born, most Americans still believed baseball was the national game. Less than half of them now take it seriously. This slide from its popularity was not a sudden downward surge as it was for one woman and others like her, but was for many Americans rather a gradual, incremental decline of interest in the game resulting from both self-inflicted wounds and robust challenges from other sports. Unlike the abrupt disillusionment of fans following the 1919 White Sox gambling scandal, the contemporary fall from grace came in stages. Major League baseball began disaffecting modern traditional fans by its migration of teams, its expansion policy which weakened the caliber of play, its periodic short-term strikes, beginning in 1972, and by its offensive-minded changes such as the designated hitter rule in the American League in 1973, followed by alterations in the strike zone. The rising popularity of professional football ultimately delivered the coup de grace to baseball's long standing preeminence.

The turning point, many commentators believe, was the 1958 televised National Football League Championship game between the Baltimore Colts and the New York Giants seen by 45 million people, not including New York City and its environs, where the game was blacked out. The Colts' sudden-death overtime victory is still recalled by one of these viewers, The *Washington Post* book critic Jonathan Yardley, as "thrilling." He had "known nothing about pro football when the game began and was hooked on it for life when it ended." In the words of Johnny Unitas' biographer, Tom Callahan, professional football "had finally staged a championship game that could hold its own with a World Series."[2] By the time of the first Super Bowl in January 1967, professional football had not only rivaled baseball, it had changed our culture. Sunday dinners were now frequently scheduled around professional football games and conversations at school and work the next day often revolved around touchdowns and yardage gained instead of double plays and strikeouts. Monday Night football and Super Bowl Sunday soon took on lives of their own, the latter virtually adding another Christmas as far as social gatherings were concerned.

This spectator sport that moved at a faster pace than baseball converged with the rise of television in the late 1950s. Together, they spelled the end of baseball's supremacy. In a 1998 essay, "The Decline of Baseball Civilization," the columnist Charles Krauthammer noted that baseball couldn't "compete on screen with the spectacles of basketball and football." Baseball's "discrete and isolated action, with its long pauses for reflection and reverie, is the quintessential radio sport, "while in an age of television, "fast, clock-driven games … were more perfectly attuned to the quick-cut world of video."[3]

In contrast to football and basketball, many sports fans now regard major league baseball games as slow-moving, boring, and too long. Even older enthusiasts have lost their interest in a game that now features frequent batter and pitcher delays, often taking more than three hours to play. One of the reasons for the game's rise as the national pastime in the late nineteenth century was that the normal two hours or less a game ordinarily took to play could fit between the end of a man's work day, or child's school day, and the family evening meal. This faster pace of baseball continued into the 1950s. One of the contributors to this volume who played semi-professional baseball recalls leaving a Baltimore steel mill at 3:15, arriving at batting practice before 5:30, and returning home by 8:30.

Now, most televised baseball games, especially in October, start in the evening and run late into the night. Krauthammer asks "how many people actually saw live" one of the most dramatic baseball moments of the previous 25 years, Carlton Fisk's 1975 World Series home run, "the one where he bounces up and down like a rabbit and coaxes the ball to stay fair. He hit it at 12:34 A.M." By contrast nearly 100 million watched the stunning conclusion of the 2008 Super Bowl about 10 P.M.

Fifteen years before Fisk's breath-taking home run, lots of kids and adults in Pennsylvania were awake to see what they would swear was the most thrilling event in their sport spectator lives, Bill Mazeroski's decisive bottom of the ninth homerun in the seventh game of the 1960 World Series against the mighty Yankees. The last time the Pirates were in the World Series had been in 1927 and in three of the 1960 Series games the Yankees had beaten up on them with lopsided scores. The Yankees, on the other hand, were in the Series so often after World War II that many New Yorkers claimed it as a birthright. In 1960 they featured the new Murderer's Row of Mantle, Maris, and Berra. If there ever was a baseball David facing Goliath, Mazeroski, the scrappy little second baseman known mostly for singles, fit the part perfectly. So, in this case, did the role of television when baseball was still king of the hill and television executives knew it, working with Major League baseball to schedule games before bedtime. In the rural Rostraver Township in Western Pennsylvania, where the Pirates were demigods, the final Series game was piped into the high school auditorium where baseball replaced the three R's that glorious afternoon and where students acquired a new mythical hero.[4] At Forbes Field, pandemonium erupted after Mazeroski's home run, requiring him to weave his way through delirious fans as he rounded the bases on the way home. Suspense had given way to the sheer joy that in 1960 could still occur in the Mudvilles of America.

It was the joy of the game, its moments of suspense, and the fan camaraderie that it builds, that first attracted a young girl in Cumberland, Maryland, in the 1950s. My wife, Earleen, acquired her love of the game in her grandmother's kitchen, listening to the play of the Pittsburgh Pirates' game on the radio. The games fit into her grandmother's meal preparation time. As she became more knowledgeable about baseball the young girl kept a box score of the games to reconstruct them for her brother when he returned from his paper route. The play-by-play flow of baseball was ideally suited to conversion to personal box scores or those that appeared later in newspapers, to creative reconstruction by radio announcers who made the game come alive in your living room, or to your presence at the park to study what Krauthammer calls "the slow, uncoiling game." In contrast, televised baseball begs for highlights and now features endless replays, multiple overzealous commentators, and close-ups superimposed on the unfolding play on the field.

Television screens also offered its viewers a growing array of other fast-moving spectator sports. Professional football's rising popularity by the 1960s continued unabated with Monday Night Football, league expansion, proliferating championship games, and shrewd scheduling. By the 1970s it supplanted baseball as the nation's favorite sport. Professional basketball also challenged baseball in popular appeal, college basketball's March Madness has become truly that, while auto racing is reaching beyond its earlier southern blue collar fan base to capture a national audience.

Basketball's rise in popular appeal can be partially explained by its rapid growth in cities. As America became more urban, so did the sport that lent itself to city playgrounds and required only a ball, an elevated basket, concrete, and as few as two players—or even just one. City basketball became especially alluring to African Americans in the inner cities who could not always afford the more expensive equipment and the playing fields that organized baseball requires. Basketball became the "cool" sport among young black Americans, while baseball's attraction declined. In 1975 African Americans comprised 27 percent of major league baseball players, but the proportion has dropped to 8.5, less than their proportional presence in the national population. The black fan base is even lower. In professional basketball the proportion of black players rose from zero in 1949 to 77 percent in 1998.[5]

One of major league baseball's hopes for the future lies in its appeal to young people in the Caribbean basin where one of the enduring themes of the social history of major league baseball still occurs. The game that first enabled poor (white) native-born Americans, and later their African American counterparts, to achieve economic success and stature, has now become the ladder for impoverished Hispanics coming from south of our border. The percentage of foreign-born major league players has climbed steadily to 29 percent in 2007. Most of them were Latino or of Latino descent. Some of them have brought with them the exciting kind of play that exists in the Caribbean region—"the quicker, passionate, even more confrontational style of play," that Tim Wendel has described in his essay on Hispanics players who don't have to overcome walls to migrate North.

Not even an ocean can stop the migration of Japanese into the American Major Leagues. While their numbers are smaller than for Hispanics, they are nonetheless prized by team owners here and by fans in Japan who forego sleep to watch their idols play on transatlantic cables. For the richest major league owners, money seems little obstacle in securing a player who can take them to their own Promised Land, and now to what is more appropriately than ever called the World Series. The Boston Red Sox recently dished out $101.3 million dollars to Daisuke Matsuzaka, veteran of the Japanese majors, and to his team's owner.

Obscured in this financial extravagance is why the game has become so popular in the country we once fiercely fought in war. In many ways, the early history of its appeal in this far away land paralleled its history in late nineteenth century America. We introduced our national game to the Japanese as part of an explosion in bilateral trade, but it took hold because the game's dynamics fit Japan's culture almost as well as it once did our own. The face-off between the pitcher and batter is another version of the face-off in Asian martial arts. Teamwork is also highly valued in Japan and is perhaps more easily attained in that homogenous country. Moreover, the Japanese belief in the ethic of practice often produces perfection. Few Japanese players exhibit this lesson better than Ichiro Suzuki, the most consistent hitter in the game over the past decade. When the Seattle Mariners offered to help him find a place to live, Suzuki requested three bedrooms, one for himself, one for visiting family, and a third one, that could be rimmed with mirrors, for practicing his swing.

American boys still dream about becoming major league players and attendance at major league games is at an all-time high. Yet, in the country of its birth, baseball is no longer the major staple in American culture, as it was a half century ago when GI's in World War II used baseball terms such as Texas leaguer as passwords near enemy lines. The appeal of certain venues such as Yankee Stadium, Chavez Ravine, Fenway Park, and Wrigley Field helps to explain the rising attendance, along with the greater number of teams and some new viewer-friendly parks that attract customers, much like shopping teenagers seeking companionship with friends at a mall, as well as loyal fans. Among the new ballpark attractions are restaurants where the games are watched on television, wine decks for casual conversations, and luxurious corporate-owned skyboxes in which employees and their families dine on fine fare. But, the cost of tickets, parking, and ball park food for an average family has grown too expensive for many fans to attend games in major league stadiums. Hence, the resurgent crowds in the minor leagues, where the prices are low and the seats are close to the field of players, some of whom live with families in the stands.

It is the fan's connection with teams and their players that was once the hallmark of major league baseball, a bond that could be almost religious in its depth. This was my wife's experience with the game in the 1950s. As a young girl she adored her grandmother, who happened to love the Pirates, the team whose games were broadcast by radio in Cumberland, Maryland. In her grandmother's kitchen she never learned much about cooking, but she certainly learned how baseball was played, found idols, and a team to love. It became the Brooklyn Dodgers, mysteriously brought to town by another radio station. She prayed at mass for those perennial World Series' chasers and as a teenager her idea of paradise was to see a game at Ebbets Field watching her favorite, Clem Labine, pitch, and even more heavenly yet, to be sitting in Ebbets Field watching her team finally win the World Series. Crestfallen by their 1958 departure for the West Coast, unfathomably far away, she nonetheless continued to keep track of her team through the local newspaper, the *Sporting News*, and, of course, the radio.

The migration of the Dodgers and their National League rival, the New York Giants, to the West Coast, both in 1958, left New Yorkers with just one baseball team to enshrine and left Yankee atheists with no secular church to attend. It also destroyed the symmetry of morning newspaper box scores in the East, ruined as it was by disparate time zones. Meanwhile, that same year, a newer religion — professional football — won millions of converts among sports loving Americans as they watched the Colts' sudden-death victory over the other Giants on television. While baseball had broken the faith of some of its fans, professional football had won legions of believers. My wife never liked football, but neither did she fall completely in love with another baseball team. For her and others, baseball's slide had begun.

My own experience with the game was different because I played it. As a boy, baseball was the alpha and omega of my summer life. Not even a finger caught in a car door on the way to a game could keep me off the field; my father simply produced a splint, and the game went on. He also put me on a bus to Comiskey Park in 1951 so that I could see my favorite team, the Chicago White Sox, play a doubleheader against the Yankees while he was attending a convention meeting.

A young John Wiseman batting with his father, Chalmer, in Idaho Falls, Idaho, in the late 1940s.

Nellie Fox, Minnie Minoso, and Chico Carrasquel were my summer heroes. The color of their skins and their background were a matter of indifference to an innocent teenager in overwhelmingly white South Dakota. What mattered was their panache and the fact that the local radio station carried the White Sox games into my bedroom. As was the case with millions of other boys, my weak hitting shortened the years of my team play. Then, during the tumultuous 1960s, when baseball paled in significance to larger, contentious, national issues, the game became for me largely an afterthought, except for the Giants-Dodgers series, fiercely competitive that they were. Willie Mays, Willie McCovey, and Juan Marichal gave me a team to be passionate about again, the way I was once about the White Sox in the days of Fox, Minoso, and Carrasquel.

Years later, in the late '70s and early '80s, my two daughters helped to keep my continuity with baseball intact by luring me into the television room to watch the Orioles. This was toward the end of the quarter century in which the Orioles reigned as the most successful — and exciting — team in baseball. We all, even Dad, viewed the game with a kind of innocence. "There were days," recalls Elizabeth, "of playing catch in the front yard with the radio facing out through our bedroom window so we could listen to the game." When Eddie Murray came to the plate in a close contest in late innings we would stop throwing the ball and join in the stadium chant — E D D I E E E. He rarely disappointed us. None of them did for more than a few moments and some of them became endearing. Elizabeth named one of her teddy bears "Flanagan" after the crafty Oriole southpaw and often fell asleep listening to the game on the radio with her companion nearby.

Then there were the" beloved trips" to the games. Under the guise of taking an historic tour of Baltimore — to placate their teachers — I took my daughters out of school so that we could arrive early at Memorial Stadium long before the evening game began. This gave us time to follow our ritual, as our trips were the same every time for nearly a decade. I carefully prepared a picnic supper that featured barbecued chicken, a drink mixture of several juices, rolls, homemade brownies, and what we came to call "obligatory" apples (usually left uneaten). We parked blocks away from Memorial Stadium (for free) and so as to allow the excitement to mount as we approached the park. Once inside and settled in our seats in Section 34, the girls would dash toward the field to get autographs. That still left us time to watch infield practice, to eat the first course of our dinner, and to get our scorecards ready before the game began.

Our presence, we believed, assured an Oriole win. On 25 consecutive games to Memorial Stadium our team won, thanks in part to an unkempt cab driver named Wild Bill Hagy, the team's unofficial cheerleader, who led the cheering from our section. In crucial games he moved closer to the field of play where he forced his overweight body into the shapes O-R-I-O-L-E-S, while standing on the Oriole dugout roof. Our catechism also required we stay until the end of the game, even when it rained and the Orioles were far ahead. Then we lingered outside the stadium for autographs despite the three hour trip home. Over the years Memorial Stadium became our home away from home.

When my daughters went off to colleges in Baltimore, this family ritual ended. Major league baseball gradually became more of a mental exercise for me rather than a do-or-die loyalty to a team. At the dwindling number of games that I attended at Memorial Stadium I concentrated on certain parts of them. In one I focused on the mound artistry of Jim Palmer at the end of his long career in 1984. In another, in 1988, I zeroed in on the bats that players used. An epiphany occurred that night in the year that nothing had gone right for the Orioles. They were playing the Red Sox and Wade Boggs, one of

Wild Bill Hagy leads his cheering section at Memorial Stadium in Baltimore (courtesy Hearst News American Photographic Collection in the University of Maryland Special Collections Library, College Park).

the game supreme hitters, went two for four. I noticed that many of the Oriole batsmen were lugging heavy bats, apparently equating their weight with home runs, while Boggs controlled his lighter weight bat more successfully. On the long drive home after another dismal Oriole defeat I decided to call Boggs the next morning. I found out where the Rex Sox slept and timed my telephone call to Boggs' room perfectly. After a quick introduction to a startled but willing listener, I asked about the size of his bat. He informed me that his bat was light in weight (as, he told me, was Ted Williams') but that the distribution of the weight was even more important to providing bat control and success. When I asked him if the team's hitting coach encouraged young players to follow Williams' and Boggs' example, he said yes, but it was their choice to make.

A multitude of choices that players, fans, and owners have made, has contributed to the game's decline. Expansion and huge salaries weakened players' loyalty to a team which in turn disaffected fans. Sports enthusiasts also had a growing spectrum of contests to select from as their favorite respite from work. The choices made by baseball club owners, beginning in the 1960s, to brake the fall of public favor may have inadvertently hurt as much as it helped. Their decisions to lower the pitching mound, to widen the strike zone, and to establish the designated hitter were all meant to add offensive power. But more runs and more hitters also meant longer games which in turn decreased the number of older viewers who constituted the largest part of traditional baseball followers.

Just as attendance and viewing audiences began to rebound in the 1970s, the Players' Association chose to mount its challenge to the owners' control over their economic lives. In the wake of the pivotal individual rebellions of the late 60s, characterized by Sandy Koufax's and Don Drysdale's salary holdouts and Curt Flood's pivotal refusal to accept a trade, the players union collectivized the revolt in 1972. The stakes—the owners' contribution to the pension plan—were small that year. But this first players' strike of the twentieth century, according to one prominent baseball historian, Steve Treder, "utterly changed the players' understanding of their own power and directly set in motion the chain of events that led to the establishment of the free agency in 1976."[6] Continued stoppages, until the number reached eight, over amounts of money that staggered most people, tried the patience of even baseball loving Americans. In the past, players' salaries had often significantly exceeded the wages of their loyal fans. But the published sums of salaries that emerged from this modern war between capital and labor accelerated to truly astronomical levels that made the minimum wage for players ten times higher than beginning teachers' salaries—with millionaire incomes to soon follow. Even former players resented the vast disparity between what they had received in the golden era of baseball in the 1950s and what the super stars now take home. One of them has calculated that Alex Rodriguez earns more for one game than this former player made in seven years in the major leagues, beginning in 1944.[7] Owners were equally insatiable for wealth in their quest for the vast television revenues, league expansions, and a surge of new stadium construction at public expense that featured new luxury suites reserved for corporate America.

This spiraling escalade of gratuitous wealth reached its most inglorious heights during the strike of 1994, one that ended the season a month and a half early and denied the nation a World Series that not even two World Wars cost us. In response to the players' hard-won right of salary arbitration and free agency, the owners called for a salary cap and special allocations to small market teams. The negotiating impasse that ensued between the players' union and the owners prompted the owners to unilaterally impose a salary cap which prompted the players' union to call the strike. To many lifelong baseball fans, the 1994 strike became the Humpty Dumpty of their favorite game.

Others took refuge in new stadiums, the exploits of some players, the nostalgic appeal of the television production of Ken Burns' series on the old ball game, some movies that captured its former place in the American imagination, and eventually fantasy baseball. Beginning with the construction of the aesthetically pleasing and intimate Camden Yards, the new parks were inviting to customers who could be closer to the game in play, if not the players' lives, the way they once were when they both lived in similar neighborhoods. Baltimore also provided lapsed baseball fans with the heroics of Cal Ripken, Jr., a player who almost single-handedly restored unadulterated honor to the game. For proud Oriole fans Ripken allowed them to forget a string of losing seasons. For others he represented our better selves, not wanting to get up to go to work some days but knowing we could and should. Here was a player who exemplified the traditional work ethic, and whose honed skills, stamina, and intelligence personified what greatness on the field almost always required. As though he were scripted for the part in a movie that would celebrate everything good about the game, Ripken was born an hour's drive from Baltimore, spent his youth at Oriole spring training camps where his father coached, and played all of his 21 years with one team, one that unceremoniously fired the manager who was his mentor and dad. For fans who hungered for player loyalty to a team, Ripken was a gift from heaven.

The homerun barrage also brought some fans back to the ballpark where attendance figures rose to record heights before the 1994 strike, and then reached even great heights in the summer of 1998 that featured the homerun-record chase of Mark McGwire and Sammy Sosa. The fans' thirst for homeruns at the end of the twentieth century revived the deflowered game the way Babe Ruth did following the Black Sox scandal eighty years before. Even my disillusioned daughter and I drove to Pittsburgh to see McGwire hit one of his towering homeruns.

Baseball has historically undergone ebbs in popularity, both in the lives of families and in the nation at large, since gambling tainted the game in the 1860s and 1870s, then more dramatically in 1919. With each ebb, corrective measures have reversed the decline, returning the flow of the game's appeal. Following the capital-labor war of the 1880s a reserve clause stabilized the business side of the game. After the fixing of the 1919 Series a stern, independent, and punitive Commissioner halted, if not ended player gambling on the outcome on a game they played. These were decisive steps that removed turmoil and scandal in the game which restored the faith of fans. Fortunately, for the national game, these decisive actions were followed by players like Babe Ruth who not only enlivened play on the field, but whose extravagant personality fit the roaring 20s. Decades later, in the aftermath of the 1994 strike, McGwire and Sosa provided excitement and Ripken embodied stamina and loyalty.

One can only speculate what will follow in the wake of the unfolding steroid controversy, the newest cheating crisis that has tainted the game. Major league baseball lacks a strong commissioner who is inclined to act decisively the way Landis once did. Nor can he act unilaterally on the drug issue because he has to deal with the head of the players' union. Senator George Mitchell's exhaustive December 2007 report on steroid usage named errant players. They were largely marginal players who needed enhancement chemicals to remain on the roster, or stars plagued by injury. Drugs gave

John Wiseman with his daughters (Caroline, left, and Elizabeth) at Caroline Brady's Camden Yards wedding reception, 2001. Elizabeth Alves was a bridesmaid.

them the added competitive edge to perform better in a game that now pays extraordinarily well. The Mitchell Report found fault with the commissioner, the union, and the owners—all who looked the other way in a kind of conspiracy of inaction lasting more than a decade. The use of performance-enhancing drugs has been too tempting for players to resist, and, unless effective testing is enforced, cheating is unlikely to go away. Moreover, new, undetectable drugs that give players a boost are apt to come along. One can argue that players and owners have often behaved selfishly in the past, as does a society that often condones cheating. This reality simply confirms baseball as a reflection of American life.

So has the divided emotional appeal of the game within my family mirrored that of the nation of baseball fans who were once united. While my own love affair—and Caroline's—with the game continues, Earleen's, and Elizabeth's has waned. Perhaps Elizabeth's sons will inspire a revival of her love for the game as she and her sister once did for me. As for Earleen, the musical chairs shuffle of players to the highest bidding teams has diminished her loyalty to a favorite team, always the hallmark of her love of the game. And while I watch parts of many major league games on television and religiously check the boxscores and standings in the morning newspaper, I am waiting for a new Willie Mays or Minnie Minoso to stir my passion again.

Until that happens I'll probably join the parade to minor league parks like the one in Idaho Falls, Idaho, where my baseball roots lie. It was in Idaho as a young boy that I marveled at Earl "Hi Ho" Silverthorne chasing fly balls in the outfield and stealing bases, always losing his cap in the process, while the fans chanted "Hi Ho." For me, and I suspect for many of the readers of this book, baseball remains the best game there is. It's there to be filled in with more major league players and owners worthy of their role. That will bring joy again to many townships of America and perhaps restore true ownership of the game to where it belongs—to us. That, after all, is how it all began.

Chapter Notes

Chapter 1

1. *Decatur* (Ill.) *Republican*, October 29, 1868.
2. Each of the examples described in this paper is explored in greater detail in my two-volume book, *A Game of Inches* (Chicago: Ivan R. Dee, 2006).
3. *Cleveland Herald*, February 21, 1884.
4. *Detroit Free Press*, May 9, 1886.
5. The *Boston Globe*, for example, wrote dismissively on September 9, 1873: "Barlow acknowledged his weakness at the bat by attempting the black game, but [A. G.] Spalding got him out twice, and the attempt, which is rather a weak one for a professional club, was a failure."
6. James Wood, as told to Frank G. Menke, "Baseball in By-Gone Days," part 2, syndicated column, *Marion* (Ohio) *Star*, August 15, 1916.
7. Clarence Deming, "Old Days in Baseball," *Outing*, June 1902, 357–358.
8. *Sporting News*, March 3, 1894.
9. *New York Clipper*, April 5, 1879.
10. Peter Morris, *Level Playing Fields: How the Groundskeeping Murphy Brothers Shaped Baseball* (Lincoln: University of Nebraska Press, 2007).
11. Hall of Fame pitcher Tim Keefe briefly tried umpiring in the 1890s after his playing career ended. But he soon resigned, explaining: "My sole reason for leaving the field and for then and there determining to sever my connection with the national game forever is that base ball has reached a stage where it is absolutely disgraceful. It is the fashion now for every player engaged in a game to froth at the mouth and emit shrieks of anguish whenever a decision is given which is adverse to the interests of the club to which he belongs. This may not be wearying to the general public, but it is certainly disgusting to the umpire who gives decisions disinterestedly and as he sees the plays. The continual senseless and puerile kicking at every decision has been infernally trying to me, and I have been considering for some time whether I had better not resign. I can evidently please nobody." The last straw for Keefe came when old friend and teammate Roger Connor protested one of his rulings (*Brooklyn Eagle*, July 13, 1896).
12. *Janesville Daily Gazette*, March 28, 1905, 2.

Chapter 2

1. The nickname was given in 1892, according to *Cy Young: Baseball's Legendary Giant*, by Ralph H. Romig (Philadelphia: Dorrance, 1964), p. 29.
2. Quoted in the *New York Sun*, republished in the *Morning Herald*, August 17, 1897, p. 7.
3. Keeler said this to Abe Yager, baseball writer for the *Brooklyn Daily Eagle*, according to several secondary accounts.
4. See *Baltimore: The Building of an American City*, by Sherry Olson (Baltimore: Johns Hopkins University Press, 1980), pp. 238–40.
5. Quoted in *The Sun* (Baltimore), December 17, 1898, p. 8.
6. *Morning Herald*, March 18, 1901, p. 4.

Chapter 4

1. Warren Brown as quoted in Jim Enright, *Chicago Cubs* (New York: Macmillan, 1975), p. 124.
2. Kostya Kennedy and Richard Deitsch, "Fine Print," Scorecard section of *Sports Illustrated*, September 23, 2002, p. 26.
3. Charles C. Alexander, *Our Game: An American Baseball History* (New York: Henry Holt, 1991), p. 90.
4. William Wrigley, Jr., the chewing gum magnate, became the principal stockholder of the Cubs in 1919 and sole owner in 1921.
5. Jerome Holtzman and George Vass, *The Chicago Cubs Encyclopedia* (Philadelphia: Temple University Press, 1997), p. 299.
6. Enright, *Chicago Cubs*, pp. 119, 121.

7. This story is told in Peter Golenbock, *Wrigleyville: A Magical History Tour of the Chicago Cubs* (New York: St. Martin's, 1996), pp. 117–118.
8. Goldenbock, *Wrigleyville*, p. 118.
9. "Chicago is Supreme," in *The Greatest Sports Stories from the Chicago Tribune*, ed. By Arch Ward (New York: A.S. Barnes, 1953), p. 75.
10. Ty Cobb, with Al Stump, *My Life in Baseball: The True Record* (Garden City, NY: Doubleday, 1961), p. 72.
11. Lawrence Ritter and Donald Honig, *The Image of Their Greatness* (New York: Crown, 1979), p. 30.
12. Quotation from Daniel Okrent and Steve Wulf, *Baseball Anecdotes* (New York: Oxford University Press, 1989), p. 61.
13. Johnny Evers, quoted in Peter Golenboch, *Wrigleyville*. p. 135.
14. Dennis DeValeria and Jean Burke DeValeria, *Honus Wagner: A Biography* (New York: Henry Holt, 1995), p. 186.
15. Charles Dryden, "A Pennant is Blown," *Chicago Tribune*, September 23, 1908, reprinted in Ward, *The Greatest Sport Stories*, p. 89.
16. Warren Brown, *The Chicago Cubs* (New York: G.P. Putnam's Sons, 1946), p. 33; Lowell Reidenbaugh, for the editors of *The Sporting News*, *Baseball's Hall of Fame: Cooperstown, Where The Legends Live Forever* (New York: Crescent, 1993), p. 44.
17. Jim Langford, *The Game Is Never Over: An Appreciative History of the Chicago Cubs* (South Bend, IN: Icarus, 1982), p. 33.
18. David W. Anderson, *More Than Merkle: A History of the Best and Most Exciting Baseball Season in History* (Lincoln: University of Nebraska Press, 2000), p. 62.
19. Frank L. Chance, *The Bride and the Pennant* (Chicago: Laird & Lee, 1910).
20. Holtzman and Vass, *The Chicago Cubs Encyclopedia*, p. 281.
21. Cited in Warren N. Wilbert, *A Cunning Kind of Play: The Cubs-Giants Rivalry, 1876–1932* (Jefferson, NC: McFarland, 2002), p. 120.
22. Evers' brother Joe also played in the major leagues, with the Giants, but only for one game in 1913 without getting an at bat.
23. John J. Evers and Hugh Fullerton, *Touching Second: The Science of Baseball* (Chicago: Reilly and Britton, 1910).
24. Okrent and Wulf, *Baseball Anecdotes*, p. 52.
25. Quoted in David Quentin Voigt, *American Baseball, Volume II: From the Commissioners to Continental Expansion* (Norman: University of Oklahoma Press, 1970), p. 33.
26. William J. Slocum and Bill Klem, "Diamond Rhubarbs," *Collier's*, April 14, 1951, p. 30.
27. Enright, *Chicago Cubs*, p. 121, 123.
28. Enright, *Chicago Cubs*, p. 123.
29. Harold Seymour, *Baseball: The Golden Age* (New York: Oxford University Press, 1971), p. 118.
30. Brown, *The Chicago Cubs*, p. 69.
31. Data from Okrent and Wulf, *Baseball Anecdotes*, p. 52; and Enright, *Chicago Cuba*, p. 124.
32. Bruce Chadwick, *The Chicago Cubs: Memories and Memorabilia of the Wrigley Wonders* (New York: Abbeville, 1994), p. 38.
33. *Baseball Encyclopedia*, 8th Edition., ed. Rick Wolff (New York: Macmillan, 1990), pp. 163–78.
34. Okrent and Wulf, *Baseball Anecdotes*, p. 52.
35. Bill James, *The Bill James Historical Baseball Abstract* (New York: Villard, 1986), p. 344.
36. James, p. 370.
37. James, 333–334.
38. Reidenbaugh, *Baseball's Hall of Fame*, p. 83.

Chapter 5

1. Lawrence S. Ritter, *The Glory of Their Times*, New Enlarged Edition, (New York: William Morrow, 1984), p. 155.
2. *Ibid.*
3. Ritter, *Glory*, p. 157.
4. Interview with Richard Johnson, March 2002.
5. *Boston Globe*, March 11, 1912.
6. *Boston Post*, March 2, 1908.
7. *Cleveland Plain Dealer*, April 14, 1915.
8. Ed Walton, *Red Sox Triumphs and Tragedy*, (New York: Stein and Day, 1980), p. 63.
9. Quote in wwwdiamondangle.com.
10. *Boston Globe*, July 9, 1912.
11. Lawrence Ritter's interview of Joe Wood, 1963 transcript, Archival Library, University of Notre Dame.
12. Joseph L. Reichler, ed., *The Baseball Encyclopedia*, Fifth Edition, (New York: Macmillan, 1985), p. 2094.
13. *Boston Globe*, October 9, 1912.
14. Glenn Stout and Richard A. Johnson, *Red Sox Century* (New York: Houghton Mifflin, 2000), p. 89.
15. *Ibid.*
16. *Ibid.*
17. *Ibid.*
18. *Boston Globe*, October 16, 1912.
19. *New York Times*, October 16, 1912.
20. *Boston Globe*, October 16, 1912.

21. Speaker's foul pop up was hit about two-thirds of the way up the first base line. Clearly, it was first baseman Fred Merkle's ball. But Matty kept on hollering for Chief Meyers, the slow-footed catcher, to make the play. Speaker always denied it, but writer Fred Lieb claimed that Speaker was hollering Chief's name, too. The ball fell untouched, giving Speaker a reprieve. Spoke promptly drove in the tying run with a long single to right.

22. Robert Smith, *Baseball in the Afternoon*, (New York: Simon and Schuster 1993), pp. 232–235. Charles Alexander, *Ty Cobb* (New York: Oxford University Press, 1984).

23. Wood-Ritter interview transcript.

24. Ibid.

Chapter 6

1. Jefferson, NC: McFarland, 1996. Other helpful biographical works on Wagner include William R. Cobb, ed., *Honus Wagner: On His Life and Baseball* (Ann Arbor, MI: Sports Media, 2006); Dennis De Valeria and Jeanne Burke De Valeria, *Honus Wagner: A Biography* (Pittsburgh: University of Pittsburgh Press, 1998); and William Hageman, *Honus: The Life and Times of a Baseball Hero* (Champaign, IL: Sagamore, 1996).

2. Lanham, MD: Scarecrow, 1998. See also W. Harrison Daniel, *Jimmie Foxx: The Life and Times of a Baseball Hall of Famer, 1907–1967* (Jefferson, NC: McFarland, 1996).

3. There are many fine statistical sources for both Wagner's and Foxx's careers. The following websites were among the sources consulted for the information contained in the next two paragraphs: Baseball-Reference.com, Major League Statistics and Information, http://www.baseball-reference.com/; CMG Worldwide, Honus Wagner, http://www.honuswagner.com/highlights.htm; Society for American Baseball Research, The Baseball Biography Project, http://bioproj.sabr.org/; David W. Smith, Retrosheet.org, http://www.retrosheet.org/; Baseball Almanac — the Official Baseball History Site, http://www.baseball-almanac.com/index.shtml; and tbi, The Baseball Index, http://www.baseballindex.org/tbi.asp.

4. "Bill Veeck," Baseball-Reference.com, http://www.baseball-reference.com/bullpen/Bill_Veeck. January 4, 2008.

5. "Babe Ruth Quotes," Baseball Almanac, http://www.baseball-almanac.com/ quotes/quoruth.shtml. January 4, 2008.

Chapter 8

1. David Alan Corbin, *Life, Work and Culture in the Coal Fields: The Southern West Virginia Miners, 1880–1922* (Urbana and Chicago: University of Illinois Press, 1981), 218; Ronald D. Eller, *Miners, Millhands, and Mountaineers: Industrialization of the Appalachian South, 1880–1930* (Knoxville: University of Tennessee Press, 1982); and John Alexander Williams, *West Virginia* (New York: W.W. Norton, 1976) provide background on the southern West Virginia coalfields.

2. John C. Hennen, *The Americanization of West Virginia: Creating a Modern Industrial State, 1916–1925* (Lexington: University of Kentucky Press, 1996), 101; Corbin, *Life, Work and Culture in the Coal Fields*, 35–37.

3. Heenen, *Americanization of West Virginia*, 104; Eller, *Miners, Millhands, and Mountaineers*, 220–21.

4. Baseball in Bluefield and surrounding areas in 1924 and 1925 is covered in Stuart McGehee, "Bluefield Baseball: The Tradition of a Century," *Goldenseal* 16 (Spring 1990) 50–51; Stephanie Siegel, "Coal Camp Baseball," *Coal People Magazine*," 27 (December 2002) 25–26; *Bluefield Daily Telegram*, May 31, June 29–July 21, August 1–September 15, 1924; May 28, 29, July 31, August 6, 1925.

5. *Welch Daily News*, October 4–7, 1924.

6. Charles C. Alexander, *John McGraw* (New York: Penguin, 1988), 242–43; *The Sporting News*, March 11, 1920.

7. Rhonda Tanney Coleman, "Coal Miners and Their Communities in Southern Appalachia, 1925–1941," *West Virginia Historical Society Quarterly* 15 (April 2001) 9; Paul J. Nyden, "Coal Town Baseball," *Goldenseal* 6 (October–December 1980) 31–39.

8. Jean Battlo, *Pictorial History of McDowell County, 1858–1958* (Parsons, WV: McClain 2003), 245.

9. *The Sporting News*, December 21, 1939.

10. Crandall A. Shifflett, *Coal Towns: Life, Work, and Culture in Company Towns of Southern Appalachia, 1880–1960* (Knoxville: University of Tennessee Press, 1991), 162.

11. Nyden, "Coal Town Baseball," 37–38.

12. Balllo, *McDowell County*, 245; Coleman, "Coal Miners and Their Communities," 1–11.

13. *Bluefield Daily Telegram*, June 14, 1987.

14. Coleman, "Coal Miners and Their Communities," 9; Nyden, "Coal Town Baseball" 31–39.

15. Siegel, "Coal Camp Baseball," 25.

16. For Raleigh County baseball in the late-'20s see *Raleigh Register*, especially April 7, 17, May 26, 31, 1927, September 1–20, 1928, April 1–September 16, 1929.

17. David S. Matz and John L. Evers, "Derringer, Samuel Paul," in David Porter (ed.), *Biographical Dictionary of American Sports:*

Baseball (Westport, CT: Greenwood, 2000), 377–78.
18. *Logan Banner*, June 21, July 19, 1929, July 29, September 12, 16, 23, 1930.
19. *Raleigh Register* and *Beckley Post-Herald* covered the Raleigh County League, and to a lesser extent the UMW League, in the 1930s. April 19, May 10, 1932.
20. Coleman, "Coal Miners and Their Communities," 8–10; Nyden, "Coal Town Baseball," 31–32.
21. Darrell J. Howard, *"Sunday Coming": Black Baseball in Virginia* (Jefferson, NC: McFarland, 2002), 37, 44, 194; Shifflet, *Coal Towns,* 164.
22. *Beckley Post-Herald,* August 24, 27, 1940; *Raleigh Register*, September 30, October 2, 7, 14, 1940. Coleman, "Miners and Their Communities," 10.

Chapter 9

1. These figures are based on a summary of quoted capacities in the Baltimore *Afro-American,* 1929 through 1936, and the *Cleveland Indian Yearbook,* 1957 edition.
2. Author's interview with Arthur G. Toll, nephew of Eddie Gottlieb, at Toll's home in Norristown, Pennsylvania, 5 April 1972.
3. James H. Bready, *The Home Team* (Baltimore: Moore and co., 1959), p. 82.
4. Author's interview with Richard D. Powell, former general manager, Baltimore Elite Giants Baseball Club, at Powell's home, Baltimore, 14 January 1971.
5. *Afro-American* (National Edition, Washington, Dec.), 2 April 1938.
6. Ibid., 17 September 1938. See also *Baltimore Afro-American,* 8 August, 30 August, and 10 September 1938.
7. *New York Age,* 27 August, 1938; *Toledo Blade,* 6 May 1939.
8. *Baltimore Afro-American,* 1 April 1939; Philadelphia *Afro-American,* 6 May 1939.
9. See *Baltimore Afro-American,* 27 May 1939.
10. *New York Age,* 10 June 1939; *Afro-American* (National Edition, Washington, D.C.), 3 June 1939; *New York Age*, 20 September 1939.
11. *New York Age*, 2 March 1940.
12. Baltimore *Sun,* 13 April 1940; *Baltimore Afro-American,* 18 May and 8 June 1940.
13. Ibid., 22 June 1940.
14. *New York Times,* 24 July 1940; *Afro-American* (National Edition, Washington, D.C.), 27 July 1940.
15. Author's interview with Powell, 14 January 1971.
16. Baltimore *Sun,* 13 March 1943; *Baltimore Afro-American,* 10 April 1943.

17. *Baltimore Afro-American*, 1 and 22 May 1943; Baltimore *Evening Sun,* 29 May 1943; *Afro-American* (National Edition, Washington, D.C.), 24 July 1943; Chicago *Defender,* 7 August 1943.
18. *Baltimore Afro-American*, 17 June and 8 July 1944.
19. Ibid., 27 June 1946.
20. Philadelphia *Evening Bulletin,* 10 June 1941; *Baltimore Afro-American,* 31 March 1945; *New York Times*, 14 April 1945; *Baltimore Afro-American,* 30 March 1946; Baltimore *Sunday American,* 5 May 1946.
21. Baltimore *Sun,* 11 May 1946; *Baltimore Afro-American,* 24 August. 1946.
22. Quoted in *Baltimore Afro-American*, 27 June 1946. See also ibid., 17 September 1947 and 25 June 1949; Pittsburgh *Courier*, 4 September 1948; Cleveland *Call and Post* 8 July 1950.
23. *Baltimore Afro-American*, 14 October 1950.
24. See Los Angeles *Sentinel,* 30 May, 18 July, and 12 September 1946.
25. Cleveland *Call and Post*, 23 July and 13 August 1949.
26. Author's telephone interview with Sam Lacy, sports editor, *Baltimore Afro-American*, Baltimore, 11 January 1971, and with Robert P. Elmer, former booking agent of Eddie Gottlieb in Baltimore, at offices of the Baltimore Clippers, Baltimore Civic Center, 14 November 1973. See also author's November-December 1970 survey of thirty-five former fans of both races who attended Elites' games. Principal question dealt with the reasons for the Elites' moving from Baltimore after the 1950 season; some responders added comments dealing with the actual experience of attending a Negro-League game at the time.
27. *Baltimore Afro-American,* 27 July 1952; author's telephone interview with Richard D. Powell, former general manager, Baltimore Elite Giants, at Social Security Administration, Baltimore, 12 January 1971.
28. Ibid.
29. Ibid.
30. Author's interview with Lacy, 11 January 1971.
31. Author's interview with Powell at Powell's residence, Baltimore, 14 January 1971.
32. *Baltimore Afro-American,* 14 May and 14 October 1950.
33. Author's interview with Powell, 14 January 1971.
34. Author's interview with Lacy, 11 January 1971, and Powell, 14 January 1971. See also fresco Thompson (Brooklyn Dodgers vice president) to Richard D. Powell, 1 May 1951, in Powell's possession, and Louis Ressin's response to survey questionnaire (dated 3 De-

cember 1971) dealing with Elite Giants' collapse. Ressin was a fan of the Elites from 1944–50.

35. Author's interview with Powell, 14 January 1971, and with Laymon Yokely, former pitching star of the Baltimore Black Sox, at Yokely's shoeshine parlor, Pennsylvania Avenue, Baltimore, 2 December 1970.

36. Pittsburgh *Courier*, 23 June 1951.

37. Author's interview with Lacy, 11 January 1971.

38. See n. 26.

Chapter 10

1. Oldpoetry.com/opoem/9777-Countee Cullen-Incident, February 9, 2007. At the outset of this essay, I must point out that my teacher has been Jules Tygiel's magisterial book, *Baseball's Great Experiment: Jackie Robinson and His Legacy* (New York: Vintage 1984).

2. Jackie Robinson, Charles Dexter, ed., *Baseball Has Done It* (Philadelphia: Lippincott, 1964).

3. Jules Tygiel, "The Court-martial of Jackie Robinson," 14–23, in his *Extra Bases: Reflections on Jackie Robinson, Race, and Baseball History* (Lincoln: University of Nebraska Press, 2002); see, too, Neil Lanctot, *Negro League Baseball: The Rise and Ruin of a Black Institution* (Philadelphia: University of Pennsylvania Press, 2004), 231.

4. Literature on the war ranges from the early John Morton Blum, *V was for Victory: Politics and American Culture during World War II* (New York: Harcourt Brace Jovanovich, 1976) to, recently, Tom Brokaw's unctuous video, *The Greatest Generation* (New York: NBC, 1999). Thomas C. Cochran, *The Great Depression and World War II, 1929–1945* (Glenview, Il: Scott, Foresman, 1968) quoted, 103.

5. Truman Gibson, *Knocking Down the Barriers: My Fight for Black America* (Evanston, IL: Northwestern University Press, 2005), 11–13, minimizes his role while providing a blow-by-blow account of black army life.

6. Harvard Sitkoff, *A New Deal for Blacks: The Emergence of Civil Rights as a National Issue: The Depression Decade* (New York: Oxford University Press, 1978), 314–17; John B. Kirby, *Black Americans in the Roosevelt Ea: Liberalism and Race* (Knoxville: University of Tennessee Press, 1980), 170–75. See George Gallup, *The Gallup Poll: Public Opinion, 1935–1971* (New York: Random House, 1972), I, March 4–9, 1939.

7. White's pressure on Wanger, see NAACP Papers, Library of Congress, and Wanger's papers, Wisconsin State Historical Society, cited in Thomas Cripps, *Making Movies Black: The Hollywood Message Movie...* (New York: Oxford University Press, 1977), 38–41.

8. On *Gone with the Wind*, see Cripps, *Making Movies Black*, 18–23; and on Lesser, see Cripps, "Langston Hughes and the Movies: The Case of *Way Down South*," in John Edgar Tidwell and Cherly R. Ragar, eds., *Montage of a Dream: The Art and Life of Langston Hughes* (Columbia: University of Missouri Press, 2007).

9. David W. Stowe, "The Politics of Café Society," *Journal of American History* 84: 4 (March 1998), 1395.

10. In Cripps, *Making Movies Black*, the substance of this paragraph forms a backbeat.

11. Cripps, *Making Movies Black*, Chap. II.

12. For a survey of this era see Thomas Cripps, *Slow Fade to Black: The Negro in American Movies, 1900–1940* (New York: Oxford University Press, 1977), as well as Clayton R. Koppes and Gregory D. Black, *Hollywood Goes to War...* (New York: The Free Press, 1987), *passim*.

13. On the tactic of integrating a lone black figure into a white circle, see Cripps, *Making Movies Black*, Chap. III, "The Making of a Genre."

14. Accessible in VHS format.

15. For *The Negro Soldier* in film history see Thomas Cripps and David Culbert, "*The Negro Soldier* (1944): Film Propaganda in Black and White," *American Quarterly* 31: 5 (Winter 1979), 616–640.

16. Truman Gibson to Gen. Lyman Munson, July 7, 1944, Civilian Aide file, box 250, Record Group 107, National Archives, Washington; Tygiel, "Court-martial of Jackie Robinson," 14–23, in *Extra Bases*.

17. Meier and Rudwick, *Black History and the Historical Profession, 1915–1980* (Urbana: University of Illinois Press, 1986), 73–74.

18. Steven A. Riess, "Professional Baseball and Social Mobility," 34–46; Jerry Malloy, "Sol White and the Origin of African American Baseball," 62–94; and Jason Pendleton, "Jim Crow Strikes Out: Interracial Baseball in Wichita, Kansas, 1920–1935, 142–59, in John E. Dreifort, ed., *Baseball History from Outside the Lines* (Lincoln: University of Nebraska Press, 2001), see baseball in a hardening racial order. Ryan Swanson, "Bases Loaded: Race, Reconstruction, and Baseball, D.C., 1865–1876," in William M. Simons, ed., *The Cooperstown Symposium on Baseball in American Culture, 2003–2004* (Jefferson, NC: McFarland, 2003); and George B. Kirsch, *Baseball in Blue and Gray: The National Pastime during the Civil War* (Princeton, NJ: Princeton University Press, 2003), carry the story back to the Civil War.

For the parallel universe of the Negro leagues, see Malloy's essay on "the Origin of African-American Baseball"; Robert Peterson's *Only the Ball was White: A History of Legendary Black Players and All-Black Professional Teams* (New York: Prentice-Hall, 1970); Neil Lanctot, *Negro League Baseball: The Rise and Ruin of a Black Institution* (University of Pennsylvania Press, 2004); Michael E. Lomax, *Black Baseball Entrepreneurs, 1860–1901: Operating by Any Means Necessary* (Syracuse, NY: Syracuse University Press, 2003); and Leslie A. Heaphy, *The Negro Leagues, 1869–1960* (Jefferson, NC: McFarland, 2003).

19. Tygiel, *Baseball's Great Experiment*, 25–31.

20. On African Americans in the New Deal era, John B. Kirby, *Black Americans in the Roosevelt Era: Liberalism and Race* (Knoxville: University of Tennessee Press, 1980); Harvard Sitkoff, *A New Deal for Blacks: The Emergence of Civil Rights as a National Issue: The Depression Decade* (New York: Oxford University Press, 1978); and Raymond Wolters, *Negroes and the Great Depression: The Problem of Economic Recovery* (Westport, CT: Greenwood, 1970).

21. See particularly Tygiel, *Baseball's Great Experiment*, Chap. III. "The Conspiracy of Silence," and 30, on Griffith.

22. Baseball is blessed with an era of fine historians, to whom I am indebted: Harold Seymour, *Baseball*, 3 vols. (New York: Oxford University Press, 1960, 1970, 1990); David Quentin Voigt, *American Baseball* 3 vols. (Vols. 1 and 2, Norman: University of Oklahoma Press, 1966; and University Park: Pennsylvania State University Press, 1983); and Benjamin G. Rader, *Baseball* (Urbana: University of Illinois, 1992).

23. Sam Lacy, with Moses J. Newson, *Fighting for Fairness: The Life Story of Hall of Fame Sportswriter Sam Lacy* (Centreville, MD: Tidewater, 1998), Chaps. 35–37. The president of the University of Maryland, Harry "Curly" Byrd was famous for his advocacy of support of black colleges and his plea to purchase Morgan College, a Methodist school for African Americans, lest black students seek entry to the segregated university. On the sociopolitical power of Owens and Louis, see Lewis A. Erenberg, *The Greatest Fight of Our Generation: Louis vs. Schmeling* (New York: Oxford University Press, 2006); David Margolick, *Beyond Glory: Joe Louis v. Max Schmeling, and a World on the Brink* (New York: Alfred A. Knopf, 2005); and Patrick Myler, *Ring of Hate: Joe Louis vs. Max Schmeling: The Fight of the Century* (New York: Arcade, 2005). On Owens as figure see William J. Baker, *Jesse Owens, an American Life* (New York: Free, 1986).

24. On FBI interest in racial affairs, see Robert A. Hill, ed. and comp., *The FBI's RACON: Racial Conditions in the United States during World War II* (Boston: Northeastern University Press, 1995), on the *People's Voice*, 190, 196; on Bostic and Rickey, see Tygiel, *Baseball's Great Experiment*, 5, 7, 38, 74, and on MacPhail, 37.

25. Tygiel, *Baseball's Great Experiment*, 40–45, is at his best in sketching Landis's guile, and the empty wartime show — tryouts. For a sense of impending tragedy in black circles, see Lanctot, *Negro League Baseball*, 9.

26. Lacy, *Fighting for Fairness*, 47–48; Tygiel, *Baseball's Great Experiment*, 42; Lanctot, *Negro League Baseball*, 220–21.

27. Tygiel, *Baseball's Great Experiment*, 79, 243.

28. Arnold Rampersad. *Jackie Robinson: A Biography* (New York: Alfred A. Knopf, 1997, 150–51. Curiously, the author cites only the *Montreal Standard*, April 28, 1946, for the "riot" story.

29. Joseph Garonzik, *Urbanization and the Black Population of Baltimore, 1850–1870* (Ph.D., SUNY Stony Brook, 1974), I-II; Leroy Graham, *Baltimore: The Nineteenth Century Black Capital* (Washington: University Press of America, 1982), Chap. VI; Benjamin Quarles, biographer of Douglass, quoted in conversation. Jeffrey R. Brackett, *The Negro in Maryland: A Study of the Institution of Slavery* (Baltimore: 1888), 107, reports that "slaves in Maryland, particularly in cities, were allowed ... to act as freemen, and also to buy their freedom."

30. Du Bois, and later his daughter, lived near Morgan College, and were part of campus lore.

31. Antero Pietila, *Race and Realty in Baltimore History*, forthcoming, see his fn. 24, "archive file," Chap. VIII, 10, 16.

32. Pietila, *Race and Realty in Baltimore*, Chaps. I-II.

33. Antero Pietila, *Race and Realty in Baltimore*, passim.

34. *Ibid.*

35. As example, see *Sun*, April 21, 1946.

36. *Sun*, February 16, 23, 1945, and March 3, 1945.

37. Tygiel, *Baseball's Great Experiment*, 74–75.

38. Tygiel, *Baseball's Great Experiment*, 74, 79.

39. Tygiel, *Baseball's Great Experiment*, 79–82 (*New York Times*, February 18, 1948). "You can't find a copy of that report anywhere," Rickey in early 1948 told a black audience in Wilberforce College in Ohio. The *Sporting News* (Feb. 25, 1948), reported the owners' denial — "false" and "ridiculous," they said — while the new commissioner, A. B.

Chandler, was wary of integration but sided publicly with Rickey's plan. The report, wrote Tygiel, is in Chandler's papers and U.S. Congress, *Organized Baseball* (Washington: Government Printing Office, 1948). For the fullest account of Branch Rickey's role in the Jackie Robinson story, see Lee Lowenfish's comprehensive biography of Rickey, *Baseball's Ferocious Gentleman* (Lincoln: University of Nebraska Press, 2007).

40. *New York Times*, April 30, 1046; April 27, 1946; *Sun*, April 27, 1946; *Sun*, May 1, 1946; Armstrong cited in Tygiel, *Baseball's Great Experiment*, 79.

41. C.M. Gibbs in *Sun*, April 28, 29, 1946; *Afro*, April 6, 1946, though reporting early "unmistakably aloofness" on the part of Southern players. Rachel Robinson, however, recalled in an interview in Rampersad, *Jackie Robinson*, 151, 475, that she heard a fan yell "nigger son of a bitch."

42. *Sun*, April 29, 1946.

43. *Afro*, May 2, 4, 7, 1946.

44. *Afro*, May 4, 1946; *Sun*, April 29, 1946. Rachel Robinson has declined an interview. Oddly, Linthicum shifted to a "lynch mob," but reported no incidents.

45. *Afro*, May 7, 1946, and on bean balls, Tygiel, *Baseball's Great Experiment*, 133.

46. Interview with Jorgensen in which Tomas is quoted; Lacy in *Afro-American*, August 3, 1946, in Tygiel, *Baseball's Great Experiment*, 129.

47. Baltimore passes almost unremarked in Jackie Robinson "as told to" Wendell Smith, *My Own Story* (New York: Greenberg: 1948), 106; then the story grows in Jackie Robinson (edited by Charles Duckett, *Baseball Has Done It* (Philadelphia: Lippincott, 1964); Art Rust, Jr., *Get That Nigger Off the Field: A Sparkling Informal History of the Black Man in Baseball* (New York: Delacorte, 1976); and Maury Allen, *Jackie Robinson: A Life Remembered* (New York: Franklin Watts, 1987); and Rachel Robinson, *Jackie Robinson: An Intimate Portrait* (New York: Harry Abrams, 1996). Only in Jackie Robinson "as told to" Charles Duckett, *I Never Had It Made* (New York: G.P. Putnam's Sons, 1972) do the heavies appear. See also Andrew Santella, *Jackie Robinson Breaks the Color Line* (Chicago: Children's, 1996); 12, a child's version in which "fans yell racial slurs at him," and, fancifully, "*every time he came up, he went down*" [emphasis added]. Falkner's *Great Time Coming: The Life of Jackie Robinson, from Baseball to Birmingham* (New York: Simon & Shuster, 1995), offers no source. See also James Bready, *Baseball in Baltimore: The First Hundred Years* (Baltimore: Johns Hopkins University Press, 1998), 212, for a return to Rachel Robinson's angle.

48. Robinson, *My Own Story*, 106. His benign view here concurs with the local press; perhaps both were by their natures as optimists and were putting the best fact on a tense moment.

49. Rampersad, *Jackie Robinson*, 150; H.L. Mencken, "Mencken's Last Stand," *Evening Sun*, November 9, 1948, in Alistair Cooke, ed., *The Vintage Mencken* (New York: Vintage, [1955], 227–30; Joseph Christopher Schaub, *Mitzi and Mencken* (DVD recording, 2007); and two conversations with Mitzi Swamm.

Chapter 14

1. *Look*, June 11, 1957; *Business Week*, October 5, 1957, *U.S. News & World Report*, September 7, 1959.

2. Robert Creamer, "The Greatest Yankee Team Ever," *Sports Illustrated*, August 25, 1958, pp. 14–16.

3. Dennis Conner and Michael Levitt, *The America's Cup* (New York: St. Martin's, 1998), p. 2.

4. Red Smith, "What Broke Up the Yankees," *Saturday Evening Post*, March 29, 1947.

5. Arthur Daley, "Casey at the Bat," *New York Times*, October 14, 1948, p. 40.

6. Arthur Daley, "A Much Too Quiet Departure," *New York Times*, October 20, 1948, p. 41.

7. Quoted in Robert W. Creamer, *Stengel: His Life and Times* (New York: Simon and Schuster: 1984), p. 212. It had been Egan who had written a few years earlier after Stengel had been sidelined by an automobile accident that "the man who did the most for baseball in Boston in 1943 was the motorist who ran Stengel down two days before the opening game and kept him away from the Braves for two months." Ibid., p. 197.

8. *Sporting News*, April 20, 1949. It would not be the last time that the Yankees would be written off too quickly. In the fall of 1995, Frank Deford dismissed the Yankees as "Steinbrenner's Whim," an "irrelevance in pinstripes," which "have descended into a jejune mediocrity." Frank Deford, "Irrelevance in Pinstripes," *New York Times*, October 24, 1995. Two springs later, as the Yanks were poised to run off three World Series consecutive titles, Keith Olbermann labeled the Yankee owner "shortsighted Steinbrenner," who was "sacrificing the future for a dubious present" through a series of questionable trades. Keith Olbermann, "Shortsighted Steinbrenner," *Sports Illustrated*, April 13, 1998.

9. *Sporting News*, April 20, 1949.

10. *Sporting News*, April 19, 1950; April 18, 1951; April 16, 1952; April 15, 1953.

11. *Sporting News*, April 14, 1954; April 8, 1959.
12. A. J. Liebling, "The Men in the Agbadas," in *A Neutral Corner: Boxing Essays* (New York: Fireside, Simon & Schuster, 1992) p. 201.
13. Roger Kahn, *The Boys of Summer* (New York: Harper & Row, 1972).
14. Bill Veeck with Ed Linn, *Veeck — as in Wreck* (New York: Ballantine, 1976 ed.), esp. pp. 266–281.
15. Roger Angell, "Farewell, My Giants!," *Holiday*, May 1958.
16. See, Roger Angell, *The Summer Game* (New York: Popular Library, 1972).
17. Quoted in *Sporting News*, August 29, 1964.
18. *Study of Monopoly Power: Organized Baseball (1951)*, pp. 1604–1605, 1608–1609.
19. *The Gallup Poll: Public Opinion 1935–1971* (New York: Random House, 1972), p. 733.
20. *New York Times*, December 27, 1950, May 22, 1951.
21. *Statistical Abstract of the United States: 1952*, p. 24.
22. *The Gallup Poll 1972–1977: Volume I*, p. 2.
23. Jules Tygiel, Baseball's Great Experiment: Jackie Robinson and His Legacy (New York: Oxford University Press, 1983), p. 294.
24. *Death House Letters of Ethel and Julius Rosenberg* (New York: Jero 1953), pp. 67, 109; James G. Ryan, *Earl Browder: The Failure of American Communism* (Urbana: University of Illinois Press, 1997), p. 145; Edward P. Johanningsmeier, *Forging American Communism: The Life of William Z. Foster* (Princeton, NJ: Princeton University Press, 1994), p. 322.
25. Arthur Mann, *The Jackie Robinson Story* (New York: Grosset & Dunlap, 1950), pp. 114–116; Jules Tygiel, *Baseball's Great Experiment*, pp. 82–86.
26. Dates on which teams integrated from Tygiel, *Baseball's Great Experiment*, pp. 211, 219–220, 285, 292–294, 328–329, 332.
27. The St. Louis Browns signed three black ball players in mid–July 1947. They were all released a month later and the Browns did not field another black ball player until 1951. Tygiel, *Baseball's Great Experiment*, pp. 219–222, 285.
28. *New York Times*, November 26, 1955; August 1, 1957.
29. The three most comprehensive accounts are Neil Sullivan, *The Dodgers Move West* (New York: Oxford University Press, 1987), Michael Shapiro, *The Last Good Season* (New York: Doubleday, 2003) and Henry D. Fetter, *Taking on the Yankees: Winning and Losing in the Business of Baseball* (New York: W.W. Norton, 2003).

30. Lindsay Nelson and Al Hirshberg, *Backstage at the Mets* (New York: Viking, 1966), p. 77.
31. Los Angeles officials put an oar in the waters stirred up by Dodger plans to replace Ebbets Field within days of Walter O'Malley's public announcement of his downtown Brooklyn stadium proposal in August 1955. *New York Times*, August 23, 1955.
32. Letter of Anna Motraytis to Mayor Robert F. Wagner, Jr., 1957, in Robert F. Wagner, Jr., Papers — New York City Municipal Archives.
33. Arthur Daley, "The Deserted Village," *New York Times*, September 27, 1956.
34. *New York Times*, October 22, 1944, p. 35.
35. *New York Times*, September 27, 1956.
36. Robert Moses, "Robert Moses on the Battle of Brooklyn," *Sports Illustrated*, July 22, 1957, pp. 26–28, 46–49.
37. *New York Times*, September 3,4, 1941; September 4, 1947. Such a move would not be without precedent. In 1915, the Boston Red Sox played their "home" World Series games in newly opened Braves Field, which had a larger seating capacity than their own three-year-old Fenway Park. Richard M. Cohen, David S. Neft and Roland T. Johnson, *The World Series* (New York: Dial, 1976), p. 57.
38. *New York Times*, September 29–October 5, 1955; U.S. House of Representatives, *Hearings before the Antitrust Subcommittee of the Committee on the Judiciary, Organized Professional Team Sports*, 85th Cong., 2d sess., 1957, p. 1859. The differential was still greater for the encounters (1952 and 1956) when the last two games were played in Brooklyn, since after four games had been played the teams alone shared in the bulk of the receipts — the player's pool being limited to the receipts from the first four contests.
39. Based on a comparison of the sports pages of the *New York Times* and the *New York Herald Tribune* in April 1957 and April 1958.
40. *New York Herald Tribune*, April 22, 1958.
41. See, e.g. Arthur Daley, "Noble Experiment," *New York Times*, August 21, 1959.
42. Roger Kahn, "Football's Taking Over," *Sport*, April 1960, pp. 18, 70–71.

Chapter 15

1. Special Thanks to Dan Mason, Ed Edwards, Neil Flynn, and Paul Worthman for their comments.
2. Neil F. Flynn, *Baseball's Reserve System: The Case and Trial of Curt Flood v. Major*

League Baseball (Springfield: Walnut Park, 2006), 184–87.

3. Brad Snyder, *A Well-Paid Slave: Curt Flood's Fight for Free Agency in Professional Sports* (New York: Viking, 2006), 332.

4. Flynn offers generous quotes from the trial testimony throughout his book.

5. Synder, 347, 351.

6. Alex Belth, *Stepping Up: The Story of Curt Flood and His fight for Baseball Players Rights* (New York: Persea, 2006).

7. Belth, 158.

8. For a good discussion of the *Federal Baseball* and *Toolson* cases, see Snyder, 25–29.

9. On the Koufax-Drysdale holdout, see Charles P. Korr, *The End of Baseball As We Knew It: The Players Union, 1960–81* (Urbana and Chicago, University of Illinois Press, 2002), 62–64.

10. Marvin Miller, *A Whole Different Ballgame: The Sport and Business of Baseball* (New York: Carol, 1991); Korr, 67–76; Belth, 121.

11. Snyder, 74; Koor, 279n.

12. Koor, 132–33; John Helyar, *The Lords of the Realm: The Real History of Baseball* (New York: Villard, 1994), 130–31.

13. Snyder, 74–75.

14. Miller, 185. See also Snyder, 75–79; Korr, 86–88; Belth, 163.

15. Snyder, 233.

16. Miller, 186.

17. Michael Lomax, "Curt Flood Stood Up for Us: The quest to Break Down Racial Barriers and structural Inequality in Major League Baseball," in J.A. Mangan, Andrew Ritchie, eds. *Ethnicity, Sport, Identity: Struggles for Status* (New York, London: Frank Cass, 2004), 45.

18. Curt Flood with Richard Carter, *The Way It Is* (New York: Trident, 1970); Snyder, 132.

19. Snyder, 58–65.

20. Lomax, 55.

21. Flood, 29.

22. Geoffrey C. Ward and Ken Burns, *Baseball: An Illustrated History* (New York: Alfred A. Knopf, 1994), 411.

23. Miller, 172.

24. Snyder, 9.

25. Snyder, 9, 67.

26. Lomax, 44.

27. Snyder, 9–10, 67.

28. Snyder, 6, 11–12, 27.

29. Snyder, 5–6.

30. Belth, 131–33.

31. Flood, 228–36.

32. Flynn, 13.

33. Flynn, 180.

34. Snyder, 6.

35. Flynn, 181.

36. Snyder 3, 35–36, 45, 60, 68.

37. Flynn, 98.

38. Miller, 196–98.

39. Flood, 189–90; Miller, 171–74.

40. Miller, 174–75, 180–81; Snyder, 24.

41. Snyder, 78.

42. Belth, 121; Snyder, 73.

43. Snyder, 73–81; Belth, 153; Korr, 89–90, 124–25.

44. Snyder, 78, 81; Korr, 89–90.

45. Snyder, 107, 110.

46. Flynn, 57.

47. Flynn, 237, 326.

48. Flynn, 225.

49. Snyder, 191.

50. Flynn, 282, 326.

51. Flynn, 259–60.

52. Flynn, 277–82; Snyder, 191–92.

53. Flynn, 289.

54. Bob Woodward and Scott Armstong, *The Brethren: Inside the Supreme Court* (New York: Simon and Schuster, 1979); Linda Greenhouse, *Becoming Justice Blackmun: Harry Blackmun's Supreme Court Journey* (New York Times, 2005).

55. Snyder, 241–48.

56. See for example, Miller, 199.

57. Snyder, 285.

58. Snyder, 298–99.

59. Snyder, 285–87, 306–7.

60. Snyder, 300.

61. Snyder, 304–5.

62. Snyder, 313.

63. U.S. Supreme Court, *Flood v. Kuhn et al* 407 U.S. 258 (1972). http://caselaw.lp.findlaw.com/scripts/getcase.pl?court=US&vol=407&invol=258 *http://caselaw.lp.findlaw.com/scripts/getcase.pl?court=US&vol=407&invol=2 58* (October, 30, 2006).

64. Ibid.

65. U.S. Supreme Court, *Flood v. Kuhn et al*.

66. U.S. Supreme Court, *Flood v. Kuhn et al*.

67. Snyder, 309.

68. Snyder, 308.

69. Helyar, 134; Korr, 122.

70. Helyar, 109; Belth, 165; Snyder, 178; Flynn, 177, 220, 311.

71. Flynn, 220.

72. Belth, 190; Kelyar, 131.

73. Korr, 133.

74. Helyar, 132–34.

75. Korr, 130.

76. Helyar, 135–36.

77. Flynn, 316.

78. Flynn, 310.

79. Snyder, 212–32.

80. Snyder, 320–22.

81. Snyder, 332.

82. Snyder, 326–27, 330.

83. Snyder, 335.

84. Snyder, 336–37, 341.
85. Flynn, 318; HYPERLINK "http://roadsidephotos,sabr.org/baseball//curtflood.htm" *http://roadsidephotos,sabr.org/baseball//curtflood.htm* (October 30, 2006).

Chapter 17

1. All the statements from my daughters, Caroline Brady and Elizabeth Alves, came from them in email messages in October 2007.
2. *The Washington Post*, October 22, 2006; Tom Callahan, *Johnny U : The Life and Times of John Unitas* (New York: Crown, 2006), p. 173.
3. *The Weekly Standard*, April 13, 1998.
4. Conversation with Frank Peto, September 25, 2007.
5. Harold J. Barrow, *The Decline of African-American Participation in Major League Baseball*, Florida State University Honors Thesis, 2006, pp. 42–54.
6. *Nine: A Journal of Baseball History*, v. 13, 2005, p. 1.
7. Clyde King's observations on changes in major league baseball presented at a conference on baseball at Frostburg State University, November 8, 2006.

About the Contributors

William B. Akin attended graduate school with the editor of this volume in the early 1960s when baseball history was rarely, if ever, considered as a subject for a dissertation. So, he waited a while to write about something he loved—baseball. Now he is the author of *West Virginia Baseball: A History, 1865–2000* and articles on the game in a variety of sport history journals. He is emeritus professor of history at Ursinus College in Collegeville, Pennsylvania, where he taught and served as an administrator. His long-ago dissertation on technology and the American Dream from 1900 to 1941 was eventually published. So was *Faculty Development in Liberal Arts Colleges: An Unfinished Agenda*.

Widely regarded as one of the nation's foremost film historians, lifelong Baltimore resident **Thomas Cripps** is also a keen student of the wide breadth of American popular culture. His stint as a semi-professional baseball player in Baltimore in the decade following World War II gave him first-hand experience with the game and the racial dynamics of the city that he writes about in his essay. His most prominent studies on American film, a subject he also incorporates into his essay, are *Slow Fade to Black* and *Making Movies Black*. He is working on a book about the 1936 Nazi Olympics.

A native of Baltimore, **Frank Deford** is best-known for his weekly sports commentary for National Public Radio. Deford defined intelligent sportswriting during his twenty-seven years with *Sports Illustrated*. His best-known writing on baseball are his mythical short story *Casey on the Loose* and *The Old Ball Game: How John McGraw, Christy Mathewson, and the New York Giants Created Modern Baseball*. In the 1980s he was voted Sportswriter of the Year by the National Association of Sportswriters and Sportscasters for eight consecutive years. He has also written a poignant biography of his daughter, *Alex*.

A long-time award-winning sports columnist for the *Baltimore Sun*, **John Eisenberg** is a free-lance writer. He has written books on the Dallas Cowboys, the Green Bay Packers, horse racing, and the modern Baltimore Orioles. His book *The Great Match Race*, describing a 1823 sectional contest between two horses witnessed by 60,000 spectators, provided a preview of modern sports. Eisenberg's oral history of the post–World War II Baltimore Orioles, *From 33rd Street to Camden Yards*, describes the making of a contemporary championship team.

Henry D. Fetter's writings have appeared in *The Journal of Sport History*, *The New York Times*, *The Times Literary Supplement*, and *Public Interest*. He contributed to *Jackie Robinson: Race, Sports and the American Dream* and to *The Encyclopedia of American Jewish History*. Fetter is also the author of *Taking on the Yankees: Winning and Losing in the Business of Baseball*. He is a graduate of Harvard Law School and lives in Los Angeles, where he has practiced business and entertainment litigation for the past twenty-five years.

About the Contributors

Timothy M. Gay has been a Washington, D.C.–based public affairs and communication specialist for more than two decades. In addition to writing hundreds of op-ed commentaries and speeches for clients, he has written extensively on history and sports. His essays and articles on the Civil War, baseball, college basketball, and golf have appeared in the *Washington Post, USA Today,* the *Boston Globe,* and other publications. *Tris Speaker,* Gay's first baseball book, was a finalist for the Society for American Baseball Research Seymour Medal.

Anyone who wants to know the archeology of baseball parks in Baltimore needs to schedule a lunch with the peripatetic advertising executive **Robert V. Leffler, Jr.** Since his graduate school days at Morgan State University under the direction of Thomas Cripps, Leffler has spent decades tracing the whereabouts of the nooks and crannies of old playing fields when he is not building sport empires through his Baltimore–based company.

Peter Morris is the author of several studies on the early history of baseball. His first book, *Baseball Fever: Early History in Michigan,* won the Society for American Baseball Research (SABR) Seymour Medal. He has also written a two-volume study, *A Game of Inches: The Stories Behind the Innovations That Shaped Baseball.* His most recent book is *Level Playing: How the Groundskeepers Murphy Brothers Shaped Baseball* (2007). He is a public health researcher for the Michigan Public Health Institute.

While a newcomer to the publishing field of baseball history, **A. Franklin Parks** is not a novice to the subject of baseball or one of his subjects in this anthology, Jimmie Foxx. He recalls his father talking about watching Foxx playing on the Eastern Shore of Maryland where Parks was raised. One of his books, *Maryland: Unity in Diversity,* was co-edited with John B. Wiseman. He is a professor of English at Frostburg State University and is the author of a forthcoming study of William Parks, a figure as important to eighteenth century colonial America as baseball was to the nation a century later.

Generally recognized as the foremost expert on sportscasting history, **Ted Patterson** arrived in Baltimore in 1973 after working for two years with the legendary Curt Gowdy. For the next thirty years he was sports director for several Baltimore radio stations, currently for WCBM. He has won nine sportscaster of the year awards in Maryland and the Chesapeake Bay area and has written six books on sportscasting, including *Golden Voices of Baseball.* His Baltimore home contains one of the best baseball memorabilia collections in the country.

Burt Solomon has written extensively about baseball history, American science, and national political affairs. His baseball books include *Where They Ain't: The Fabled Life and Untimely Death of the Original Baltimore Orioles* and *The Baseball Timeline: In Association with Major League Baseball.* He is a contributing editor for the *National Journal,* where he has covered the White House and other aspects of Washington life. His most recent book is *FDR v. The Constitution: The Court-Packing Fight and the Triumph of Democracy.*

Paul D. Staudohar's many publications include *Diamond Mines: Baseball and Labor, Playing for Dollars, Labor Relations and Sports Business,* and *The Business of American Sports.* He is a member of the National Academy of Arbitrators, co-founder of the *Journal of Sports Economics,* and is president of the International Association of Sports Economists. He has also served on the board of editors of the *Journal of Sport and Social Issues.* He is retired from the faculty of the School of Business and Economics at California State University–Hayward. Practicing what he has written, Staudohar is a veteran labor-management negotiator.

About the Contributors

Jules Tygiel attended his first baseball game in 1956 at Ebbets Field, where he witnessed three consecutive home runs in the bottom of the ninth for a Dodger victory. What else could he have become but a distinguished baseball historian? The beginning point for students investigating the cultural importance of Jackie Robinson's racial integration of baseball is Tygiel's 1983 classic *Baseball's Great Experiment: Jackie Robinson and His Legacy*. His other books on modern baseball include *Past Time: Baseball as History*, and *Bases: Reflections on Jackie Robinson, Race, and Baseball History*. Until his death in 2008, Tygiel was a professor of history at San Francisco State University.

Tim Wendel is an award-winning novelist, journalist, and historian of Latino baseball. His books include *Castro's Curveball*, a novel set in Old Havana that explores the legend that Fidel Castro could have been a major league pitcher. He has written a history of Hispanics in baseball, *The New Face of Baseball*, and more recently *Far from Home: Latino Baseball Players in America*. He writes on this subject for *Baseball Weekly*. Wendel teaches fiction and non-fiction writing at Johns Hopkins University. His latest book, *Red Rain*, is a novel set in World War II about Japanese fire balloons.

Before his retirement in 2007 as professor of history at Frostburg State University, **John B. Wiseman** taught American history for forty years. In his last decade he specialized in organizing conferences, including one on the history of baseball in November 2006. As an assistant editor of *The Maryland Historical Magazine* he edited a special issue on baseball in Maryland. His published books include *The Dilemmas of a Party Out of Power: The Democrats, 1904–1912*, co-authorship of *Allegany County: A History*, and co-editorship of *Maryland: Unity in Diversity*. He has also written articles on race and the Democratic Party as well as Hollywood movie history. Wiseman is working on bringing a minor league baseball team back to Cumberland, Maryland, where he lives.

Index

Aaron, Hank 151
Adams, Franklin P. 55
Adams, Willie 112
Alexander, Grover Cleveland 68
Alexander, Will 123
Ali, Muhammad 166, 181
Allen, Ethan 99
Allen, Mel 86–88
Altobelli, Joe 202, 207
Altrock, Ned 48
Alves, Elizabeth 211–212, 218, 222
amateurism 35–36
American Association 17
American Football League 167
American League 32, 38, 173–174
Anderson, Marian 110, 124
Angell, Roger 163
Angelos, Peter G. 206, 208
Anson, Adrian "Cap" 28, 45, 52
Aparicio, Luis 202
Archer, Frank M. 99
Arlin, Harold 78
Armstrong, Herb 133
Atlantic League 72–73
Ayala, Benny 205

Baker, Frank "Home Run" 5, 45, 50, 73
Baker, Roger 90
Ball Four 164
Baltimore Afro-American 109
Baltimore Black Sox 107–9
"Baltimore chop" 22
Baltimore Elite Giants 6
Baltimore Grays 112
Baltimore Orioles: decline 205–209; 1890s 4, 25–33, 38; modern dynasty 199, 203; modern franchise 200–205; 1966 World Series 203
Bamberger, George 202
Barber, Red 80, 83–85, 88
Barney, Rex 148
Baseball Assistance Team (BAT) 176
Baseball Has Done It 123
Baseball Writers Association of America 79
Baseball's Reserve System: The Case and Trial of Curt Flood v. Major League Baseball 177
basketball 215

Battle of Blair Mountain 97–98
Baylor, Don 204
Beadle's Dime Baseball Book 20
Beattie, Jim 209
Bedient, Hugh 66
Belanger, Mark 201
Belle, Albert 208
Belth, Alex 177
Beltran, Carlos 155
Benitez, Armando 209
Birth of a Nation 126
Black, Joe 116, 118
Black Sox Scandal 129
Black Yanks 111, 113, 133
Blackmun, Harry 188–189, 190
Blair, Paul 201
Blake, Fred "Sheriff" 104
Blakely, John 103
Blefary, Curt 202
"Bloomer Girls" 59
Bluefield Blue-Grays 98–9
Boddiker, Mike 204
Boggs, Wade 218–219
Bolden, Ed 108
Bostic, Joe 130
Boston Braves 53
Boston Red Sox 5, 7, 59, 70
Boswell, Thomas 75–76
Bouton, Jim 164
Bowman, Bob 100
"Boys of Summer" 144, 163
The Boys of Summer 147
Brady, Caroline 211–212, 218, 222
Bramham, W.G. 130, 222
Bramwell, West Virginia (Indians) 105
Breton, Marcos 151
Bridgeforth, William S. 119
Bridwell, Al 50
Britt, Jim 90
Brooklyn Brown Dodgers 113
Brooklyn Dodgers 6–7, 170–172
Brooklyn Trolley Dodgers 26, 30–31
Brown, Mordecai "Three Fingers" 45–46, 48
Brumbry, Al 204
Bugle Field (Baltimore) 107–9, 112
Bunker, Wally 201
Bunting 17–18, 21

Index

Burger, Warren 188–189
Burns, Ken 150, 220
Busch, August 182–183
Butts, Tom 112

Cambria, Joe 107, 109, 113
Camilli, Dolph 84
Camp, Walter 34
Campanella, Roy 112–113, 118, 130, 147
Carrasquel, Chico 151, 217
Carter, Art 109
"Casey at the Bat" (poem) 4
Cashen, Frank 205
Cepeda, Orlando 151, 153–154
Chadwick, Henry 15, 21–22
Chance, Frank 4, 44–45, 47, 51–54
Chandler, A.B. "Happy" 130
Chapman, Ben 142
Chase, Hal 62–63
Chicago American Giants 112
Chicago Cubs: 4–5, 74; 1906 season 48; 1907 season 48–49; 1908 season 49; 1910 season 49–50
Chicago White Stockings 28
Chick Webb Memorial Recreation Center 111, 119
Cicotte, Eddie 67
Cincinnati Red Stockings 36
Cincinnati Reds 73, 178
Clarke, Fred 45, 49
Clemente, Roberto 7, 151
Clendenon, Don 179
Cleveland Buckeyes 115
Cleveland Indians 5, 60, 115
Cleveland Spiders 31
Coalfield (West Virginia) League Association 99
Coalwood Robins 103
Cobb, Ty 5, 26, 49, 59–60, 66–68, 71, 74
Cochran, Thomas C. 123
Cochrane, Mickey 71, 74
Coffee, Mary 135
Cole, Len "King" 50
Coleman, Tome 118
Collective Bargaining Agreement (CBA) 179, 185
Collins, Eddie 50
Comiskey, Charlie 129
Comiskey Park 111
Cooper, Irving Ben 176, 187
Corbin, David 97
Crawford, Sam "Wahoo" 49
Cricket 17
Cripps, Thomas 123
Crisfield Crabbers 74
Crosley, Powell, Jr. 84
Cuadros, Paul 155
Cuellar, Mike 203
Cullen, Countee ("Incident") 123
Cullop, Nick 99
Cumberland (Maryland) Colts 74

Curt Flood Act 195
Curt Flood v. Bowie Kuhn, et al. 176

Daily Worker 130
Daley, Arthur 162
Dalton, Harry 200, 202, 205
Damn Yankees (Broadway play) 163
Dark, Alvin 153
Dauer, Rich 204
Davis, Ossie 127
dead ball era 11, 44–45, 71
Dean, Dizzy 82, 129
Dean, Wayland 103
DeCinces, Doug 204
de Coubertin, Baron 35
Delgado, Carlos 155
Dempsey, Rick 205
Derringer, Paul 99, 103
Desmond, Connie 85, 87, 91
Detroit Tigers 49
Dexter Park (Brooklyn) 107
Dihigo, Martin 151
DiMaggio, Joe 26, 148
Dobson, Pat 203
Doby, Larry 115, 152
Dr. Peppers 109
Douglas, Phil "Shuffling" 99, 103
Douglass, Frederick 131
Douglass, William 190
Downing, Al 179
Drabowski, Moe 203
Dreyfus, Barney 80, 82
Drysdale, Don 178
Du Bois, W.E.B. 131
Duquette, Jim 209
Durocher, Leo 88, 130

East-West All-Star Game (Comiskey Park, 1943) 111
Eastern Shore (of Maryland) League 73, 78
Easton Farmers 73, 74
Ebbets, Charlie 31, 47
Ebbets Field 107, 170–172
Edgewater Giants 111
Edison, Thomas 25
Egan, Dave 162
Elite Giants 133
Elmer, Bob 116
Elson, Bob 80–81
Erskine, Carl 7, 121, 138–139, 142, 144, 146–147
Etchebarren, Andy 201
Ethiopian Clowns 111
Evers, Johnny 4, 44–45, 47, 53–54

Falkner, David 134–135
Federal Baseball Club of Baltimore, Inc. v. National League of Professional Baseball Clubs 178, 184–187
Federal League 54–55, 72
Finley, Charles 192

Index

Fisk, Carleton 213–214
Fitzgerald, "Honey Fitz" 64
Flanagan, Mike 204, 209
Flanagan, Pat 89
Flood, Curt: artist 182; child of the 60s 180–183; civil rights 7; contract negotiations 183; end 193–195; lifestyle 182; mental state 181; player 182; reserve clause 7; Supreme Court 184, 187–188
Flynn, Neil F. 177, 184
football 12, 35–36, 213–214
Fox, Nellie 151
Foxx, Jimmie 5, 12, 68, 70–71–6, 73–77
Frey, Jim 201
Fullerton, Hugh 53

Gaherin, John 190–191
Galloway sisters 117
Gambling 5, 15, 63–67
Garagiola, Joe 176
Garland, Wayne 204
Gary, West Virginia 99; Golddiggers 103
Gehrig, Lou 68, 74
German Americans 36, 38
Gibbs, C.M. 133
Gibson, Bill 114
Gibson, Bob 151, 181
Gibson, Josh 68, 120, 151
Gibson, Truman 124, 127
Gilliam, Jim 113, 116, 118
Gillick, Pat 208
Gmelch, George 155
Goldberg, Arthur 184, 186, 188
Goldberg, Lawrence 88
Gomez, Leo 208
Gone with the Wind (movie) 124
Gorman, Lou 205
Gottlieb, Eddie 108, 110, 116
Gowdy, Curt 87
Graham, Don 205
Graney, Jack 82, 89–90
Grant, Charlie 129
Green, Vernon 108, 113, 115–116
Greenlee, Gus 108–109
Grich, Bobby 204
Griffith, Clark 52, 89, 129
Griffith Stadium 107–109, 112
Grigsby, John 109
Griner, John 110
Grove, Robert Moses "Lefty" 68, 71, 74
Guerrero, Vladimer 150, 155
Guillo, Nemesio 150

Hagy, "Wild" Bill 218
Hall, Dick 202
Haney, Larry 201
Hanlon, Ned 4, 11, 25–29
Harding, Warren 97
Harrelson, Ken "Hawk" 180
Harris, A.N. 100
Harris, Bernard 117

Harwell, Ernie 85
Hastie, William 123, 127
Hemond, Roland 154
Hemus, Solly 181
Heurich Brewers 11
Hispanics: 7, 150–156; *see also* Latinos
Hittner, Arthur D. 68, 72
Hodges, Russ 85, 88
Hoey, Fred 81
Hoffberger, Jerry 207–208
Hoffman, Solly 80
Holiday, Billie 125
Holmes, Oliver Wendell, Jr. 178
Holmes, Tommy 115
Homestead Grays 102–3, 109–111, 113
Hornsby, Rogers 68
Horst, Harry von der 30
How to Play Baseball the Oriole Way (manual) 205
Huff, Sam 175
Hughes, Langston 124
Hulbert, William A. 15, 45
Hunter, Jim "Catfish" 192
Husing, Ted 81, 87

"inside baseball" 25
Interstate League, 111
Irish Americans 36–38
Island Stadium (Harrrisburg, Pa.) 111

Jabar, Kareem Abdul 138
Jackson, Howard, 11
Jackson, Joe "Shoeless" 68
Jackson, Reggie 151
Jacobs, Eli 208
James, Bill 57
Jennings, Hughey 23, 25, 31, 39
Jennings, Kelsey 103
Johnson, "Ban" Byron 4, 32, 38
Johnson, Davey 201, 208
Johnson, Walter 62, 68
Jones, Fielder 48
Jordan, Michael 151
Jorgensen, John 134

Kahn, Roger 139, 163
Kansas City Blues 59
Kansas City Monarchs 6, 128
KDKA (Pittsburgh radio station) 78, 82
Keeler, "Wee Willie" 26–28, 31–33, 39
Kelley, Joe 25, 28, 31–32, 39
Kelly, Mike 37
Kelly, Pat 205
King, Clyde 202
King, the Rev. Martin Luther, Jr. 147
Klein, Alan 155
Klem, Bill 53
Kling, Johnny 46, 48–49
Knowles, Darrold 201
Koufax, Sandy 179
Krauthammer, Charles 213

Index

Kroh, Floyd "Kid" 50–51
Kubiski, Al 205
Kuhn, Bowie 170

Labine, Clem 138, 142, 146
Lacy, Cecil 101
Lacy, Sam 109, 114, 117, 119, 129–130, 134
LaGuardia, Fiorello 111
Landis, Kenesaw Mountain 67, 79, 81, 110, 129–130
Lardner, Ring 79
Latinos: 7, 150–156; *see also* Hispanics
Laux, France 81, 87
Leonard, Dutch 66
Leonard, Eddie 119
Lewis, Grover 105
Liebling, A.J. 163
Linthicum, Jesse 133
Logan, Rayford 125
Louis, Joe 124, 127, 132
Louisville Colonels 73
Lowenstein, John 205
Lundgren, Carl 48
Luque, Adolpho 150
Lyle, Sparky 192

Mack, Cornelius "Connie" 68, 73, 74, 79
MacPhail, Andy 209
MacPhail, Larry 80, 84–85, 130
MacPhail, Lee 200, 202
Major League Baseball Players Association 179, 185–187, 193
Major League owners 6
Manley, Abe 109–10
Manley, Effa 109, 114
Mantle, Mickey 75, 163
Marichal, Juan 153, 217
Marris, Roger 166
Marshall, Thurgood 189–190
Martin, Earl "Red" 105
Martinez, Dennis 204, 209
Martinez, Pedro 155
Martinez, Tippy 205
Maryland Park 107
Matheson, Christy 4, 12, 38, 41–43, 50–54, 63, 66, 68, 79
Matsuzaka, Daisuke 88
Mays, Willie 138, 151, 217
Mazeroski, Bill 214
McCormick, Harry "Moose" 50
McCovey, Willie 217
McDonald, Arch 87, 89
McDuffie, Terry 113
McGheehan, W.O. "Bill" 78–0
McGinnity, Joe "Iron Man" 31–32, 50
McGraw, John 4, 12, 25, 27–28, 38, 40–43, 51, 63, 68, 99, 129
McGreevey, Ned "Nuf Ced" 64
McGwire, Mark 70, 221
McKeldin, Theodore 112–113, 132
McLaughlin, Jim 200–201, 205

McLendon, Gordon 90–91
McNally, Dave 192, 200–201, 203
McNamee, Graham 79, 81
McQuade, Needy 103
Meany, Tom 162
Memorial Stadium 117, 218
Mencken, H.L. 135
Merkle, Fred "Bonehead" 49, 50–51
Merriwell, Frank 49
Messersmith, Andy 192
Middle Atlantic League 110
Miller, Marvin 176, 179, 181, 184–187, 190–191
Millikin, Mark R. 68
Mills, Okey 101
Milner, Holt "Cat" 103
Minaya, Omar 155
Minor League baseball 92
Minoso, Orestes "Minnie" 122, 151–153, 155
Mitchell, George 221–222
Montreal Royals 6
Moreno, Arturo 155
Morgan, J.P. 29
Morris, Willie 91
Morrison, Guy 99
Moses, Robert 172
Moulton, Lyle 76
Municipal Stadium (Baltimore) 107, 117
Murphy, Charles W. 46–47, 50, 52–54
Murphy, John 22
Murphy, Tom 22, 28
Murray, Eddie 200, 204, 211, 218
Myrdall, Gunnar 125

Nash, Ogden 53
Nashville Elite Giants 108
National Association for the Advancement of Colored People (NAACP) 123–124, 126–128, 130
National Basketball Association 165, 167
National Football League 167; championship game (1958) 213
National Hockey League 165
National Labor Relations Board (NLRB) 186
National League 4, 7, 15–16, 45, 169, 174
National Negro League 109
Negro American Baseball Association 110
Negro Leagues 6, 23
Negro National League 110
The Negro Soldier (film) 127
Nelson, Lindsey 90, 171
New World A-Coming 123, 125
New York Giants 4, 7, 26, 30–31, 38–42, 50–51, 170
New York Yankees: 7, 32, 38, 214; attendance 162, 165–166; racial integration 167–169; titles and dominance 159–161
Newark Eagles 111
Noboa, Junior 153–154
Norworth, Jack 42

Oates, Johnny 208
O'Day, Hank 51
Office of War Information 126–127
O'Malley, Walter 170–172
Oriole Park at Camden Yards 120, 206
Oriole Park at 29th and Greenmount 108–109, 111–113
Ortiz, David "Big Papi 154–155
O'Toole, Colonel Edward O. 99
Ottley, Roi 123, 125
Overall, Orval 46–48
Owens, Jesse 124
Oxon Hill Aztecs 111

Paige, Leroy "Satchel" 115–116, 118, 120, 129, 138, 151
Palmer, Jim 199, 201–203, 218
Pappas, Milt 202
Parkside Field (Philadelphia) 107
Parksley Spuds 74
Pasquel, Jose 152
Perlozzo, Sam 209
Perry, Charles 110
Pfiester, Jack 46, 48
Philadelphia Athletics 5, 50, 53, 70, 74
Philly Stars 111
Pitching and pitchers (evolution) 18–20, 22, 26, 45
Pittsburgh Crawfords 102, 109
Pittsburgh Pirates 69, 73, 214
Pittsburgh Steelers 212
Plank, Eddie 50
Plessy v. Ferguson 128–129
Poitevint, Ray 205
Poitier, Sydney 128
Pompez, Alex 109, 118
Posada, Jorge 156
Posey, Cum 108, 112
Powell, Adam Clayton 132
Powell, Boog 199–202, 204
Powell, Lewis 188–189
Powell, Richard D. 108, 115–117, 118–119
Power, Vic 151
Pries, Don 205
Prince, Bob "The Gunner" 82
Protho, Doc 113
Pujols, Albert 150

Radio stations 80, 83
Raleigh Coal and Cake Company 98
Raleigh (West Virginia) Clippers 105
Ramirez, Manny 154
Randolph, A. Philip 124
Reagan, Ronald "Dutch" 89
Reese, Pee Wee 138, 141, 142, 146
Rehnquist, William 188–189
Reserve clause 176–178, 187
Reulbach, Ed 46, 48
Rheinholt, Matt 116–117
Rice, Grantland 78–79
Richards, Paul 200–201

Richardson, Marty 114
Rickey, Branch 84, 113, 128, 130–132, 135–137, 138–140, 145, 147
Ripken, Cal, Jr. 200, 204, 206–207, 221
Ripken, Cal, Sr. 200, 202
Ritter, Lawrence 67
Ritterpusch, Dave 205
Rivera, Mariano 150, 156
Roberts, Brian 208
Robeson, Paul 125
Robinson, Brooks 199–202
Robinson, David 141
Robinson, Frank 199–203
Robinson, Jack 141
Robinson, Jackie 6–7, 84, 113, 116, 121–135, 151, 156, 183–184
Robinson, Rachel 134, 141, 146
Robinson, Sharon 141
Robinson, Wilbert 40
Rodriguez, Alex 150, 220
Rodriguez, Francisco 150
Rodriguez, Richard 151
Roenicke, Gary 205
Roosevelt, Eleanor 124
Roosevelt, Franklin D. 110, 124
Roosevelt, Teddy 36
Rosewell, Rosey 82
Rossiter, George 118
Rostraver Township (Pa.) 214
Royal Giants 110
Rules of play 16–20
Ruppert Stadium 111
Russell, Bill 138–139
Russo, Jim 200
Ruth, George Herman "Babe" 13, 60, 68, 74

Saberstein, Abe 110
St. Louis Browns 199
St. Louis Cardinals 178
Samm, By 81
Sampson, Tommy "Toots" 105
Santana, Johan 150, 155
Saunders, Jack 114
Schmeling, Max 124
Schmidt, Charlie "Butch" 49
Schuerholz, John 205
Schulte, Frank "Wildfire" 46
Scott, Glenn 79
Scully, Vince 80
Seattle Mariners 48
Seitz, Peter 192
Selee, Frank 47
Shannon, Walter 205
Shaw, George Bernard 4, 39
Sheckard, Timmy 46
Shibe Park 107
Silverman, Al 143
Silverthorne, Earl "Hi Ho" 222
Simmons, R.S. 114
Simmons, Ted 191
Sinatra, Frank 125, 128

Smith, Bob 99
Smith, Chick 99
Smith, Kate 125
Smith, Red 162
Smith, Wendell 114, 130
Snodgrass, Fred 51, 66
Snyder, Brad 177
Soccer 35
Sorrell, Vic 99, 100
Sosa, Sammy 155, 221
Spalding, Albert Goodwill 15, 45
Spanish-American War 29
Speaker, Tris 5, 59–62, 68, 74
Sport Magazine 136, 141, 143
Sporting News 130, 132
Stage, Billy 23
Stahl, Jake 66
Steinfeldt, Harry 46, 48–49
Stengel, Casey 162
Stepping Up: The Story of Curt Flood and His Fight for Baseball Players Rights 177
Steroids (and other enhancers) 221–222
Stewart, Potter 189
Stoneham, Horace 88
Strikes 8, 211–212, 220
Strong, Nat 108
Stuart, John "Stud" 99
Sudlersville, Maryand 5, 73
Suicide squeeze 27
Sullivan, John L. 12, 37
Sullivan, Mark 34
Sutton, Artie 142
Suzuki, Ichiro 216
Swann, Mitzi 135

Taft, Charles P. 46
Take Me Out to the Ball Game (song) 4, 12, 42
Tams, Walter P. 98
Taylor, Ben 111
Television 85, 91–93, 165, 203
Thomas, Dave 113
Thomas, Joseph 109–110, 112
Thomas, Tommy 134
Thompson, Bobby 89
Tiant, Luis, 151
Tinker, Joe 4, 44–45, 47, 54–55
"Tinker to Evers to Chance" (poem) 4
To Secure These Rights 128
Toney, Sebert, Jr. 101
Toolson case 178, 184, 186–187
Totten, Hal 80
Totten, S.G. "Garson" 105
Tremblay, Dave 209
Tri-State League (West Virginia) 103
Trout, Robert 87
Truman, Harry S. 128
Tuckey, Russell T. 111

Umpires 19–20, 22–23
Uniform Player Contract 178, 185
United Mine Workers 103–4
United States League 113
Updike, John 163

Veeck, Bill 75, 130, 163

Wagner, Honus 5, 12, 49, 68–77
Walsh, Ed 48
Walton, Ed 62
Wanger, Walter 124
Washington Black Senators 109
Watt, Eddie 201
The Way It Is 180
WBBM (Chicago radio station) 80
Weaver, Earl 150, 202–203, 205, 207
Webb, Earl 104
Weber, Bill 105
Weeghman, Charles 45
A Well-Paid Slave: Curt Flood's Fight for Free Agency in Professional Sports 177
Welsh West Va (Senators) 103
WENR (Chicago radio station) 80
Westport Stadium 117–118
WGN (Chicago radio station) 80
White, Byron "Whizzer" 188, 190
White, Paul 76
White, Walter 124–126
WIL (St. Louis radio station) 83
Willkie, Wendell 126
Williams, Edward Bennett 207
Williams, Frank 141
Williams, Kenny 141
Williams, Stan 144
Williams, Ted 75, 152, 166, 219
Wills, Maury 180
Wilson, Jim 201
Wilson, Tom 108–10, 114–115, 119
Winchell, Walter 125
WIND (Chicago radio station) 80
Wiseman, Earleen 214, 216–217
WJJD (Chicago radio station) 80
WMAC (Chicago radio station) 80
Wood, "Smoky" Joe 5, 58–59, 61–67
Woods, John 99
Workman, Harry "Hoge" 99
World Series: 1912 63–67; 1960 214; 1972 172
Wright, Bill 113
Wrigley, William, Jr. 80
Wrigley Field 45
WSAI (Cincinnati radio station) 80

Yankee Stadium 109–11, 172
Yardley, Jonathan 213
Young, Denton "Cy" 26, 52, 63, 68
Young, Ralph 111

www.ingramcontent.com/pod-product-compliance
Lightning Source LLC
Chambersburg PA
CBHW051218300426
44116CB00006B/623